I0095145

Images of Africa

MANCHESTER
1824

Manchester University Press

Images of Africa

Creation, negotiation and subversion

EDITED BY
JULIA GALLAGHER
WITH A FOREWORD BY
V. Y. MUDIMBE

Manchester University Press

Copyright © Manchester University Press 2015

While copyright in the volume as a whole is vested in Manchester University Press, copyright in individual chapters belongs to their respective authors, and no chapter may be reproduced wholly or in part without the express permission in writing of both author and publisher.

Published by Manchester University Press
Altrincham Street, Manchester M1 7JA
www.manchesteruniversitypress.co.uk

British Library Cataloguing-in-Publication Data
A catalogue record for this book is available from the British Library

Library of Congress Cataloging-in-Publication Data applied for

ISBN   978 15261 0742 8   hardback

First published by Manchester University Press in hardback in 2015

This edition first published 2017

The publisher has no responsibility for the persistence or accuracy of URLs for any external or third-party internet websites referred to in this book, and does not guarantee that any content on such websites is, or will remain, accurate or appropriate.

Typeset by
Servis Filmsetting Ltd, Stockport, Cheshire
Printed in Great Britain by
Lightning Source

Contents

Figures

The author and editor have made every reasonable effort to contact the
owners of the websites Abidjantalk.com and Gbagbout.over-blog.com
to request permission to use images 7.1 and 7.2. In the absence of a
response the images have been included; however, the author and editor
would welcome copyright discussion with the owners of these websites.

Contributors

Lizzy Attree has a PhD from SOAS, University of London on 'The Literary Responses to HIV and AIDS from South Africa and Zimbabwe from 1990–2005'. Lizzy's collection of interviews with the first African writers to write about HIV and AIDS from Zimbabwe and South Africa was published in 2010 by Cambridge Scholars Publishing, and is entitled *Blood on the Page*. In that same year she was a visiting lecturer in the English Department at Rhodes University in South Africa. Lizzy is the Director of the Caine Prize for African Writing.

Mel Bunce is a lecturer in Journalism at City University, London. Mel is interested in the political, cultural and technological forces that drive international news production and she has done extensive fieldwork in east and west Africa exploring these phenomena. She holds a doctorate in Politics from the University of Oxford, where her thesis examined foreign correspondents in east Africa. She has previously worked at Birkbeck, University of London, and the University of Otago in New Zealand.

Emmanuel Fanta is currently working on a PhD thesis on African states' foreign relations, focusing on the negotiations with external actors in cases of peacekeeping missions. He previously worked as a project researcher for the United Nations University Institute on Comparative Regional Integration Studies (UNU-CRIS). He has since been working in different peacekeeping missions in west Africa. Emmanuel edited, with Timothy Shaw and Vanessa Tang, the volume *Comparative regionalisms for development in the 21st century: insights from the global South* published by Ashgate in 2013.

Jonathan Fisher is a lecturer in the International Development Department, University of Birmingham. His research focuses on the place of Africa in the international system and how regional and international relationships are managed and mediated by African states and leaders. He is particularly interested in eastern Africa and security and has published a range of articles on Uganda (*African Affairs* 2012; *Third World Quarterly* 2014), Kenya (*Journal of Modern African Studies* 2013) and the Great Lakes (*Conflict, Security and Development* 2013). Between 2010 and 2012 he was involved in a donor-funded study of the 2011 Ugandan elections and from 2013–14 was an Honorary Research Fellow in the Foreign and Commonwealth Office's Africa Directorate. He is currently writing a book on state-building in Uganda.

Julia Gallagher is a lecturer in the Department of Politics and International Relations, Royal Holloway, University of London. Julia's research focuses on Africa in international politics, and particularly on ideas of Africa and of the international. Her first book, *Britain and Africa under Blair: in pursuit of the good state* (Manchester University Press) was published in 2011, and she has published in *African Affairs*, *Millennium*, the *Review of International Studies* and *International Theory*. Julia is currently writing a book exploring Zimbabwean ideas of the international.

Georgina Holmes is a lecturer in International Relations at the University of Portsmouth, an honorary research associate in the Department of Politics and International Relations at Royal Holloway, University of London and a visiting lecturer in the Centre for Gender, Culture and Development in the National University of Rwanda. Georgina received her BA and MA in Interdisciplinary Gender Studies from the University of Warwick, before completing her PhD in International Relations at SOAS in 2010. She is the author of *Rwandan Women and War: Gender, Media and the Representation of Genocide*, published by IB Tauris in 2014.

Wanja Kimani is a visual artist, writer and researcher with an MA in Human Rights from the University of Essex. Current research interests lie between art and politics in the Horn of Africa, particularly Ethiopia where she is based and engaged in documenting contemporary art. Her work has been featured in international exhibitions in Africa, Asia, Europe and the USA and is featured in private and corporate collections.

George Ogola is a senior lecturer in the School of Journalism and Media, University of Central Lancashire, Preston. He has published widely on the political economy of the media in Africa, (African) popular culture and the impact of new media on the broader media ecology in the developing world. He is also interested in how ICTs address questions of power and democratisation in Africa. His latest book (co-edited with Peter Anderson and Michael Williams) called *The Future of Quality Journalism: A Cross-Continental Study* was published in 2013 by Routledge.

Clare Paine holds an ESRC-funded MPhil from Aberystwyth University and currently works for Christian Aid. She is interested in the intersection between discourses of international development and the resurgence of traditional authorities in sub-Saharan Africa, and has carried out extensive fieldwork in northern Uganda.

Anne Schumann received her PhD from the School of Oriental and African Studies, University of London in 2011 with a dissertation on the political and social dynamics of popular music in Abidjan, Côte d'Ivoire. Since 2012 she has worked as a postdoctoral fellow at the University of the Witwatersrand in Johannesburg, South Africa. Her research interests include African popular culture and the interaction between digital technologies, popular music, and cultural entrepreneurship.

Foreword

One should be thankful to Julia Gallagher for this project on *Image and Africa*. The title is a programme on the creation, negotiation, and subversion of images. The introduction dwells on the complexity and politics of image, collectively known in the profession as 'imagology', a strange concept that refers to the technique and aims of representation. What is an image? It brings to mind the concept of representation. Should one consult everyday dictionaries, to represent is to picture, to portray, and to delimit by rendering an image. But, in actuality, the representation is a symbol of something else. It stages something, and describes, in words and symbols, a projection, deliberately created. The questions that recur throughout the book are: how has it been created, and by whom?

This book presents a critique of a more traditional approach, represented for example by my own book, *The Invention of Africa* (1988). Its key argument is about the significance of 'the outside world and African images' and the idea of images as spaces of motivation in dialogues. It does this, first, by presenting, across its contributions, a critical ethnography of the processes that produce images, from within news offices to state houses, from party headquarters to artists' studios. In doing this it provides an analysis of representations motivated by local policies and their structural references, and the complexity of the African presence in the world, revealing how images of Africa are inscribed internationally.

The contributions themselves come from a remarkable variety of disciplines, and the international dimension of the project can be seen from the list of contributors. One could regroup them into three sections. There are, after the introduction theorising the very concept of image by Dr Gallagher, contributions that dwell on the process of imaging. These conceptual contributions include a chapter by George Ogola on what it would mean to construct an image of the continent of Africa; one by Mel Bunce about the struggles between African and foreign journalists over the representation of images of Africa, which qualifies itself as a new way of storytelling – in actuality, narratives; and a chapter by Jonathan Fisher on the political management of images for the benefit of foreign donors.

The second tranche concentrates on case studies. They include Emmanuel Fanta's work on Ethiopia's images, then Clare Paine's chapter on Acholi in Uganda, Anne Schumann's on Ivoirian electoral politics, and Georgina Holmes' on the eastern DRC. These contributions themselves bring together success and failure stories, addressing the competitive interests of international donors and investors, as well as the internal contradictions that together give birth to a plethora of images on a wide canvas, externalising political contest to address and shape the perceptions of outsiders, from donors to diasporas.

A third group discusses projects that reflect themselves in the editor's theorising Introduction, and include Wanja Kimani's 'Re-imagining Ethiopia', and then, Lizzy Attree on representations of the body in South African literature, fiction, and films. It is thus at the level of individual artists and authors that we are returned to larger questions about agency and relationships.

Throughout, one notices the strong originality of the argument. It resides in the attention paid to representations by African administrations and African actors, including political parties, militia groups and individual artists and authors. A number of case studies (Uganda, Rwanda, Kenya, Ethiopia, DRC, Côte d'Ivoire) dwell on the specific management of representations and the procedures for selling them to international donors. One should also note the importance accorded to the dialectic between types of African political authority (traditional and modern) and the politics of integration in the wider world.

Indeed, one reads these contributions from a background. It relates three main spaces. The fundamental space, which is dominant and at the same time very discreet, concerns the interrelation between processes of production and the social relations that explain the representations. A second space is political. It is present in descriptions, and one can see the correlations between the organisation of production within societies, and its impact on social relations. And, finally the book itself comes to represent in actuality a third space, by establishing the correlations between an intellectual background and concrete disciplinary practices.

The model is known. It can be linked to an intellectual Marxian tradition. The book actualises in effect such a capacity through figures, judgements, registrations, and the visibility of effects, according to the tension between what is true versus its negation, what is good versus what is bad, and what is a beautiful image versus a negative one.

A careful reading of the complementarity of angles and chapters made me go back to Michel Foucault's idea of uncovering a specificity in terms of an archaeology of knowledge. This is an unexpected key to a way of facing the project. You ask yourself how different elements and entries are organised in this analysis, from the existent chapters and their groupings. Then you look at variations and ways of applying rules from different disciplines. One does that through concepts and viewpoints about the origin and manipulation and evolution of images, thus, facing the complexity of subordination reflexes.

These are points of entry that lead one to understand the complexity and the diversity of this contribution and its powerful originality in presenting today's images of Africa.

Gallagher's project from London reflects, in my mind, that of Dietrich and Marlene Rall about images of Mexico in Germany, *Mira que si nos miran: imágenes de México en la literatura de lengua alemana del siglo XX* (Universidad Nacional Autónoma de México, 2003). Three main thematics impose themselves. One, representations from voyage diaries; two, images of Chiapas in German and Mexican narratives; and three, alterity and interculturality, including perceptions of Germans in Mexico. The two books meet and testify to what is our present day world, intercultural, and acknowledging and transcending preconceptions, frontiers, thanks to images.

V. Y. Mudimbe
Duke University, Durham, NC
11 April 2014

Preface

Chinua Achebe, in his essay, 'An Image of Africa', discusses the Western desire (and need) to depict Africa as the antithesis of Europe. He illustrates it in a withering critique of Joseph Conrad's *Heart of Darkness*, a book that projects an entirely European image of Africa, one that fails to see or engage with Africa, but merely confirms existing notions of Africa as '"the other world", the antithesis of Europe and therefore of civilization, a place where man's vaunted intelligence and refinement are finally mocked by triumphant bestiality' (*An Image of Africa*, 1983: 3).

The way in which images of Africa are put to such uses has a long pedigree, as V. Y. Mudimbe has discussed in his influential book, *The Invention of Africa*, and it continues for many in the West to dominate depictions of the continent as corrupt, malnourished, full of diseased children, conflict and crime, from internet scams to piracy. In such an analysis, it seems that outsiders – once travellers, missionaries, anthropologists and colonial officials; now development agencies, well-meaning pop stars and foreign journalists – are the chief shapers of African image, while African agents are passive or impotent.

One way to challenge this idea would be to write about Africans' images of themselves and their countries and continent – as Daniel Mengara does in his book *Images of Africa*. Such a project would involve replacing 'artificial', imposed images of the continent with 'authentic', home-grown ones.

This book, however, takes a different path, exploring the ways that image is created through relationships between Africans and the wider world. It challenges the idea that Africans are powerless in the creation of self-image. It explores the ways in which image creation is a process of negotiation entered into by a wide range of actors within and beyond the continent. And it examines the extent to which images, once created, take on a life of their own, coming to shape realities underneath. In doing this, the book is an attempt to challenge the ideas behind either a purely Western or a purely African invention of image.

The book began life as a collection of papers for the European Conference of African Studies in 2011. The ambition was very loose: it was simply to bring together scholars from different disciplines around a concept and see what happened. It worked. We had contributions on politics, media, art and literature, exploring between them images of the continent, of regions and countries, and of individuals, from African and European scholars. Alongside various theoretical and disciplinary approaches, we found fascinating themes in common, largely relating to the ways in which images are created within the tensions of relationships, between elites and grassroots in Africa and beyond. It was evident that the theme of image was propelling a wide range of rich work on Africa. We decided to continue to pool ideas, and this book is the outcome of two years of discussion, writing and reflection.

It has been a tremendously enjoyable process, thanks largely to the energy and creativity of the contributors. The first chapter – which outlines the theoretical framework for the book – developed out of those early discussions and subsequent 'conversations' between a range of fascinating research projects. It is a response to many ideas, and has been strengthened by the juxtaposition of rich work in many different African contexts, and from different disciplinary perspectives. One of the great delights of seeing a project grow in this way is the unpredictability of it. It has been organic, a creation achieved between ten people, all engaged in different research projects, rather than the outcome of an original conception.

I am extremely grateful to Professor Mudimbe who has generously supported the project throughout, and contributed the Foreword to this book. Others have helped along the way, especially Laura Routley and Stephen Chan, as well as the anonymous reviewers who provided many thoughtful and helpful suggestions for improvement. Thank you to my university, Royal Holloway, which supported the work with a grant, and to the superbly professional team at Manchester University Press.

Julia Gallagher
London
April 2014

Theorising image: a relational approach

Julia Gallagher

This book is about images of Africa – how they are produced, by whom and for what purposes; and about how they are understood. These questions are fraught because of the continent's relationship with the wider world, particularly the European world, which for many years assumed the right to create images of Africa, in fiction, travel writing, anthropological research, maps, missionary accounts, colonial records and reports produced by aid agencies. Since the middle of the twentieth century, when the majority of African states began to move towards independence, this domination of image has been challenged by those who argue that Africans should reappropriate their own images and restore their authenticity.

But images of Africa never have been, and never could be, owned in either of these ways because the point of an image is communication. Image is relational – a co-creation of those whom it represents, and those who are trying to understand the representation. Without engagement from both parties, an image is pointless. Image is subjective, yes, but it is subject to both sides of a relationship.

This is not to say that images cannot be manipulated, and do not serve some interests or damage others. The creation and negotiation of images of Africa in the wider world has usually been achieved on an uneven playing field. Moreover, when it comes to creating images of a continent containing fifty-four countries and more than a billion people, there is going to be a lot of competition as to who gets a hand in the shaping. Therefore part of this story is about the ways in which image is created, negotiated and subverted within relationships between actors in Africa and the wider world; and another part is about the diversity and contests over image that happen within Africa itself.

In order to get into these difficult questions about the role of ownership, power and manipulation in image, I am going to begin with a BBC debate entitled 'Should Africa employ lobbyists?' (2011), which asked whether creating particular images of the continent's countries was a useful or a damaging deception. Writing in favour of brand management in the case of the Democratic Republic of Congo, PR consultant Joel Frushone argued:

> For countless reasons, including a label of 'rape capital of the world', an unheralded position near the top of Transparency International's most corrupt nations rankings and more than four million lives lost during years of civil war, DR Congo badly needed to overhaul its reputation if it were to attract the development funds required to rebuild its shattered self. (Ibid)

On the other side of the argument, human rights campaigner Thor Halvorssen focused on the ways in which some African dictators use PR to hide and continue their abuses and crimes:

> '[R]eputation management' can be a euphemism of the worst sort. In many cases across Africa, it often means whitewashing the human rights violations of despotic regimes with fluff journalism and, just as easily, serving as personal PR agents for rulers and their corrupt family members. But they also help governments drown out criticism, often branding dissidents, democratic opponents and critics as criminals, terrorists or extremists. (Ibid)

This debate highlights a number of prevalent assumptions about image and Africa. First, it is clear on both sides of the argument that 'image' is conceived as being radically different from 'reality', beyond the assumption that image merely offers a surface or superficial depiction. Image for both is a deception: the difference between Frushone and Halverssen centres on whether the deception helps change reality, or merely covers it up. For Frushone, re-forming image might eventually enable the reordering of (a better) reality. The DRC is shattered, but by employing more positive images, it can create connections with the outer world that will help it to remake itself. For Halverssen, a false image is used to hide reality; the image is opaque, corrupt and its role is to keep the outside world in the dark, away from understanding and attempting to do something about 'the truth'. This leads to two further assumptions: first, that image is very powerful; and second, that image is malleable and can be controlled. Image can draw in aid, it can hide crime; potentially, an image can even change reality. Images can also be manipulated and changed. It therefore matters who controls them: African elites, who Frushone argues can use them to rebuild their country, or Western agents who, as Halverssen implies, can better promote the interests of 'ordinary' Africans? The debate is heated because of the power and malleability of image.

However, there is a contradiction at the heart of this debate. Its focus on image as controllable is at odds with the underlying and unexplored relational nature of image. It reinforces an idea of Africa outside the world, separate from its complex international relationships, where African actors can choose what to display. And yet, every conception of the image of the DRC – from its definition by international organisations as corrupt, to its reconstitution to 'hide' reality as a way to generate foreign aid – is shaped by its place in and relationships to the wider world. At its most minimal, the DRC's image is created in response to external demands and expectations. Pushing the idea further, image is a product of relationships between the place, the people being imaged, and those on the outside who are engaging with them. Image, presented in the BBC debate as something created by particular actors, should rather be viewed as something jointly created between actors on both sides of a relationship.

According to even the baldest dictionary definition (these are drawn from the *Shorter Oxford English Dictionary*), 'image' comes from two directions. First, it is an expression of a thing, or its counterpart; a copy, symbol, emblem, representation, type, typical example or embodiment. It is an approximate account of the thing – an 'artificial imitation' for instance – but it emanates from it and is shaped by its relation to it. Second, though, an image is something held in the mind of an outsider or observer: it is a mental picture or impression; an idea, or a conception. In other words, an image is characterised both by its (imperfect) connection to the thing – its artificiality, its imitative quality – and by its existence in the imagination of an other – as an idea, conception, or mental picture. Image, when you get down to it, is something that is shaped between a thing and its observer: it is a product of the relationship between the two.

In the context of countries and continents, the story is far more complex. The DRC is not a 'thing', but rather it is many 'things', and also nothing. The many actors and bodies comprising the 'thing' engage, in various ways, with actors and bodies beyond it. Creating a unity of such a 'thing' is particularly artificial, contingent and malleable.

This book is an attempt to think about these complex images of Africa in relational terms. The authors explore questions about the agency of the various actors involved in image creation – state elites, journalists, local leaders, political parties, militia groups, artists and authors – and their relation to ideas, actors and forces beyond Africa. For all of them, image is certainly both malleable and important. By starting with image, and by treating it as relational, we aim to examine the power of image to shape both the thing and the observer, as well as the relationship between the two.

The purpose of this chapter is to outline a theoretical approach to image, based on the idea that it is relational. I am interested in exploring ideas of image in art and how these can be brought to bear on an understanding of image in politics. I do this, first, by discussing various ideas about image, from maps to brands and masks. Second, I draw on the works of Achille Mbembe and Jean-François Bayart which address the complex juxtaposition of image between those it represents and those who consume it within political relationships. Third, I discuss these ideas in relation to a piece of sculpture, *Scramble for Africa* by Yinka Shonibare. This depiction of the Berlin Conference establishes an ambiguous image of Africa and Europe as intertwined in the 'creation' of the continent. Finally, I offer some conclusions on the relational nature of image and also introduce the rest of the book, outlining how these ideas are developed and illustrated in the chapters that follow.

A schematic history of images of Africa: maps, brands and masks

For centuries the dominant European image of Africa was an outline scattered with a few peripheral cities and ports, with roads leading to a dark, dangerous and exciting interior. Rumours of slave traders, cannibalism and peculiar fetish rituals gripped European audiences from the time of Heroditus to the accounts of adventurers, traders and missionaries into the eighteenth and nineteenth centuries (Mudimbe, 1994). The map outline was far from enlightening, rather its apparent opacity presented an image of a shadowy, barely-grasped world, one that invited projected fantasies of horror and adventure. It was this sense of the 'dark continent' that particularly exercised Western imaginations as they constructed the alter-ego to European enlightenment (Achebe, 1983; Mudimbe, 1994). Images of Africa seemed to serve as a way for Europeans to help make sense of themselves.

In 1884–5, European powers gathered in Berlin to get a grip on Africa, both literally, in the carving up of the continent between them, and figuratively, in the new image they had created of a continental map. The undefined interior was now filled in. The shapes of various countries and domains were fixed, the continent's mysteries were made visible. The map of Africa was an exercise in which Europe put itself into Africa and attempted to illuminate it, to make it clear, clean, bright and good, possibly in an attempt to control and subdue anxieties about its own projected irrationality (Bhabha, 2004).

Maps are images that describe or represent a place as closely as they possibly can. The image they create is ostensibly scientific – drawing on data collected by explorers and cartographers – and rational – aimed at making a place clear, open, navigable. As well as being rational and instrumental, maps are also prescriptive images, a 'formal ensemble of abstract places' that squeeze out interpretation and story-telling (Certeau, 1984: 121). They require the reader to master the language and skills of map-reading, to bend their own idea of a place to that of the map-maker. Maps seem to say: I must be understood as my maker intended, otherwise I will not be understood at all. Maps demand that the viewer enters into the world of the maker or she will literally be lost.

This map had enormous effects on Africa. Its shapes defied local cultural, linguistic and religious rationalities as foreign governments put in alien ideas, rules and 'traditions' that came to determine the continent's politics, culture and history. The European image of Africa was artificial and constraining, it subverted and twisted the thing it represented by forcing it to fit an idealised European image.

It is a rejection of a 'European' Africa that has animated much of the thinking about images of Africa since the colonial period, leading to demands that Africans reclaim management of image in order to restore authenticity. Daniel Mengara makes this argument in the introduction to his book, *Images of Africa: stereotypes and realities*, in which he states: 'Clearly the Africa that we know or hear about today is, essentially, a European-made Africa' (2001: 8). The foreign manufacture of Africa's image means that Africa 'has been able to offer to the mirror of the world only a pale reflection of its true self' (Ibid: 11). Mengara argues that the only way to reclaim the 'authentic' Africa is to 'deconstruct' the effects of colonial systems, and he calls for a 'peeling away of this legacy in order to reveal the true essence of the African world' (Ibid: 12).

Mengara argues for a rebalancing of image by assigning it a different ownership through which it will achieve authenticity. In doing so, he implicitly buys into a rational, prescriptive conception of image: it is still defined by who owns it. Africans, instead of outsiders, get to draw the map and make up the rules of how it should be navigated. This approach to image underwrites much conventional thinking in IR and foreign policy analysis, and has been described by Robert Jervis in his seminal book, *The Logic of Images in International Relations*. He argues that the creation and projection of image is a tool available to state elites, providing them with a particularly cheap way to achieve foreign policy objectives. He describes his approach as one of framing 'the foundations of a theory of deception in international relations' (1989: 10). The image may well not be a representation of the 'real', but a deliberate concoction designed to confuse or dissemble. Jervis deals with this process on the level of rational state elites, and conforms to a conventional IR approach that assumes that such actors control states as units involved in a game in which each unit plays its hand as best it can, given its own objectives and the partial information it possesses about the other units. Deception is a particularly useful tool in the game.

More recent work on branding in IR builds on this premise, providing another way to play Jervis's 'game'. As reflected in the BBC debate, many governments spend large sums on branding strategies to try to improve or shift their international image. Country brands are created to project specific images – the peace-loving nation, the fiscally prudent investment bet, the slightly unpredictable powerhouse – designed to achieve desired foreign policy objectives (van Ham, 2001). Creating particular images is seen as an effective way to control or at least direct international 'consumption', that is, the way in which other states calculate how best to deal with you.

African governments have engaged in marketing for many years, partly in a bid to wrest their image from outsiders. Newly independent African states employed Western PR firms to help improve their image (one is described in Chinua Achebe's 1968 novel, *A Man of the People*). The South African and Rhodesian regimes employed PR companies throughout the 1970s to help them overcome negative international images that associated them with racism and internal conflict, with some success (Manheim and Albritton, 1987). More recently, African governments have attempted to create 'brand personalities', devoting hefty resources to promoting them in the attempt to win investment, tourism and aid. Thus, South Africa is 'Alive with possibilities' (Opoku and Hinson, 2006); Uganda is 'Gifted by nature' (Kahn, 2006); and in 2004 Nigeria was the 'Heart of Africa' (Nworah, 2006) but has more recently become a 'Good people great nation' (Adebola *et al*, 2012).

But there are difficulties with this way of thinking about image. It rests on the problematic fantasies of control and authenticity. Control is expressed by the map, an image that defines the thing in a prescriptive way that can only be understood using the language of the map-maker. Discussions of brands likewise imply that images can be created and projected by state elites, more or less well depending on their skill at playing the 'game'. Authenticity is a reaction to this, the notion that an image can be made closer to the thing if its past is wiped out, if it is de-Europeanised and returned to its rightful authors. The problem with fantasies of control and authenticity is their ontological individualism, the denial of the relational nature of image. They imply that image can be self-generated. Whether image is created by external colonial authorities, or by African political elites, the process is limited, prescriptive and essentially static. This immediately leads to two challenges. First, images are limited by their credibility: how far can we push a particular image in the face of contradictory ideas, or an engrained image already held by others? On the most superficial level, for example, Nigeria is widely perceived as highly corrupt and badly managed, its image 'battered before the world' (Adebola *et al*, 2012: 426). There is only so much that the government can do to counteract this because the evidence and prejudices of the world is against a substantial change. The image of Nigeria is something that must comprise ideas and content from both inside and outside, the realities, desires and prejudices of each. Second, at a deeper level, ideas of 'authenticity' posit a self that exists outside its relation to others. Feeding on ideas of overcoming history and an implicit individualism, it seeks to remove Europe from Africa, setting up an alternative author of control. But image cannot be purely generated by the self, the 'thing', it must comprise expectations already formed of it and already existing in the wider world or it will only ever be alien and peripheral.

A different type of image – a mask – might help us to look at this rather differently. Masks present an overtly fabricated, distorted idea of the person underneath to the outside world. The particular potency of a mask comes from the way it both embodies the barriers between the person wearing it and the observer, and helps mediate between the two. To some extent it conveys what the wearer wants it to. The mask is designed to hide the 'reality' beneath, and project a distorted or idealised representation. However, if masks are to resonate, to connect in a meaningful way to the observer, they must also become imbued with her fantasies and desires. The observer must recognise something true in the mask, and in order for this to happen, she needs to put something of herself into it. The fact that masks are an artifice is clear on one level to everyone; their ability to convey deeper meanings is only made possible by the complicity of both wearer and observer in a collective suspension of disbelief. Both parties must make an investment.

Writing about masking ceremonies in Côte d'Ivoire, Sasha Newell describes the way in which men put on masks to 'perform as supernatural beings (ancestors, forest spirits, deities) for women and children, who at least pretend not to know that the beings before them are their own husbands, fathers, and brothers, wearing costumes in order to deceive them' (2013: 140). The audience and the wearers of the masks all enter into the idea that the theatre is real, that spirits have come among them. 'Everyone acts as though the masks were real creatures, even though everyone knows it is a human production, and by virtue of that, the mask takes on real, non-human powers' (Ibid: 143). Newell suggests that the masks cannot do their work unless they are able to embody the projections both of the wearer and the observer. This involves the imagination and fantasies of each which, together, give them a deeper significance than that contained in their mere materiality.

Masks provide a compelling account of image because they illustrate one of its key characteristics, that it is jointly created and negotiated as part of a relationship, carrying the thoughts and desires of both those who initiate and those who receive. This is possible because of the social context in which masking ceremonies are performed. The people involved share an understanding in which they agree that masks are to be imbued in this way. This understanding of image then demands a public space. For images of Africa in the wider world, such an understanding demands a global public space. Such a space – so large, diverse and riven with power imbalances – is necessarily going to raise further complexities and qualifications to the notion of image. I will begin to address this idea in the next section, and it is a notion that runs implicitly throughout the rest of the book.

A relational approach to image

Image as understood so far straddles the interface between underlying 'truth' and outlying expectation. But the chapters in this book all begin from the assumption that this straddling is not neutral. This can be approached by exploring three levels or planes involved in thinking about image. First, there is the inner level, the self or the 'thing'; then there is the image of the self that encircles it; finally, beyond the image is the outer level, the other. None of the three planes are fixed, all are related to and affect each other. The image acts like a contact plate between the other two, the site on which each negotiates itself in relation to the other. But the image is not a passive site of negotiation, it appears to have autonomy or a life of its own because it profoundly affects both inner and outer levels. To think like this is to treat image as an encapsulation of the 'thing' that somehow gathers fragments and gives them a shape. The shape, as we have seen, is necessarily contingent and artificial but it becomes our shorthand for seeing and understanding the 'thing'.

How are the thing, the image and the outsider related to each other? Two conceptual perspectives can be brought to bear on this question: Achille Mbembe's work on the visible and the invisible (2001); and Jean-François Bayart's theory of extraversion (2000). Mbembe, in a discussion of the role of image in Camaroonian politics, describes the image as endowing the reality beneath it with rich meanings drawn from the imagination of onlookers:

> [T]he invisible was not only the other side of the visible, its mask or its substitute. The invisible was in the visible, and vice versa, not as a matter of artifice, but as *one and the same*, and as external reality simultaneously – as the image of the thing and the imagined thing, at the same time … To the extent that there was no representation of the real world without a relation to the world of the invisible (and hence without relation to a ghost), the image could not but be the visible and constructed form of something that had always to conceal itself – a reality that the often widely used categories of *fantasy* or '*double*' must fail adequately to comprehend. Because the image referred, endlessly, to the multiple and simultaneous functions of life itself, it was, in autochthonous thought, charged with disturbing powers. (2001: 145–6)

This passage describes how the observer sees the invisible inside the visible image. The observer endows the image with far richer meaning, putting into it its own creation of the 'invisible' and the 'imagined', 'bring[ing] to life the thing for which the image was a metaphor' (Newell, 2013: 143). For Mbembe, the outside world projects all sorts of imagined fantastical depths onto the image and ascribes to it 'disturbing powers'. Image thus becomes at least as much about the ideas, desires and fantasies of the other as a depiction of the self.

He goes on to explore how autochthonous notions of power and image inform modern Cameroonian political life. In a discussion of critical cartoons of President Paul Biya, Mbembe explores the extent to which, despite the cartoonist's attempts to 'exorcise' the magic of the autocrat, he instead manages to increase his 'omni-presence', adding to his 'pile of magics' (Mbembe, 2001: 155). As a result, the autocrat manages to:

> abolish and maintain distance at one and the same time, since he is both remote and close, the obverse and the reverse, that 'something' that *is present for us* not only because it is displayed and we experience it – *we experience the thing* – but, more decisively, because it is the very thing of our *experience*: tangible, palpable, and visible, but at the same time secret and distant – in short, a 'non-localized universal presence'. (Ibid: 153, original italics)

Similar notions of image saturate west African artistic traditions. In Western traditions, writes Nooter, art is for display, to be analysed, to impart information; it is open, displayed in galleries and on walls, meant to be grasped. In contrast, African 'art' is meant to remain mysterious, ambiguous; it is deliberately kept hidden:

> Meaning is elusive, in part because secret knowledge is organic, always in the process of change, and also because its interpretation will vary ... . No matter what level of initiation you may have achieved ... your particular understanding of that knowledge will differ from another's (Nooter, 1993: 57).

Writing about Côte d'Ivoirian Baule art, Vogel highlights the importance of keeping objects hidden inside houses, wrapped in blankets. This is part of an approach that sees the materiality of the objects as superficial and secondary: it is the way in which the observer remembers and imagines the object that conveys its essence. Because the objects are rarely seen, mental images of them are paramount. Night, darkness and obscurity are part of this, and not to be regretted (in sharp contrast to the Enlightenment European approach to art which demands light, exposure, transparency):

> Obscurity is both accepted as a normal inconvenience and experienced as positive, useful, and pleasurable ... It constitutes an alternative domain, a medium. Night and darkness provide a way of knowing and experiencing in which *understanding is actually deepened by ambiguity and fed by imagination and memory* (Vogel, 1997: 74, my italics).

Vogel also writes:

> The incompletely seen objects of the Baule suggest that there are ways to experience art that require a more active collaboration between artists and observer than will be familiar to many Westerners. Memory and imagination are central to this experience; the viewer's mind supplies what is visually withheld, creating lasting images to satisfy its own tastes, moods, desires, and psyche' (Ibid: 72).

In a similar way, Mbembe's description of the African autocrat presents an image that is incomplete, fluid and intangible. Its potency – and in Vogel's terms, the degree to which it is understood – lies in the way it carries the ideas and fantasies of the onlooker and the degree to which they internalise it and carry it around inside themselves (Mbembe, 2001: 156).

Mbembe is describing images of an African autocrat, and in particular the ways in which his subjects create his image. Although his image is about their fantasies, he holds the upper hand. Even if image is more about the other's preconceptions, it can still serve the self. There is perhaps a conscious playing by the autocrat on the subjects' fantasies. However, when Mbembe turns to images of Africa created in the West, his perspective shifts, and image becomes emasculating, its 'special feature is to be nothing at all' (Mbembe, 2001: 4). Here his ideas about image are more in line with those of Mengara, arguing that the West's preoccupations come to define African images, and do so in ways that flatten and disempower. This could be a question of balance, or the-mutual investment in the image. As with Côte d'Ivoirian traditions of masking and art, there is an acceptance of mutual creation and the complicity in a suspended disbelief – what Newell calls 'public secrets' (2013: 144) – in the domestic example, whereas this may be much weaker in the relationship between Africans and Westerners.

However, it may be possible to overplay the lopsidedness of Western agency in the creation of images of Africa. This is an area Bayart tackles in his work on extraversion. Here he presents both a slightly shifted idea of image creation, and an exploration of the effects of the image on the African state, or the 'inside'. Here, the image is designed for external consumption, calculated to please. It is both more consciously crafted and projected, and exposed, or 'extraverted'. Although shaped within the constraints of disparate power balances, it can work in favour of the weaker protagonist. Bayart at first appears to separate ideas of the surface, or image, and the real. He argues that the difference between them is deliberately created by African elites in order to better reflect external expectations. He describes the surface idea as 'institutions and nodes of power which are tantamount to a décor of *trompe l'oeil*' (Bayart, 2000: 29) and he discusses the difference between the '*pays legal*, a legal structure which is the focus of attention for multilateral donors and Western states, and … a *pays reèl*, where real power is wielded. In extreme cases this duplication can lead to the existence of a hidden structure which surrounds, or even controls, the official occupant of the presidential throne' (Ibid: 229–30).

Bayart underplays the (perhaps unconscious) Western understanding of the *pays reèl*, the extent to which its hidden qualities are recognised, if only obscurely, as part of the subliminal image. The veneer created by strategies of extraversion could be viewed as a cover for the 'public secret' – after all, it plays right into European fantasies of the 'dark continent' – enjoyed by both subjects and observers in the creation of African image, but he does not explore this aspect.

Bayart's next step is to lay out the way in which the *pays legal* acts to create a form of governmentality. Part of the African 'self', is, in Bayart's depiction, always in and of the world:

> The ideological and cultural relationship which sub-Saharan Africa has with the rest of the world is profoundly baroque. It proceeds by re-using existing practices, or by juxtaposing them; by processes of sedimenta-tion, transfers of meaning and the manufacture of identities which are

subsequently deemed authentic. The effects of hybridization are all the more ambivalent in that they take place directly in the realm of the imagination. In this respect, the relationship of Africa and overseas remains rooted in simple fantasy ... . We hasten to add that the imagination (*imaginaire*) is not to be understood as that which is 'unreal', but rather as 'the domain in which the real and the unreal become indistinguishable from one another'. (Ibid: 251–2)

While the image presented to the outside world is in a sense false, it also creates what is real, what is inside. So here is a very powerful reinforcement of the idea of the straddling image as controlling and shaping both the outside world's perceptions, but ultimately also the inner world's reality.

For Mbembe and Bayart, image is deeply impregnated with the ideas and preoccupations of the internal and external worlds, and at the same time acts upon them. Mbembe's image is potent because it is partially hidden, 'wrapped in blankets' like the Baule artefacts. It is powerful because it is fleshed out by the observer; it appears to suck her in. If the image was held up to the light, it would lose its power. Bayart's far more instrumentalist understanding of image has it deliberately crafted and exposed. Instead of drawing the observer in, it has been shaped around her notions, prepackaged and ready for consumption. While Mbembe's leader, who looks inwards towards his people, is glimpsed, mysterious, Bayart's state looks to the outside world, presenting to it a smooth exterior; plausible, persuasive, complete. For Mbembe, the image is a conduit for outsiders' fantasies, and yet the image can project power onto the self. For Bayart, the self creates a false image to project onto the world, but the image ends up shaping the self, perhaps in unexpected ways.

Both Bayart and Mbembe support the idea that the person being imaged derives power from the image, even if they are also shaped and to an extent controlled by it. Moreover, this power can be exercised in conscious and unconscious ways; certainly Mbembe's work can be understood in conjunction with Freudian ideas of the uncanny in which unconscious feelings and fantasies are projected onto an other who is then encountered as strange and alien, appearing to possess supernatural powers or malevolent intent (Freud, 2003). It is also possible, as I have suggested, that the mask-like quality of Bayart's extraverted image works because it is understood as such, and invested in, by Western observers too.

Image, therefore, is significant not just as a way into understanding or seeing something, but as a shaper and site of negotiation between inside and outside. Image faces both ways, conveys different meanings outside and back in. Yet at the same time, it must encompass shared ground. It also shifts and changes, is pulled and pushed from both sides.

An exploration of image through sculpture

I now want to illustrate this relational idea of image creation through a discussion of Yinka Shonibare's sculpture, *Scramble for Africa* (2003), a depiction of the Berlin Conference of 1884–5. Contemporary accounts of Berlin depict a room full of white, bearded, frock-tailed diplomats gathered around a map of the continent, assessing how it should best be divided (Pakenham, 2001). It is a historical moment that suggests the total subjection of a continent to foreign powers which, thousands of miles away, determine the fate of several million people with pens, rulers and the idea of reaching a civilised agreement within the rules of European power games. It also conjures up the process by which the 'blank space' within the outline of the continent's map was filled in. European diplomats put themselves into the outline, the particular vanity being that they were thus animating it and making it real.

In Shonibare's sculpture, twelve men are seated on mahogany chairs around a table bearing the famous map. They are engaged in lively, perhaps tense discussion. The figure at the top of the table is making a point, dramatically underlined by his raised arm and pointing finger. Some sit with arms folded or hands clasped – are they in agreement? Some lean back or even away from the table – perhaps they are marginalised players? The figure at the bottom end of the table is angrily about to get to his feet – perhaps he disagrees with the point being made? His neighbours put their hands on him to restrain him, apparently trying to keep the peace.

Of course none of this is what first strikes the viewer because two jarring features confront her immediately. First, the figures are headless, their necks smoothly ending as they emerge from their frock-coats. This does nothing to detract from the animation of the figures who are expressive, but expressionless. They have been uncannily deracinated. Without colour or facial features, these figures possess an indeterminate identity. Second, this unnerving feature is further reinforced by the fact that Shonibare's figures are dressed in a variety of brightly coloured, loudly patterned Java prints. The fabrics of orange, green, blue, purple, yellow and gold suggest Africanness rather than the expected black clothes of nineteenth-century European gentlemen. Are these figures actually European at all?

This is part of Shonibare's point. Java prints are not of African origin, but were first produced in Dutch Indonesia and imported to west Africa, part of a wider European cloth manufacturers' competition for African markets. As Christopher Steiner explains, these markets were lucrative and competitive, and the European cloth makers worked hard to try to represent an Africanness that would appeal to their consumers, leading to a 'back and forth process in which European textile producers responded to African desires, and in which African consumers reacted to European stylistic and commercial proffers' (1985: 91). The success of the fabrics, he argues, suggests that the manufacturers achieved a far more subtle interpretation and image of Africa than that found in the European travel, missionary and official literatures. These prints are now worn throughout the continent and have come to represent an authentic 'Africanness', seeming to outsiders to encapsulate a vibrant, multiply-coloured, exotic continent. Shonibare, in using Java fabric, thus plays with ideas about authenticity. As Anthony Downey suggests, his work is about the 'fabrication' of Africanness (2004: 31).

The headless figures and the Java prints are Shonibare's hallmark and his wider work also explores the themes of authenticity and fabrication. Okwui Enwezor has suggested that the work challenges two stereotypes. The first is the 'colonial fantasy' of the separation between European civilisation and African barbarity: the use of 'African fabrics' upsets the idea of an 'arms' length relationship', putting the 'unsavoury elements within the midst' of European scenes (1997: 11). Shonibare expresses the tension between European fantasies of the dark continent, their attempts to subdue them through the drafting of a scientific, rational map, and the inevitable failure of this attempt at creating distance. The second idea that Shonibare unsettles is an Afrocentric desire for cultural authenticity, and a widespread lack of understanding of the 'problematic site of cultural appropriation', its inevitable hybridity (Ibid).

These echo two approaches to image creation I outlined earlier, namely the European ideas of a purely self-generated image created by state actors for external consumption; and the notion that African images have been created purely by outsiders and need to be reclaimed and shaped along properly African lines. The European vanity rests on the notion that the individual is self-determining, her challenge is only how to convey herself to the outside world. The Africanist fantasy is that of a de-Europeanised, 'authentic' Africanness.

Shonibare's sculpture expresses the embededness, implication and mutual constitution of Africa and Europe. It is assembled of bits from inside and outside the continent, the Victorian gentlemen on their mahogany chairs, the representation of diplomacy and discussion, subverted by apparently African fabrics. In the end, who can tell where Africa starts and Europe ends: the two are inseparable, each appropriating and re-projecting the other. The image – the map, perhaps – of Africa is a creation achieved within the relationship.

However, for me the most dramatic feature of the sculpture is the headlessness of its figures. The depersonalisation of their headlessness puts the figures firmly into the past, stuck in a museum or fixed in time. They are animated, but they are also horribly static, like shop dummies or automatons. Looking at them, one can imagine Shonibare manipulating their limbs to give them the semblance of life. In fact, it is the process of creation, rather than the events of 1884–5, that dominate the viewer's interaction with the sculpture. The abrupt disjuncture between animated, life-scale bodies and absent heads won't let us suspend disbelief or imagine ourselves back into the Berlin Conference. Instead, our impressions focus on the collection and assembling of dummies, fabrics and furniture, their incongruence and artificiality.

There are aspects of this headlessness that speak to ideas about the relationality of image. On one level is the idea that the headless figures demand that we decide who they are and fill in the empty shoulders for ourselves. In this way, Shonibare's sculpture is an image that is constituted by everyone who looks at it: *Scramble for Africa* implicates its viewers in the division of the map. On another level, this idea is underlined by the uncanny feel of the sculpture, its horrible shop-dummy quality. Freud suggested that something is uncanny because it is both 'homelike' and 'unhomelike', familiar and strange (2003: 124). The unnerving, menacing characters of fiction or real experience are created by the projection of our own repressed fantasies that then appear to come from someone else. In this way the 'bogeyman' is particularly terrifying because he represents our own unacceptable fantasies and desires. The bogeyman is 'out to get us' and punish us for our own destructiveness. Freud argues that most particularly we experience this as the terror of being blinded or castrated. The viewer's fascination then with Shonibare's headless (or perhaps blinded or castrated) figures is due in part to her own relationship with it. Its ability to disturb is a measure of what she must put into it of herself, and that disturbance is a measure of the way in which it affects her idea of who she is.

Here then is an image that proceeds in stages and through the relationships between the events and people it depicts, the materials it is made up of, its artist and its viewers. It suggests a dynamic and involved idea of image-creation, one where many actors put parts of themselves into the image; and where 'authenticity', 'reality' and 'separation' are substantially undermined. Moreover, this image becomes a thing that reflects back on the actors themselves, disturbing preconceptions, reformulating self-image and identity.

Conclusions and introduction to the rest of the book

I have discussed ideas of images as maps – prescriptive, filled in with bits of Europe – and as masks – potent because they are constructed in viewers' imaginations and memories. I have argued that these relational ideas of image are more powerful and persuasive than the static approaches presented in International Relations literature on deception and branding. These emphasise the power of the subject or self in creating and projecting particular images, and fail to account for how image is shaped by the viewer. Their uses by those advocating an African ownership of image, while understandable in the context of the way foreigners have appeared to monopolise images of Africa, also fail to capture the relational aspect of image.

So what does a relational approach to image offer? First, it restores agency, but in a conditional, negotiated form, in which African actors have a role in image creation, but one that is continually moderated by its observers or consumers. Bayart's extraversion dwells on the fabrication of image for external consumption, a projection of something false that fits external preconceptions and desires. This is balanced by Mbembe's approach which sees image creation as a drawing in of the observer's fantasies, an introjection of something external. Together, Bayart and Mbembe depict a dynamic process in which image is the receptacle or holder of elements from both the inside/object and the outside/observer.

Second, this approach moves us beyond the valourised individual towards a more historically nuanced account of African images in the world. Image, in its relation to the self via the relation to the other resonates better with African conceptions of selfhood than the Western individual. I would also argue that this approach is one that applies beyond images of Africa and might be used more widely to understand the creation and role of image in IR more generally.

The chapters in this book draw in various ways on these ideas. Through nine sub-Saharan African case studies, the book explores image on a range of levels, beginning with the challenge of creating images of the whole continent, and moving on to the shaping of national images, of sub-national, regional and local images, and ending with images created by individuals of their communities and of themselves. Inevitably the question comes full circle back to the way in which these more dispersed images together create new ways of imagining the continent and its countries. Between them, the chapters explore the medium of image, image in the media (conventional and new), political images of countries, 'traditional authorities' and parties, NGOs and militia groups, and images created in art, literature and film.

The chapters broadly address a number of themes. First, a challenge to the idea that Africans are powerless in the creation of self-image. The authors explore different ways in which image creation is a process of negotiation entered into by a wide range of actors within and beyond the continent. Images of Africa thus reflect ideas and preoccupations from both the inside and the outside. Second, the contributors explore the extent to which images, once created, take on a life of their own, coming to shape the 'thing'. Image, we find again and again, is powerful in its ability to change what is underneath. Images, once created, can influence and alter Africa. Third, there are spaces within Africa for a variety of alternative images to emerge, and these often compete with and subvert 'official' images. Images are seen to emerge from a variety of relationships between actors in and beyond the continent.

The book opens by addressing the way in which the media creates images of the whole continent. George Ogola writes about the difficulties of setting up pan-African television networks that can encompass the continent, and explores the possibilities of alternative ways of conceiving the continent through more diffused images. He asks, how can 'Africa' be defined? Can political ideas of the continent – focusing on pan-Africanism, for example – do more than offer a static, flattened image? Ogola turns to the Africa served up by Nollywood, and suggests that its strength lies in its ability to convey many Africas that are open to interpretion by many observers. This disrupts fantasies of an organised, centralised control of image, and offers far richer and more resonant images of the continent.

Mel Bunce explores the processes of contestation and negotiation over the creation of images of Africa that are played out between foreign correspondents and African journalists in an international agency newsroom in Kenya. She looks particularly at the difference between insider and outsider representations of Africa, describing the conflicts between them and how these are resolved. A key theme here is the idea of attachment – Bunce explores the Western ideal of a detached reporter, and how this is challenged by local journalists with very different conceptions of how news should represent and shape events.

The next two chapters explore the ways in which African governments create images of their countries that conform to, or succeed in shifting donor expectations. Jonathan Fisher compares the ways in which the governments of Uganda, Rwanda and Kenya project their countries on the world stage, and in particular towards donors. He traces the effective strategies employed by the governments of Yoweri Museveni and Paul Kagame who have created images that are congenial to donor countries, comparing them with those of Mwai Kibaki and

Daniel Arap Moi who have been less successful. He explores how far these processes of extraversion have constrained or enabled the governments concerned.

Emmanuel Fanta explores similar efforts in Ethiopia, in particular the government's uses of 'bad' and disturbing images in pursuing its objectives in international engagement. He argues that the government has drawn on Western images of Africa to shape its relationship with donors, using ideas of mimicry and subversion. In a discussion of state failure, he describes how Meles Zenawi's government successfully manufactured an image that worked to unsettle and disturb, playing on guilt and fear to achieve its foreign policy objectives.

The subsequent two chapters look at images created by sub-state groups, again for, and in conjunction, with foreign consumers. Clare Paine discusses the creation of a 'traditional' authority in Uganda, describing the way in which an image of a traditional Ugandan kingship is revived and refurbished with support from Western donors. This process has involved a (not always successful) balancing act in which claims to authenticity based on 'tradition' are combined with assumptions about what a progressive NGO should look like. Paine's exploration of the relationship between image and culture leads to conclusions about the ways in which the subjectivity of both donors and recipients can be created through the manipulation of image.

Georgina Holmes describes the way in which a militia group located in the east of Congo – the FDLR – constructs 'strategic narratives' using the medium of the internet to shape its international image in a PR battle. She discusses the way in which discourses on sexual violence and human rights are taken up by the FDLR, and addresses the extent to which a deliberate creation of a narrative for external consumption shapes relationships with the diaspora and foreign governments.

Anne Schumann's chapter focuses on the creation and use of images within Côte d'Ivoire, tracing the image battles between the candidates in the 2010 presidential elections. Partly played out to an international audience on the internet, the candidates' images are closely tied to ideas of the external (both positive and negative). Schumann discusses the importance of foreign audiences and foreign relationships, as well as the use of an international medium, to establish images of political figures for domestic consumption.

Finally, the book concludes with two chapters detailing the ways in which individuals create images of their communities and themselves, challenging official representations. Wanja Kimani tells the story of photographic images in Ethiopia, beginning with the introduction of photography as an elite-driven modernisation programme. She discusses how the medium has become a popular way for Ethiopians to describe themselves, and to counter the Western-dominated aid industry images which they find disempowering. Kimani describes the work of several contemporary Ethiopian photographers and artists who have reappropriated images of Ethiopia, discussing the ways in which relationality draws on pity, objectification or complicity, affecting image creation in a variety of ways.

Lizzy Attree looks at depictions of the sick body in South African fiction and film, increasingly asserted after years of official avoidance. In particular, she is concerned with the ways in which official representations of a confident, vibrant South Africa have rested on a denial of frailty, and she explores the ways in which images of sick bodies create new national imaginaries, rupturing, but also restoring new forms of subjectivity. Throughout, authors rely on the complicity of the reader to help shape images of AIDS and people with AIDS.

As the authors show, images of Africa continue to be shaped through the history of its relationships with the wider world. This includes the way in which Africans reject overly-determined images created by outsiders, and attempt to re-determine their self-image, but also the way in which Africans play on outsiders' fantasies, desires or subliminal fears to serve up palatable images and achieve particular ends. They explore struggles within the continent over who can determine its images – the colonial power, the benevolent donor, the news reporter, the nationalist government, the traditional authority, the militia group, the political party or the individual artist and writer.

References

Achebe, Chinua (1983): *An Image of Africa: racism in Conrad's* Heart of Darkness (London: Penguin).

Achebe, Chinua (2001): *A Man of the People* (London: Penguin).

Adebola, Olakunle Igbekele, Felix Olajide Talabi and Ishola Kmorudeen Lamidi (2012): 'Rebranding Nigeria: the role of advertising and public relations at correcting Nigeria image', *Educational Research* 3(5): 424–8, http://interesjournals.org/full-articles/rebranding-nigeria-the-role-of-advertising-and-public-relations-at-correcting-nigeria-image.pdf?view=inline.

Bayart, Jean-François (2000): 'Africa in the world: a history of extraversion', *African Affairs* 99(395): 217–67.

BBC (2011): 'Should Africa employ lobbyists?', BBC Africa, 18.10.11: www.bbc.co.uk/news/world-africa-15109351.

Belting, Hans (2005): 'Image, medium, body: a new approach to iconology', *Critical Inquiry* 31(2): 302–19.

Bhabha, Homi (2004): *The Location of Culture* (London: Routledge).

Certeau, Michel de (1984): *The Practice of Everyday Life*, trans. S. Rendall (Berkeley: University of California Press).

Downey, Anthony (2004): 'Yinka Shonibare in conversation', *Wasafiri* 19(41).

Enwezor, Okwui (1997): 'The work of Yinka Shonibare', *Nka: Journal of Contemporary African Art* 6–7: 10–11.

Freud, Sigmund (2003): *The Uncanny* (London: Penguin).

Jervis, Robert (1989): *The Logic of Images in International Relations* (New York: Colombia University Press).

Kahn, Jeremy (2006): 'A brand-new approach', www.jeremy-kahn.com/articles/NovDec06–NationBranding.pdf, cited 26.4.13.

Manheim, Jarol B. and Robert B. Albritton (1987): 'Insurgent violence versus image management: the struggle for national images in Southern Africa', *British Journal of Political Science* 17(2): 201–18.

Mbembe, Achille (2001): *On the Postcolony* (Berkeley: University of California Press).

Mengara, Daniel M. (2001): *Images of Africa: stereotypes and realities* (Asmara: Africa World Press).

Mudimbe, V. Y. (1994): *The Idea of Africa: African systems of thought* (London: J. Currey).

Newell, Sasha (2013): 'Brands as masks: public secrecy and the counterfeit in Côte d'Ivoire', *Journal of the Royal Anthropological Institute* 19: 138–54.

Nooter, M. H. (1993): 'Secrecy: African art that conceals and reveals', *African Arts* 26(1): 55–102.

Nworah, Uche (2006): 'Rebranding Nigeria: critical perspectives on the Heart of Africa Image project', www.brandchannel.com/images/papers/40_rebranding%20nigeria%20–%20critical%20perspectives.pdf, cited 26.4.13.

Opoku, Robert and Robert Hinson (2006): 'Online brand personalities: an exploratory analysis of selected African countries', *Place Branding* 2(2): 118–29.

Pakenham, Thomas (2001): *The Scramble for Africa, 1876–1912* (London: Phoenix).

Steiner, Christopher B. (1985): 'Another image of Africa: toward an ethnohistory of European cloth marketed in west Africa, 1873–1960', *Ethnohistory* 32(2): 91–110.

van Ham, Peter (2001): 'The rise of the brand state: the postmodern politics of image and reputation', *Foreign Affairs* 80(5): 2–6.

Vogel, S. M. (1997): 'African art/Western eyes', *African Arts* 30(4): 64–77.

2

Constructing images of Africa: from troubled pan-African media to sprawling Nollywood

George Ogola

In March 2012, the Atlanta-based international news channel CNN was forced to pull a video from its website following online 'protests' criticising the organisation's coverage of a story in Nairobi, Kenya. CNN's Nairobi correspondent David McKenzie had covered an incident in downtown Nairobi where suspected Al-Shabaab militants threw grenades into a bus terminus, killing and injuring several people. The story was introduced with a bold banner that read: 'Violence in Kenya', superimposed on a graphic of the Kenyan flag. The story was quickly picked up by the rest of the international media. Seemingly enraged by the coverage, the Kenyan online community condemned McKenzie and CNN on Twitter, Facebook and other social networking websites. Many demanded that McKenzie and CNN apologise for 'poor reporting' and for (mis)representing the country. McKenzie however insisted that the report was factually accurate, as did CNN, their removal of the video notwithstanding.

Importantly, the dispute centred on the perceived (deliberate) construction of a problematic image of Kenya as 'violent'. Informing this disagreement were arguments variously appealing to the producers and the imagined audiences which offered very different renderings of the same event. On the one hand was CNN inserting the story within a much broader narrative framework, informed in part by Kenya's recent history of electoral violence but also (arguably) by the largely invisible discursive frames used throughout international news that tend to totalise 'African' stories and strip them of their complexity. On the other hand were Kenyans, aware of the implications of allowing an image of Kenya as 'violent' to be defined elsewhere and portrayed as 'common sense'. They wanted to (re-)define that image and create a new narrative framework within which the story could be interpreted.

This brief anecdote is of fundamental importance in two ways. First, it lays bare the notion of image as a contested construct that is defined as much by its producers as its consumers. Second, it reveals how international news is a site in which assumed centres and peripheries are constantly involved in a struggle over the construction of an interpretive habitat against which events should be understood. As Gurevitch *et al* observe, foreign news is made intelligible to primary audiences by 'casting faraway events in frameworks that render these events comprehensible, appealing and relevant to domestic audiences … and by constructing meaning of these events in ways that are compatible with the "dominant ideology" of the society they serve' (1991: 206). The Kenyan story was a complex one which had to be made accessible to a world audience. To do so, CNN silently but deliberately invoked a 'familiar' narrative frame that made the story 'easy' to comprehend. In the process the story was rendered both true and untrue. It is this contradiction that is at the heart of this discussion; the politics around the making and unmaking of the image.

The struggles over 'ownership' of international news narratives have generated heated debates over its ability to represent Africa. A number of studies on international news coverage seek to show how the world is not only unevenly represented but also how it is implicated in much broader ideological and political contestations (Van Ginneken, 1998; Shoemaker and Cohen, 2005; Sreberny *et al*, 1997; Nyamjoh, 2005). These studies argue that Africa and much of the developing world feature less in international news, relative to the more affluent global North.

More significant however is the widely cited contention that poorer parts of the world are routinely 'misrepresented' in international news. A number of critical works on representation in international news contend that Africa's coverage in particular is often broadly located within a discursive regime of Otherness, a paradigm of difference that consistently relies upon pre-determined news templates and many unqualified generalisations (Van Ginneken, 1998; Thussu, 2007; Ebron, 2002, Williams, 2011). Ebron, for example, argues that the continent often 'enters a global imagination through news accounts of ethnic wars, famine, and unstable political regimes' (2002: 2). In global news, she writes, 'a cycle of destruction and unrest encircles sub-Saharan Africa like a swarm of bad omens that, more often than not, fails to distinguish national differences or historical moments. Africa is often portrayed as a timeless story of tribal rivalries, intended to invoke in the minds of its spectators the pre-modern' (Ibid). The Kenyan writer Binyavanga Wainaina captures this coverage in a satirical essay 'How to write about Africa':

Always use the word 'Africa' or 'Darkness' or 'Safari' in your title. Subtitles may include the words 'Zanzibar', 'Maasai', 'Zulu', 'Zambezi',

'Congo', 'Nile', 'Big', 'Sky', 'Shadow', 'Drum', 'Sun' or 'Bygone'. Also useful are words such as 'Guerrillas', 'Timeless', 'Primordial' and 'Tribal'. Note that 'People' means Africans who are not black, while 'The People' means black Africans. (2005)

But not all agree with this argument about negative representation. Indeed, writing in *The Africans*, nearly two decades ago, David Lamb complained that those who criticised negative coverage seemed instead to desire:

> a style of advocacy journalism that concentrates on civic centers and ignores the warts. It wants a new set of journalistic guidelines for covering the underdeveloped world, one which, if used in the West, would tell journalists to disregard the Watergates and Charles Mansons and concentrate on the positive and uplifting. It wants to be covered by historians not journalists ... . I am not sure who would really benefit if foreign correspondents wrote about Africa as some people wish it were rather than as it is (cited in Cavanagh, 1989: 250–1).

In other words, Lamb suggests that calls for a more 'sensitive' coverage of Africa merely amount to a cessation of criticism and the presentation of an Africa designed to support African elites and vested interests.

These diametrically opposed meta-narratives, while both open to criticism, have nonetheless continued to shape debates on the image of Africa in international news. Beyond that, they have played a critical role in ideologically shaping several pan-African media initiatives primarily aimed at contesting and redefining international news narratives on and about the continent. Using pan-African(ist) media initiatives, including Pan-African News Agency (PANA), SABC Africa, and South Africa's Multichoice Limited as illustrative and explanatory examples, this chapter seeks to do three things. First, to examine and challenge the ideological frameworks within which some of the media initiatives are anchored. Second, to explore some of the political, economic and institutional challenges these media initiatives face, and finally, to propose an embryonic 'third way' for conceptualising the increasingly elusive pan-African(ist) media agenda.

Explaining that which is called Africa

Discussions on pan-African media typically employ a familiar if sometimes problematic conceptual vocabulary. The discussions are often dominated by references to concepts such as 'contraflows', 'counter hegemonic narratives', 'African values', and 'Western values' among others – terms which generally delete nuance and contradiction in favour of simpler binaries. While these terms do in fact have some analytical purchase, they also consistently totalise experiences without adequate qualification. I would argue that the apparent failure or the deliberate refusal to unpack or problematise the conceptual vocabulary around which the pan-African media agenda is primarily anchored is a fundamental weakness manifest in some of the failed interventionist media projects.

For instance, let us linger on one of the key legitimating arguments in this project – the idea of 'contraflows'. To be sure, 'contraflows' is a term broadly used to refer to 'mass media programming that reverses the dominant (Western, First World) direction' (Kavoori, 2007: 50). At its core is the assumption that within international news is an 'unreflexive Western dominance and its natural result: global cultural homogenization' (Ibid). Contraflows, Kavoori argues, 'in the end are placed in the specific diacritical space of localism with only one of two options available to it: assimilation or defiance. Little attention is given to the range, diversity and complexity of such programming and to the world they are shaping' (Ibid: 51).

Pandurang expresses similar objections to the range of conceptual vocabulary cited above, arguing that some of these analytical models 'are not adequate for exploring new forms of multi-culturality that are in the process of emerging' (2001: 2). He argues that 'what is needed is a theoretical framework that goes beyond formulations of cultural imperialism and simplified binaries and speaks from the affective experience of social marginality and from the perspective of the edge – they offer alternative views of seeing and thinking, and thereby allow for narratives of plurality, fluidity and always emergent becoming' (Ibid).

The other related conceptual problem is the belief in the existence of 'a set of stable empirical referents – of spatial location and spatial exclusivity of cultural products' (Kavoori, 2007: 49). For example, a number of African media initiatives assume a common existential empirical constant – that which is called Africa and of things African, authentic and unadulterated. From a theoretical perspective, the task of defining and therefore understanding Africa is a difficult one. This is because Africa, particularly as it is mediated or mediatised is neither obvious nor uniformly perceived across its users and referents. V. Y. Mudimbe's books, *The Idea of Africa* (1994) and *The Invention of Africa* (1988) provide us with historical references of Africa as an ambiguity which must be unpacked and explained. In *The Invention of Africa*, he explains that

> Africa as a coherent ideological and political entity was invented with the advent of European expansion and continuously re-invented by traditional

African and diasporan intellectuals, not to mention metropolitan intellectuals and ideological apparatuses, educational institutions and then atten-
dant disciplines, traveler accounts, popular media and so forth. (1988: 23)

This argument may be contentious, not least because it tends to deny
the constructed Other any agency in shaping its form and narratives, as
critics such as Ogude have argued. Ogude contests the idea that Africa
was 'formed' 'on the terms set by colonialism/modernity' (2012: 6). But
as Julia Gallagher argues in the introduction of this book through her
reading of Shonibare's 'Scramble for Africa' (2013), Europe and Africa
are connected in ways that make it impossible to tell where Africa starts
and where Europe ends. This relationship strongly calls into question
the legitimacy of arguments that limit agency only to the colonial project and Africa's reaction to it.

Whether 'created', 'invented', 'negotiated' or indeed 'imagined' as
Anderson (1991) suggests, the indigenes have since taken ownership of
the continent; it is therefore far from being merely a fantastical ambiguity. However, this does not necessarily qualify its assumed monolithic,
coherent and homogenous existence. Africa remains internally incoher-
ent both as an idea or set of ideas and as a 'thing'. The two should not
be conflated. Be that as it may, the belief in its 'existence' has been so
widely and powerfully circulated that there is now a tendency to ignore
the chaos of its historical formation and the impact of globalisation on
it; its hybridity, plurality and indeed fluidity (Pandurang, 2011) both as
an idea and as a 'thing'. Recognising these factors, fraught with contradiction as they must be, should allow us to begin to understand why
Africa's 'story' is so difficult to tell; why the pan-African media therefore remains, in many ways, a dream deferred.

It is germane therefore to point out that a number of pan-African
media initiatives often start off by validating the very contentious narrative they seek to contest. The failure to acknowledge the instability
of the referent – Africa – partly legitimises the very essentialisation of
a diverse continent as an undifferentiated space and culture. Precisely
because of this, we paradoxically end up with its misrepresentation in
the very attempts to revise the same in the international news media.

Erasing differences to create an *Africana* – the idea and the thing – is
problematic because it recreates a 'narcissism of sameness'. Difference is
'subjugated under the imperialism of the same' (Xie, 2000: 2–3). These
arguments seek to underscore the problematic theoretical and ideological premises upon which some of these pan-African media initiatives are
usually anchored. For while they correctly identify Othering in international news, they seem to lack the conceptual vocabulary to offer

an alternative. They invent a problematic *Africana*, one that fails to acknowledge the inherent difficulties imposed by an imagined sameness.

Constructing the 'African voice': from NWICO to PANA

The 1970s saw heated debates about the uneven flows of international news from the global North to the global South within the International Telecommunication Union (ITU) and UNESCO. Although the idea of a pan-African media had already been canvassed, it was these debates that led to the first major proposals for new continental news agencies to address the international news flow imbalance between the global North and South.

The debates at ITU and UNESCO were about correcting the uneven international communication structures, but they were also hugely political and ideological. Many countries from the global South had raised concerns over the domination of international communication by Western-based transnational news agencies, principally Associated Press (AP), United Press International (UPI), Reuters and Agence France-Presse (AFP). These concerns ranged from fears about 'cultural imperialism' to accusations of Western media 'encroachment' on national sovereignty. Newly independent states were particularly anxious about the implications of these uneven news flows on their 'independence'. For these countries, the control of the media and news flows was considered an important variable in their new matrices for national development.

The debates that took place at UNESCO, broadly pitting developing nations with the support of Moscow against Western news agencies, eventually led to a series of contested proposals on a new communication order called the New World Information and Communication Order (NWICO). It was developed by the MacBride Commission chaired by the Irish politician Sean MacBride. Political, economic and ideological interests invested in international news meant that most countries remained divided over NWICO. Western news agencies and organisations solicited support from their governments to reject the project, many arguing that the new order was 'a barely disguised edict condoning censorship and denying freedom of expression' (Cavanagh, 1989: 354). In protest, the UK and the US decided to withdraw their funding for UNESCO, effectively ensuring that the NWICO proposals could not be implemented.

Although the NWICO project never quite came to fruition, it did lead to the establishment of a number of news agencies in the developing world including InterPress Services (IPS), Non-Aligned News Agencies Pool (NANAP) and Pan-African News Agency (PANA). However,

PANA's establishment was also partly the fulfillment of a political dream by the Organisation of African Unity (OAU), which quickly appropriated it to its cause. The setting up of an African news agency was one of the key proposals set out by the OAU in its inaugural assembly in 1963 (Cavanagh, 1989: 354). PANA was therefore expected to help pursue the OAU's pan-African political project. On paper, PANA was to play the dual role of pooling information fed by Africa's state-owned media while also carrying news from its own pool of correspondents to cover the continent. Its central mandate was to 'correct the distorted picture of Africa, its countries and peoples resulting from the partial and negative information published by the foreign press agencies and to assist in the liberation struggles of peoples against colonialism, neo-colonialism, imperialism, apartheid, racism, Zionism and all other forms of exploitation and oppression' (Cavanagh, 1989: 354). This nationalist orientation was to become one of its major weaknesses.

This overtly political mandate weakened PANA's ability to succeed as a news agency. By becoming a platform for various national state media, which mainly covered 'protocol' news, the agency was seen as a mouthpiece for several repressive governments within the continent and was quickly discredited. Not only were its stories not used by the international media, they were also disregarded by most news organisations within the continent.

PANA also faced other equally significant challenges. Poorly financed, the agency was confronted by the logistical nightmare of covering a continent with nearly fifty states, hundreds of languages, and varied political and economic interests. By 1988, PANA was barely financially solvent, as most states failed to honour their budget contributions to the organisation. Indeed, in the late 1980s, PANA was already operating on a budget deficit running into millions of dollars and was on the verge of collapse (Cavanagh, 1989). Unable even to pay its own correspondents, it relied mainly on news sent by state news agencies, most of which were unedited government press releases. Much of the news from PANA was also dated by the time it was sent out to media houses, having already been covered by other international news agencies with the technical capacity and finances to collect and disseminate news. Indeed, a report published by the *New York Times* in 1988 found that nearly 70 per cent of news used by African news organisations was supplied by Western news agencies. PANA reports were the least used, if used at all (Van Ginneken, 1998).

PANA's agenda thus remains largely unrealised. The agency lacked and still lacks the necessary financial resources and expertise to cover the continent, and while it is no longer necessarily exploited by national governments, ideologically it remains trapped in a political time-warp. PANA's nationalism was the product of a specific historical juncture and over time its role has become increasingly ambiguous. The political consciousness that the 1960s Pan-Africanism evoked was ideologically tied to the fight for self-governance. The period demanded a specific fabrication of Africa and of a discourse that would create political solidarities and turn Otherness on its head. The broader narrative of political emancipation demanded a stylisation of a very specific image of Africa that found space and relevance in organisations such as PANA. Africa today is a radically different continent with new political and economic realities which demand new response.

A case of two 'African brands': South Africa's SABC Africa and Multichoice Limited

As the continent's largest economy and with some of the most vocal Pan-Africanist leaders, South Africa has played its part in the calls for an 'African media voice', not least because it also has arguably the most developed media infrastructure in the continent. Former president Thabo Mbeki's calls for an 'African Renaissance', codified in his brainchild the New Partnership for Africa's Development (NEPAD), was a case in point. But South Africa also provides two interesting if contrasting images of Africa. The two pan-African media initiatives, SABC Africa and Multichoice, provide varied readings and approaches to the pan-African (media) agenda.

SABC Africa was created as the external arm of the state-owned SABC. It was formed following the 'amalgamation of two previously separate channels – its namesake SABC Africa which was a news, current affairs and documentary channel beamed to the rest of the continent, and Africa-2–Africa, an all entertainment channel made in Africa for Africa' (Teer-Tomaselli, 2007: 159). The symbolic import of the channel's adoption of the name Africa was instructive. At one level it gestured at a very nationalistic orientation. Indeed, it stated as its 'philosophy' the need to 'celebrate the positive side of Africa and being African' (Ibid).

SABC's 'African(ist) ambition' was manifest in its rapid expansion in Africa and around the world. In 2007, it set up Africa's first 24–hour rolling news channel SABC News International and opened bureaus in Beijing, Dakar, Brussels, Sao Paulo, New York, Jamaica, the DRC, Washington DC, Harare, Lagos, Nairobi, London and the UN.

The locations of the bureaus clearly indicated the organisation's conscious attempt to cover the global South even as it maintained a presence in the more established news capitals of Europe and the US. But statements made by Mbeki at the launch of SABC News International in 2007 seemed to suggest that the station had a very specific political and ideological agenda. Mbeki's words were particularly unambiguous with regard to SABC's international vision:

> For far too long we have relied on others to tell us our own stories. For that long we have seemed content to parrot the words and stories of others about us as if they were the gospel truth.
> This is not a lament about some dim and distant past but the contemporary reality facing Africa and all its citizens. As a result of this, most of the time we are unable to tell our own stories; we are afraid to sing our own songs and are thoroughly intimidated to respect our cultures and honour our true heroes and heroines.
> We become incapable of articulating our own reality and celebrating our own achievements because we are told that the few setbacks relative to our many successes, should forever define our existence.
> Colonial and apartheid legacies abound. A telephone call from Ghana to Nigeria may have to go first to Europe before being rerouted to its destination in the neighbourhood. Often, the news and stories in our publications seem to be following the same colonial routes even if not physically, at least philosophically.
> The international broadcast news landscape is not only dominated by a few resource-rich channels, but even when African broadcasters participate in the dissemination of news it is always in the context of stories filed by foreign news agencies, with headquarters in Atlanta, New York, London and other major cities of the powerful nations.
> Accordingly, we trust that the new SABC News International will tell the African story in as much depth and contextual detail as possible and physically get around the continent identifying the successes and reverses so as to reflect what is really happening on our continent. (2007)

Mbeki went on to say that SABC News International would also 'serve as one of the critical building blocks that should help us to realise the vision of the African Renaissance' and become 'our dependable mirror reflecting to us our African actuality and which, through its high quality journalism, news-gathering operations, pursuit of truth and correct contextualisation of events and processes liberate us from those who, for too long, have told half-truths and lies that have served to magnify a negative image of Africa'(Ibid). In a similar speech delivered while opening SABC International's East African Bureau in Nairobi, then Deputy President Phumzile Mlambo-Ngcuka said the bureau would help generate news 'with the right African perspective' (2007).

Almost, *a la* PANA, SABC Africa and its News International channel was ideologically oriented to serve a political project. But the market seems to have judged this political project rather harshly, for in just two years, the bureaus in Beijing, Dakar, Brussels, Sao Paulo, Jamaica and DC had all been closed with the rest reportedly put under constant evaluation (Bailey, 2009). Before long, many of the international stories, even those within the continent, were increasingly sourced from the major international news agencies. The only 'local' touch was the introduction of voiceovers by SABC journalists on agency footage.

There were fundamental problems with SABC's approach to its African news project, failures which the relative success of the Naspers-owned Multichoice Limited puts into sharp perspective. Rather than venture into the cut-throat market of 'spot news', Multichoice went for more general content creation and delivery. Multichoice grew out of M-Net, South Africa's first private TV channel. M-Net began as a joint venture of four newspaper publishers, which included Naspers, Republican Press, Allied Publishing and Times Media Limited, aimed at breaking SABC's broadcasting monopoly in the country (Teer-Tomaselli, 2007: 155–6). It first introduced an analogue service distributed to more than twenty African countries in 1992. However, its subscriber division was later launched as Multichoice Limited (MCL) in 1993. In 1998 Naspers acquired control of the company, which was now Multichoice Investment Holdings (MIH), MCL having been separated from M-Net. Having bought MIH from the other press groups, the MIH conglomerate, which now comprised Multichoice, M-Net and M-Web, became a wholly owned subsidiary of Naspers in 2001(Teer-Tomaselli, 2007).

Fundamentally, Multichoice looked at Africa not necessarily as an ideological and political construct but as a market. Its 'products' were targeted at consumers – rather than Africans – mainly the burgeoning middle-class within the continent, but also beyond it, expanding into the Middle East, Asia and Latin America. But the success of this company can also be explained by the advantages brought about by the vertical and horizontal integration within the subsidiary itself and its parent company Naspers. Multichoice became a broadcaster, publisher and subscription manager exploiting the economies of scale availed by its various products and parent company. It now owns operations ranging from entertainment to interactive and e-commerce services across more than fifty countries in Africa, the Mediterranean, Asia, Europe and Latin America. By owning the content delivery and distribution platforms, Multichoice has been able to create narrowcasted channels which it uses to promote 'products' marketed as 'African'. These include the Africa Magic Channel and Africa Magic Plus, among others. In part, PANA and SABC-Africa's struggles point to their failed attempts to construct a centralised undifferentiated image of Africa, one whose various textures and contradictions were deleted in its rendering, an Africa divorced from the realities of multiculturality, hybridisation and fluidity – an incomplete Africa.

Invisible borders: barriers to world news market entry

There are other reasons why it has been so difficult for pan-African news agencies to become established and viable. The debate on Africa's misrepresentation in global news has focused attention on the need to create continental news organisations, fronted in many cases by nationalist politicians and policy-makers as seen in some of the examples above. But little attention has focused on the international communication infrastructure which remains critical in understanding the production and distribution of the uneven world news flows. It is important to recognise that the real powers behind world news coverage are not necessarily the Anglo-American news organisations but the transnational news agencies (TNAs), who are themselves owned by much bigger corporate concerns.

World news is generally defined, produced and distributed by TNAs, the most dominant of which are principally based in New York, London and Paris. As noted above, in the 1970s and 1980s, debates on NWICO revolved mainly around anxieties over the world news agenda being defined by a cartel of news makers seen to represent the interests of the developed world and only responsive to the needs of Western markets (Samarajiwa, 1984: 119). The TNAs operate mainly as business concerns interested in maximising returns on their product – news, protecting their markets and creating new ones. TNAs do not operate as news organisations but as 'firms that mobilise resources for the production and distribution of a commodity in economic markets' (Samarajiwa, 1984: 120). Samarajiwa argues that 'considerations of profit-seeking and market control are held to be as relevant to the analysis of TNAs as they are to other business firms' (Ibid). Indeed, on its website (www. AFP.com), AFP describes its users as 'clients'. The TNAs have over the years created an impregnable wall in the news business, particularly involving the production and distribution of international 'spot news'. In an illuminating discussion on how these TNAs operate, Samarajiwa teases out three key issues which act as entry barriers to similar agencies from the developing world. These include what he describes as the 'economies of replication', pricing policies, market control and diversification (1984: 130).

Samarajiwa explains how world news flows comprise three levels, the first and most important being 'spot news', referring to the immediate reports of an event happening. The second level refers to the more detailed reports that follow and expand on 'spot news', while within the third level are the 'finished products'. Level one is considered the most important as it is at this stage that news is framed (Ibid: 121). The first to 'break' the news thus very often becomes the one who defines the news narrative. TNAs dominate the production of 'spot news', hence their inordinate influence in constructing the international news agenda. This is mainly because news organisations may have reporters or correspondents around the world, but they are too thinly spread to be everywhere at all times. TNAs on the other hand have extensive worldwide networks capable of producing and distributing news at the speed in which the news is needed by news organisations and other 'clients'. For example, AP has over 240 bureaus around the world while AFP produces more than five thousand stories every day in English, French, German, Spanish and Portuguese (www.AFP.com).

Samarajiwa argues that one of the main barriers to entering coverage of 'spot news', and therefore the world news market, is the 'first copy costs'. These are the costs involved in 'delivering a complete news report with the required promptness and accuracy to a hypothetical first buyer – that is, the costs of the worldwide news production network, transmission, correspondent etc' (1984: 130). Setting up the necessary infrastructure to deliver world news efficiently and promptly is extremely expensive. Further, the recurring expenditures are even higher and could be double or treble the capital costs (Ibid).

Since replication costs are usually low, as the producer retains exclusive control over the product, TNAs practice what is known in economics as 'price discrimination'. The costs of subscription are not the same across the world. It is important to note that TNAs also act as domestic news agencies in their countries of origin where they charge premium amounts for their products. This is also their most valuable market. The price paid by a US newspaper for AP news reports is substantially higher than what a European newspaper pays for the same report. Sales to developing countries are generally regarded as spin-offs and are therefore much cheaper. A number of news organisations in the developing world are therefore able to purchase these products at far lower rates than would possibly be charged by their own local news agencies. The implication is that Western TNAs are therefore able to shut out potential competitors from the developing world. But since the domestic media in the West are the TNA's main clients, it is their interests that are of primary importance to the TNAs.

The American and European TNAs also have very privileged positions in their home markets, which cannot be easily accessed by foreign TNAs. Examples of the difficult experiences of IPS-Interlink and Al Jazeera in the US are cases in point. IPS-Interlink, for instance, was almost hounded out of the US market while Al Jazeera was frustrated at various levels including being barred from reporting from the New York Stock Exchange because of its perceived negative representation of the United States (Sakr, 2007). Furthermore, the TNAs are almost without exception part of much larger corporate organisations, which also own the domestic news organisations which buy their news. The news organisations must therefore source their news from the TNAs as they are in most cases part of the same corporate families. For example, AP is owned by its buyer news organisations in the US, including various newspapers, radio and TV organisations. Reuters is owned by Thompson Reuters, a corporate organisation with interests in the global equities market, health and information solutions, and which only sold its education subsidiary Thomson Learning in 2007. Likewise, AFP is part of a larger integrated media enterprise which includes subsidiaries such as AFP–GMBH, its German language service which produces graphics, text and internet products, SID, the German language sports service, and Citizenside, a site where 'thousands of amateurs and professionals sell newsworthy videos and photos' (www.AFP.com).

TNAs thus have unparalleled leverage in the production and distribution of news and are unlikely to be threatened by any new pan-African media news agency or media organization, particularly those aimed at the production and distribution of 'spot news'.

Can the empire strike back?: the case against an 'African Al Jazeera'

What then are the chances of a successful pan-African media enterprise? Is such a medium feasible? More importantly, is it even necessary? These questions invite varied responses. The relative success of the Qatar-based Al Jazeera has prompted some to talk about the possibility of setting up an 'African Al Jazeera'. Thabo Mbeki once noted that there was no reason why an 'African Al Jazeera' cannot succeed (cited in Gouveia, 2005: 4). Philip Fiske de Gouveia of the London-based Foreign Policy Centre, a European think-tank, also proposed to the UK Foreign Office to establish a Pan-African media project along the same lines as Al Jazeera (Ibid). There is little doubt that Al Jazeera's growth since its establishment in 1996 has been phenomenal. Indeed, in 2005, an industry website conducting a poll involving nearly two thousand advertising executives in seventy five countries identified Al Jazeera as the world's fifth most recognised brand (Clark, 2005, cited in Sakr, 2007: 116). But how does one assess Al Jazeera's 'success'? Could the model be a blue-print for a similar venture in Africa?

Al Jazeera was founded by seed money provided by the Emir of Qatar with an initial five-year grant of nearly US$137 million, but the station has also had to rely on regular supplementary grants from Qatar. The station's International Division, now Al Jazeera English, has increased its world profile but with considerable financial implications. The sta-tion's financial independence remains elusive as it has found it difficult to generate the requisite advertising revenue. It is also significant to note that while the organisation focuses on 'spot news' and therefore gener-ates much of its own content, it also significantly uses footage provided by Anglo-American TNAs. This only serves to demonstrate just how difficult it is to challenge the dominance of the TNAs in the production of international news, even for well-funded news organisations.

Lauded as an organisation 'striking back at the empire', Al Jazeera's alleged success has also been subject to much debate. To what extent, for example, has the organisation actually managed to challenge the monop-oly of the Anglo-American TNAs over discursive practices in inter-national news? Note for example that senior editorial managers have continued to come from established Western news media organisations. For instance, the English division was first headed by Nigel Parson who had been a director at APTN. He came with a cast of seasoned journalists from major news organisations in North America and Europe including BBC, ABC, ITN, CNN, SKY and CBC. The effect of such editorial domi-nance by journalists and managers from Europe and North America cannot be ignored even if their precise 'effect' may only be conjectured.

Al Jazeera thus continues to polarise opinion. Indeed, Sakr observes that as world opinion shifted following 9/11 and the invasion of Iraq, the station's messages continued to elicit contradictory responses, with both the West and the Arab world castigating it. She notes that being allied to the Qatar government, the station was put on the defensive in a way that seems to have altered the nature of the 'Al Jazeera pro-ject'. The station announced it was going 'to build a communication bridge between the East and the West' and much later, to 'promote certain values' (2007, 127). The decision does raise important points for discussion. Sakr asks whether 'by self-consciously articulating a rationale for its own existence based on building bridges, the station moved from being a transparent media outlet to becoming a political actor in its own right' (Ibid: 127). Has it or will it go the way of IPS, which, as Thussu once observed, 'by putting developmental concerns on the UN agenda ... soon morphed from news agency to pressure group'

(Thussu, 2007: 252). Al Jazeera's ownership profile, editorial direction and business model make it highly unlikely to be used as blue-print for a successful pan-African media project.

Al Jazeera has been a political actor in an historical epoch of immense political import in the Arab world. It is a period when the assertion of a particular identity and the self-creation of that image are of critical importance. Pan-Arabism has been central to the politics of Al Jazeera's self-positioning as an alternative to the dominant Western international press. Arab journalism has taken up the role of 'border guards of an imagined Arab *Watan* [nation]' (Pintak, 2009: 193). It is a journalism that 'reflects a worldview that largely transcends borders, a sense of self-identity that sets region above nation and religion above passport' (Ibid) As I argue in a separate discussion of Arab media, 'fuelled by feelings of Otherness in the face of perceived international, mainly Western anti-Arab sentiment, Arab journalists seek to forge a shared consciousness of pan-Arabism' (Ogola, 2014: 300). But this image of an Arab *Watan* also means that internal contradictions, the complicated textures that inform Arabness, are ignored. As a consequence, we have seen the emergence of a number of radical TV stations in the region such as Al-Majid and Al-Manar that violently unsettle the Al Jazeera narrative. Similarly, that same narrative of the Arab *Watan* has also been dominated by organised and powerful political outfits such as the Muslim Brotherhood who style it in their own image. An 'African Al-Jazeera' would most likely falter as it would be yet another attempt to centralise the production of an image of a *thing* too diverse to be solely defined as something coherent and homogeneous.

Searching for a Third Way?: Nollywood, the 'identity economy' and the making of a new pan-African consciousness

The key to a successful pan-African media project seems to lie in the recognition of the complex relationships within the various 'scapes' that constitute and shape media texts, and the various structures that enable their international mediation. It must also acknowledge the relationship between producers and consumers as active participants in image creation. Fundamentally, there is an immediate need to reconceptualise our understanding of the *pan-African consciousness* in the *pan-African* media. That consciousness is a child of many worlds – history, culture, economics, politics and others. There are important lessons to be learnt from the Nigerian Nollywood film industry in relation to this consciousness. How does Nollywood construct a pan-African narrative which is now capable of negotiating its own space in the global cultural arena?

PANA, SABC-Africa, and even the much talked about but unrealised 'African Al Jazeera' have all tended to gesture towards a nationalism with roots in much older pan-Africanist movements such as Pan-Africanism, Black Consciousness and Negritude. These movements 'shared a concern with transcending self-conceptions based either on localised tribal identities or national boundaries imposed through colonisation' (McCall, 2007: 97). But McCall observes that although historical experiences can evoke a sense of unity, what many pan-Africanists have longed for is to 'discover and cultivate a common cultural core – a poetics that could ring as true in a Congo village as on the streets of Johannesburg' (Ibid: 92). It is this poetics that has been elusive.

McCall describes the 'rise of Nollywood with its prolific output, its spectacular popularity and its unprecedented ability to reach remote and non-elite audiences' as 'the most radical development to date in the history of African media' (Ibid: 94). While it has gained from a better communications infrastructure, enabled by the growth of ICTs in the continent, the liberalisation of the region's media sector, with it the expansion of private media, and the growth of African diasporas in Western metropolises, there are other equally significant explanatory factors. The growth of Nollywood cannot be explained as having been driven by a pan-Africanist agenda invented by a government or a group of elite pan-Africanists. It is not as McCall avers, 'concerned with advancing a developmental agenda or political movement ... instead it gives voice to a broad spectrum of cultural views – Christian, Muslim, traditional, folkloric' (Ibid: 94) and has remained relatively immune to exploitation by powerful Nigerian kleptocrats. Instead, 'every time a governor or lascivious clergyman is exposed, the scandal is dramatised and folklorised as a Nollywood drama' (Ibid). It acknowledges its audiences' everyday experiences and fluid identities, which necessarily evade capture.

As is common with popular cultural productions, views on Nollywood remain mixed. Its critics have complained that it fetishises wealth and violence, emphasises glamour over substance, is sexist and lacks a specific ideological orientation capable of making it effect political and social transformation (Okwori, 2003; Adesanya, 2000; Garritano, 2000; Lawuvi, 1997). Yet its critics, McCall observes, are also its most voracious consumers. As such, he suggests, as many other scholars of popular culture have done, we need to 'rethink what constitutes the political in Africa' (2007: 94). Nollywood does not provide a coherent philosophy or worldview that might be called 'pan-African' but is a primary catalyst in an emergent continent-wide popular discourse in what it might perhaps mean to be African. Its audience in Africa and beyond is huge and growing and it is beginning to crack world film markets on its own terms – a *Naijanica* morphing into an *Africana* unendorsed by an African elite keen to cultivate a specific 'African culture'. McCall further argues that what 'positions Nollywood as a catalyst for a pan-African discourse is precisely [that] it has no particular view, no specific agenda and certainly no discernible coherent ideology', describing it instead as 'a sprawling marketplace of representations' (Ibid: 96).

The example of Nollywood reminds us of Comaroff and Comaroff's idea of 'ethno-futures', a concept they use to explain how the 'identity economy' functions. In their book *Ethnicity Inc.* they argue that 'the sum of "our ethno-episteme"' … appears to be morphing into exactly the opposite of what social sciences would once have had us believe' (2009: 1). While ethnicity 'remains the stuff of existential passion, of the self-conscious fashioning of meaningful, morally anchored selfhood, it is also becoming more corporate, more commodified, more implicated than ever before in the economics of everyday lives' (Ibid). In other words, ethnicities or the differences pan-Africanists are so keen to deny, index belonging and, increasingly, these differences are being acknowledged as they are corporatised and become capable of competing in the global marketplace. More importantly, they assert legitimacy through a process that invokes difference, not sameness.

Comaroff and Comaroff cite several illustrative examples including the corporatisation of the Catalan identity in Spain, the Shipipo in Peru and the metamorphosis of Kenya's Gema (Gikuyu, Embu, Meru Association) into a venture capital called Mega. Culture, they argue, is now also 'intellectual property, displaced from the museum and the anthropological gaze no longer naked or available to just anyone pro bono' (Ibid: 30). Could it be, they ask, that 'contra to much social science orthodoxy, one possible future – perhaps the future of ethnicity – lies, metaphorically and materially alike in ethno-futures, in taking it into the marketplace? In hitching it, overtly, to the world of franchising and finance capital? In vesting it in an identity economy' (Ibid: 8). The commercialisation of identity, as is seen with Nollywood and the broader notion of the 'identity economy', the focus on difference instead of sameness, is a project in need of more critical engagement.

Nollywood contests attempts to centralise our meanings about what is Africa and what it means to be African. Instead, it elaborates on the elusiveness of that identity. It captures its hybridity, its ability to appropriate and to cannibalise. It is aware that audiences bring to bear their experiences in their consumption of Nollywood. These experiences are both personal and communal and it is in their negotiation that meaning is derived. Its weaknesses notwithstanding, Nollywood does not celebrate a non-existent *Africana*. It doesn't even strive to create one. Instead, Africa and what it means to be African emerges from its various stories and the many ways in which they are consumed. Africa as both the *thing* and the idea emerges out of this diversity. As a result, around the continent and beyond, Nollywood has become the African movie industry. From Guangzou, China to London in the UK, Nollywood videos are being sold and consumed as 'African'.

Conclusion

Pan-African media initiatives have faced many challenges, both ideological and practical. The challenges raise key questions: What does the emerging or emergent pan-African(ism) mean? What is 'African news'? How do we reconcile the politics of image production and news production, particularly within existing international communication structures? As Carlsson observes, 'contemporary society is far too complex ... and discourages the thought of 'a new international order' of the sort envisaged in the 1970s' (2005: 213). The kind of pan-African discourse that attended the NWICO debates was the product of a specific historical juncture. That history and those arguments may still have some purchase but we now face radically different challenges. For example, we cannot ignore the fact that we now live in an 'era of multilevel governance of the media system', an era of 'different actors, public and private, on multiple levels, from the local to the global' (Carlsson, 2005: 213). To use the words of Appadurai, 'the media and its texts, one would argue, are now structured by a complex overlapping disjunctive order, one constituted by a number of "scapes" that cannot only be interpreted territorially – the ethnoscape, technoscape, the infoscape, financescape, all interconnected and overlapping' (1990: 296).

Discursively, there is a need to rethink the propensity to homogenise Africa when the basis of these interventions is very often predicated on the need to confront totalising narratives that essentialise the continent and its people. I have argued that the internal imagination of a homogenous Africa actually legitimises its essentialisation as an undifferentiated space and culture. Pan-African media initiatives must therefore begin by first acknowledging the continent's diversity, even its incoherence. The deletion of internal differences undermines the very attempts to develop counternarratives capable of telling 'African' stories. Difference within must therefore be rehabilitated. Media policies and debates on the pan-African media agenda must be located within a broader and more complex matrix that transgresses current populist imaginations of the continent. The relative success of both Multichoice Limited and

Nollywood demonstrate two ways which this project might be pursued. It is clear that the market, the affective experience of the consumer, too, plays a critical role in the construction or the shaping of image – of Africa as of anything else. That role cannot be ignored by a pan-African media enterprise. The pan-African consciousness does indeed exist, but it does not necessarily reside in an imagined sameness, it could very well exist in difference, the kind manifested in Nollywood's 'sprawling marketplace of representations' that McCall (2007) talks about.

References

Adesanya, A. (2000): 'From film to video', in J. Haynes (ed.), *Nigerian VideoFilms* (Athens, OH: Ohio University Centre for International Studies).

Anderson, B. (1991): *Imagined Communities: reflections on the origin and spread of nationalism* (London: Verso).

Appadurai, A. (1990): 'Disjunctures and difference in the global economy', *Theory, Culture and Society* 7(2): 295–310.

Archetti, C. (2010): 'Comparing international coverage of 9/11: towards an interdisciplinary explanation of the construction of news', *Journalism: Theory, Practice and Criticism* 11(5): 567–88.

Bailey, C. (2009): 'SABC closes foreign bureaus', IOL News, www.iol.co.za/news/south-africa/sabc-closes-foreign-offices-1.439704#.U-oV0fldW_E, accessed 27.11.11.

Carlsson, U. (2005): 'The Macbride Report in the rear-view mirror', *Quaderns del CAC* 21 (January–April): 59–63.

Cavanagh, K. (1989): 'Freeing the Pan-African news agency', *The Journal of Modern African Studies* 27(2): 353–65.

Comaroff, J. and J. Comaroff (2009): *Ethnicity, Inc.* (Chicago: University of Chicago Press).

Derrida, J. (1982): *Margins of Philosophy*, trans. Alan Bass (Chicago: Chicago University Press).

Ebron, P. (2002): *Performing Africa* (Princeton, NJ: Princeton University Press).

Garritano, C. (2000): 'Women, melodrama, and feminist critique: a feminist reading of hostages, dust-to-dust, and true confessions', in J. Haynes (ed.), *Nigerian Video Films* (Athens, OH: Ohio University Centre for International Studies).

Gouveia. P. (2005): *An African Al Jazeera?: mass media and the African renaissance* (London: Foreign Policy Centre).

Gurevitch, M., M. R. Levy and I. Roeh (1991): 'The Global newsroom: convergences and diversities in the globalization of television news', in P. Dahlgren and C. Sparks (eds), *Communicationand Citizenship* (London: Routledge).

Kavoori, A. (2007): 'Thinking through contra flows: perspectives from postcolonial and transnational cultural studies', in D. Thussu (ed.), *Media on the Move: global flow and contra flow* (London: Routledge).

Kavoori, A. and A. Malek (eds) (2000): *The Global Dynamics Of News: studies in international news coverage and news agenda* (Stamford, Conn.: Ablex Publishing).

Lawuyi, O. (1997): 'The Political Economy of Video Marketing in Ogbomoso, Nigeria', *Africa: Journal of the International African Institute*, 67(3): 476–90.

Mbeki, T. (2007): 'Address by President Mbeki at the launch of SABC International' available at www.anc.org.za/show.php?id=4295, cited 27.11.11.

McCall, J. (2007): 'The Pan-Africanism we have: Nollywood's invention of Africa', *Film International* 5(2): 92–7.

McKinnon, R. (2008): 'Blogs and China correspondence: lessons about global information flows', *Chinese Journal of Communication* 1(2): 242–57.

Mlambo-Ngcuka, P. (2007): 'Address by Deputy President of the Republic Of South Africa PhumzileMlambo-Ngcuka at the South African Broadcasting Corporation (SABC) East Africa Bureau launch, Nairobi' available at www.polity.org.za/article/sa-mlambongcuka-sabc-east-africa-bureau-launch-07072007-2007-07-07, cited 27.11.11.

Mohanty, C. (1987): 'Under Western eyes: feminist scholarship and colonial discourses', *Feminist Review* 30: 61–88.

Mudimbe, V. Y. (1988): *The Invention of Africa: gnosis, philosophy and the order of knowledge in African systems* (London: James Carrey).

Mudimbe, V. Y. (1994): *The Idea of Africa* (Bloomington: James Currey).

Nyamjoh, F. (2005): *Africa's Media, Democracy and the Politics of Belonging* (London: Zed Books).

Ogola, G. (2014): '(Re-)framing the 'quality' debate: the Arab media and its future journalism', in P. Anderson, G. Ogola, and M. Williams (eds), *The Future of Quality News Journalism: a cross-continental study* (New York: Routledge)

Ogude, J. (2012): 'Whose Africa? Whose Culture? Reflections on agency, travelling theory and cultural studies in Africa', *Kunapipi*, 34(1): 12–27.

Okwori, J. Z. (2003): 'A dramatized society: representing rituals of human sacrifice as efficacious action in Nigerian home-video movies', *Journal of African Cultural Studies* 16(1): 7–23.

Pandurang, M. (2001): 'Cross-cultural texts and diasporic identities', *Jouvert* 6.

Pintak, L. (2009): 'Border guards of the "imagined" Watan: Arab journalists and the New Arab Consciousness', *The Middle East Journal*, 63(2): 191–212.

Sakr, N. (2007): *Arab Media and Political Renewal: community legitimacy and public life* (London: I.B. Tauris).

Samarajiwa, R. (1984): 'Third-World entry into the world market in news: problems and possible solutions', *Media, Culture and Society*, 6 (92): 119–36.

Shoemaker, P. and A. Cohen (2005): *News around the World: content, practitioners and the public* (London: Routledge).

Sreberny-Mohammadi, A, D. Winseck, J. McKenna, and O. Boyd-Barrett (1997): *Media in global context* (London: Arnold).

Teer-Tomaselli, R. (2007): 'South Africa as a regional media power', in D. Thussu (ed.), *Media on the Move: global flow and contra flow* (London: Routledge).

Thussu, D. (2007): *Media on the Move: global flow and contra flow* (London: Routledge).

Van Ginneken, J. (1998): *Understanding global news: a critical introduction* (London: Sage).

Wainaina, B. (2005): 'How to write about Africa', *Granta 92*.

Williams, K. (2011): *International Journalism* (London: Sage).

Xie, S. (2000): 'Rethinking the identity of cultural otherness: the discourse of difference as an unfinished project', in R. McGillis (ed.), *Voices of the Other: children's literature and the post-colonial context* (New York: Garland Publishing, Inc.).

3

International news and the image of Africa: new storytellers, new narratives?

Mel Bunce

The international news coverage of Africa has long been criticised for its episodic, simplistic and relentlessly negative content. Commentators argue that news content homogenises the continent, places an over-emphasis on African humanitarian issues, simplifies ethnicity and identity, and highlights Western-led rescue efforts (see de B'Beri and Louw, 2011; Hawk, 1992; Keane, 2004). Scholars have argued that these representations are both powerful and dangerous: they perpetuate negative stereotypes, reinforce neo-colonial power imbalance, and undermine inter-cultural empathy and connectedness (Mbembe, 2001; Silverstone, 2007).

An underlying assumption – and a source of concern – for these critics is that the international news coverage of Africa is written and produced by outsiders: Westerners writing from an occidental perspective. Drawing on the critical tradition of Orientalism, discourse analysts note that Africa is frequently presented as the object of a Western gaze, and this gaze objectifies, exoticises, and lingers on traits that are different, noteworthy, and 'other', by contrast to the safety, prosperity, and enlightenment of a Western 'home'. As Mengara suggests: 'the Africa that we know or hear about today is, essentially, a European made Africa' (2001: 8). Cumulatively, such news coverage creates what Mengara describes as 'the systematic and systemic manufacturing of a continent', based on binary oppositions that juxtapose a civilised, democratised West, with a savage Africa: 'Superiority versus inferiority, civilised versus uncivilised, pre-logical versus logical, mythical versus scientific among other epithets' (Ibid: 2). Or, as Spencer writes in relation to Western foreign correspondents in Rwanda, there is a 'positional superiority adopted in news coverage' and this reaffirms 'the images of dependency which have become symbolic of the African experience' (2005: 85–6).

Structural changes in the way international news content is collected, however, complicate this characterisation. Over the past two decades, news outlets around the world have systematically cut their foreign news budgets, leading to a radical reduction in the total number of Western foreign correspondents posted abroad (Carroll, 2007). Rather than expensively-posted foreign correspondents, many news outlets now contract local journalists to provide them with news content. The result is that international news – an important source of images and texts in the semiotic construction of 'Africa' – is to a large extent, discovered and written by journalists from the region.

This chapter explores the important role these local journalists play, and asks whether their presence is starting to change how Africa is depicted in the international news media. This question was explored as part of a larger research project looking at the international news coverage of Africa, and the factors that influence foreign correspondents as they go about their work (Bunce, 2013). It draws on fifty-one semi-structured interviews with local and international correspondents working in Sudan, Uganda and Kenya, between 2007 and 2011. The interviewed journalists worked across all of the major international newswires and news organisations operating in the region, as well as a wide range of newspapers and news magazines. Some chose to speak on the record, and others wished to remain anonymous.

The interviews reveal that local journalists frequently disagree with Western correspondents about what news should be produced: they pursue more localised and empathetic depictions of their countries. However, there remain a number of structural and organisational barriers that prevent their views from being included in final news content. To explore how these dynamics play out in practice, and shape news content, the chapter presents a case study of the international news coverage of election violence in Kenya in 2007–8, and a discussion of how news production patterns have changed since this period.

The chapter problematises Mengara's claim that, 'the Africa that we know or hear about today is, essentially, a European made Africa' (2001: 8). But it also questions the idea of image control more generally. In the international news industry, where the global and local are becoming increasingly intertwined, notions of image ownership are highly problematic. News production today is a site of struggle where journalists from diverse backgrounds contest the way in which news events should be framed; and their news stories are consumed by an international audience who are themselves active in writing, commenting and disseminating news. It is in the webs of these relationships that the image of Africa is constructed, and imbued with meaning.

The rise of local journalists

One of the most striking trends in foreign news production over the last twenty years is the increased centrality and importance of local 'foreign correspondents': journalists who report on their home country for global news outlets. In the early 1990s, Kliesch found that 63 per cent of the journalists providing foreign news for American outlets were American nationals posted abroad (1991). Ten years later, a comparable survey found only 31 per cent, a dramatic shift that reflected growth in contracts for local journalists who already lived in the news site (Wu and Hamilton, 2004: 521). Large news outlets such as the BBC have announced their intention to further reduce their posted staff in the future and recruit cost-effective local journalists in their place. Local journalists now provide substantive portions of day-to-day reporting, particularly in dangerous contexts such as Somalia and Iraq where Western correspondents may be less free to move around (Borden, 2009).

Local journalists play a particularly important role in reporting on east Africa, where there are now very few traditional Western correspondents posted abroad. In this region, the most prolific and important news outlets are the newswires Reuters, AFP and AP and, to a lesser extent, the international outlets BBC, CNN and Al-Jazeera (Williams, 2011). Local African journalists constitute approximately half the staff at the Nairobi bureaux of these major newswires and news outlets. At the time of this study, none occupied management positions, but they did play significant roles as senior correspondents and shift managers, overseeing the commissioning and editing of news from around the region.

Local journalists also play an extremely prominent role as 'stringers' (contracted journalists) for these outlets in countries around east Africa. The Reuters newswire, for example, has its east African headquarters in Nairobi, and a network of sixteen text stringers in countries around the region. Of these sixteen journalists, thirteen were local nationals: a Tanzanian national reports on Tanzania, a Burundi national on Burundi, and so on. Similarly, at the AFP newswire, eleven of thirteen text journalists in the east Africa region are local nationals.[1] These local-national FCs are often the only journalists in the field when an important event takes place. As a result, local journalists are the primary front-line agents who discover and suggest news from east Africa for the world's media consumers.

The stories are then edited in Nairobi bureaux, and put on 'the wire' to be disseminated around the world, providing the raw news content for thousands of newspapers and television channels who cannot afford their own foreign correspondents. Their stories also dominate news flows in the online news world, where news amalgamators rely heavily on newswire copy (Paterson, 2006). Finally, they play an important agenda-setting role for the remaining handful of traditional, Western FCs who are working alone to cover the whole African continent from their Nairobi and Johannesburg postings, and are often deskbound.

New correspondents, new narratives?

Initial responses to the rise of local journalists have been mixed. Some commentators have expressed concern that local journalists may be more vulnerable to the persecution of repressive governments (see also Bunce, 2011). More positively – and also the focus of this chapter – is the suggestion that the rise of local journalists represents a welcome break to the historic domination of Western perspectives in the international news. As the BBC's James Miles stated: 'I welcome them as colleagues who will give us a fresh perspective on the news from their countries ... many see the advent of local reporters as a welcome step towards a post-colonial reporting world' (quoted in Sambrook, 2010: 50). For Anthony Borden, 'the real key to inspired reporting on the world is a well-trained, well-supported local journalist who has finally been empowered to tell his or her own story' (2009: 144).

But to what extent are local journalists able to challenge traditional representations of Africa? Faced with organisational pressures, and the intense editorial demand for news that will sell in international markets, will local nationals simply replicate the writing of their Western colleagues? As Nyamnjoh suggests:

> Financial hardship leads many African journalists to seek positions as stringers for the major Western media. To be accepted, they have to think, see and write as Westerners do. Their principles are informed by Western epistemological assumptions about truth and practice, even if the reality of the ground should entail a more contextually appropriate system of meanings. (2005: 87)

Hamilton and Jenner are also circumspect:

> These 'foreign' foreign correspondents offer the potential for greater international perspective in their reporting, but will they deliver, or will foreign nationals instead end up seeing the world through the lens of the home countries of the media companies for which they are reporting, with the only advantage being that they work for less money? (2004: 138)

My interviews in east Africa suggest a mixed answer to this question. At the traditional Western newswires (AP, AFP and Reuters) and outlets

(BBC and CNN) a difficult synthesis is taking place. Local perspectives are increasingly included in news stories, resulting in more nuanced coverage. However, structural and organisational barriers mean the news continues to be dominated by a Western-centric mode of reporting, particularly during crises. It is only at alternative media – Al-Jazeera English and the unmediated platforms of Twitter – that local voices provide a consistent and genuinely alternative perspective on news events.

A localised perspective

The local journalists interviewed in this research felt that their nationality and background distinguished their reporting in three positive ways: it meant they had excellent contacts and trusted sources; they had a greater knowledge of the economic, political and historical context in which events took place; and they had a high level of emotional investment in their region, which made them both committed to their work, and in some instances, very sensitive to the local reception of their news.[2] The interviews – both with local and Western-born journalists – suggested that these differences informed the local journalists' news work: they chose different issues and gave different emphases.

The local journalists felt they had more background knowledge of the events that occurred in their country; they were able to place an event in context, and evaluate its significance. Importantly, local journalists felt that their insider knowledge made them more likely to describe stories in ways that reflected – rather than reified – local realities. As Samson Ntale, a Ugandan stringer working in Kampala for the CNN, stated:

> Internationals don't always know as much about the background and history of this place. So for example, yes, we have traditional dress – but that was brought in by outsiders – it hasn't been here forever. They don't know things like that, and so they're more likely to write a simplistic version of things. It's not malicious or racist – it's just not knowing. (Interview, Kampala, 31.8.10)

Andrew Cawthorne, the English-national bureau chief of Reuter's East Africa noted this was the case with his Somali stringer, who suggested and lobbied for stories that he had not considered important:

> She will say, 'this is happening, this leader's been replaced by this leader in this town'. And I say, 'well, the fact that this Sheik has taken over this Sheik isn't very interesting to the world' …. And she'll say, 'well actually it is important, because this leader is more pro-government', or 'they might want to introduce this type of new Sharia law'. And I think, oh, ok, so maybe that's important (Interview, Nairobi, 2.8.09)

The chief described this as a common occurrence at his outlet, where he felt there was a 'happy symbiosis' between the deep local knowledge of his outlet's journalists born and raised in east Africa, and the international perspectives of the Western correspondents in the Nairobi office.

In a similar vein, Andrew Simmons, a senior British-born producer for Al-Jazeera English (AJE) described the way Kenyan journalists' perspectives challenged Western reporting stereotypes. Simmons recalled writing a report on soaring food prices in Nairobi. His instinct had been to go to the city's slums and see how the food crisis was affecting Kenya's poorest; however, his Kenyan producer stopped him, saying: 'Hang on – the crisis is affecting the middle class too – let's go to Nakumatt [a large supermarket chain] and see how people are coping.' (Interview, Nairobi, 14.8.09). The producer's intervention resulted in a story that directly challenged – or provided a counterpoint – to the representation of Africa as exotic and 'other'. The middle-class supermarket shoppers in the report have more in common with their international news audience than the struggling occupants of slums; the subjects are like 'us' – not foreign or 'other' – and, as such, occupy a space that encourages a response of empathy rather than mere sympathy. Roger Silverstone called this the 'proper distance', and argued it was essential if the news media was to help foster an ethics of care, 'a sense of the other sufficient not just for reciprocity but for a duty of care, obligation and responsibility, as well as understanding' (2007: 46).

Local journalists also felt that their deep networks, cultural capital and language enabled them to draw on a wider range of sources in their work, meaning there were more local perspectives. The British-national correspondent for the BBC in Khartoum could not speak Arabic, and noted that this limited her potential sources: 'Things you need access to like government officials, you can't' (Interview, Khartoum, 29.8.07). Without Arabic, and in the absence of a deep network of local sources, international FCs were dependent on translators, who might be difficult to find, and who varied in quality and transparency. Without accessible sources, visiting journalists might find themselves relying on NGO spokespeople for information and quotes, as they are easy to access, and speak.[3] Local journalists, by contrast, often had very deep networks of trusted contacts and sources who were particularly valuable in countries where repressive governments – and fear of government repression – might inhibit individuals from speaking to journalists.

Some local journalists also described feeling highly invested in their country, and noted that this influenced their work. They described feeling driven to place events in their political context, and to hold elites to

account. Ben Simon, a Canadian stringer at AFP Kampala, described a
Ugandan-national BBC reporter:

> He writes important, follow-up stories whenever he has the chance. A
> group of us were going to cover an LRA [Lord's Resistance Army] story
> up north. And he decided instead to go to follow up on a landslide story
> and ask, has the government delivered on its promise to help? I thought
> that was good – he pitched the less sexy story, but one that's important,
> and to try and hold people accountable. (Interview, Kampala, 29.8.10)

Mike Pflanz, foreign correspondent at the UK's *Daily Telegraph* in
Nairobi, thought that his Kenyan predecessor at the newspaper was
emotionally involved in the local political/media ecology, and driven to
hold local elites accountable:

> He was consistently angry. About corruption, about the situation in Kenya
> and so on, and I think that bled into his reports occasionally. No bad
> thing – he had a great following ... I would have been able to write it, but
> I wouldn't necessarily have had the same compulsion to do it. (Interview,
> Nairobi, 4.8.09)

Pflanz by contrast, although concerned with the local situation, felt
that his primary ethical obligation – and the purpose of his work – was
to describe events to readers 'back home' in terms they could readily
understand.

Structural constraints: audiences and news epistemologies

Local journalists are able to influence the content of news stories in a
variety of ways. However, their ability to challenge dominant narratives
should not be overstated. All journalists operate within the constraints
of wider political, economic and organisational pressures. Shoemaker
and Reese influentially suggested that there was a 'hierarchy of influences' (1996). In this hierarchy, the contributions of the individual journalist was at the bottom; above them are the organisational values and
demands of their news organisation; and above that, factors external to
the media world, such as politics, economics, ideology and so on. These
organisational and external factors constrain the autonomy of individual correspondents and their ability to shape news content. Thus, even
where local journalists want to make a difference – and to tell stories
from a more localised perspective – they may not be able to.

Foreign correspondents in east Africa drew attention to two main
restrictions to their reporting. The first was the need to produce news
stories that sell. This is a particularly strong constraint for stringer
journalists who are paid by the story. In order to be commissioned,

they must pitch and write stories that cater to their specific news out-let's editorial position and audience interests. Today the international news market is tight, profits are low or absent, and outlets (newswires in particular) are locked in fierce competition to be first with the news. Williams notes that, in this context, 'rather than a set of news criteria, the values of news should be seen in terms of what clients and subscribers are willing to pay for. Giving customers what they want is crucial' (2011: 78).

One of the most significant implications of this customer-orientated approach has been, Williams suggests, a focus on news that is Western-centric: the majority of newswire customer are based in the Global North, they pay for the news, and it is to them that the newswires cater. As a Kenyan newswire reporter in Nairobi commented: 'Ultimately, we've still got to feed London and that's the bottom line.' This meant it was difficult to publish stories that were not of interest to international clients: 'I could send them the story "twenty people died in a car crash" and they would still come back with "twenty people die every day in car crashes". It's very depressing. African lives just don't matter' (Interview, Nairobi, 11.8.09).

A second major constraint on the work of local journalists is the conventions and professional norms that guide international journal-istic production. Chief amongst these is the notion of objectivity, often described as a definitional component of professional journalistic work (Schudson and Anderson, 2009). Objectivity refers to a package of ideas that includes the notion of 'retreatism' or non-involvement, whereby journalists are expected to be disengaged from their news stories, acting only as a witness to events. The norm of objectivity emerged in European and American news markets, but it has been expanded to the sphere of international news production, where it is so strong that those journalists or news outlets that do not abide by the principle are seen as 'unprofessional' in their work.

Journalistic objectivity is not always the first – and certainly not the only – news value embraced in media systems outside the Global North, however. Research on journalists' news values in Tanzania (Ramaprasad, 2001), Uganda (Mwesige, 2004), Ethiopia (Dirbaba, 2006) and Ghana (Hasty, 2006) reveal that journalists also value pro-fessional objectives such as explaining government policy to citizens, giving marginalised people a voice, creating a space for nation-building discourse, supporting peace processes and development aims and acting as an advocate for citizens. These aims are often at odds with the notion of the 'objective journalist', who is supposed to be an uninvolved observer, and who purports to have no agenda.

Reporting post-election violence in Kenya, 2007–8

The Kenyan post-election violence of 2007–8 provides a good opportunity to explore how the divergent values of local journalists interact with, and are constrained by, the news needs and epistemologies of global news outlets. The conflict created a complex situation for the news bureaux in Nairobi, where many of the Kenyan journalists took a different position from their Western peers regarding how the conflict should be reported. Ultimately, however, the Western voices in the newswires, enforced through hierarchical chains of command, prevailed over and above dissenting opinions of local journalists.

On 30 December 2007, incumbent Mwai Kibaki was declared the winner of the Kenyan presidential election, amid widespread claims of vote rigging from both local and international electoral monitors. Within an hour, supporters of Kibaki's opponent, Raila Odinga of the Orange Democratic Movement, began rioting across the country and attacking Kibaki supporters. The violence began as an expression of outrage at the fraudulent elections but quickly became ethnically oriented, with Luo (Odinga's tribe) mobs venting their anger on Kikuyu (Kibaki's tribe) neighbours. By the end of February 2008, post-election violence had left more than 1,200 dead and some 350,000 displaced.

The post-election violence displayed what the International Crisis Group terms 'a serious ethnic character', but ethnic differences were by no means the single root cause of the conflict (2008: 1). Tribal groupings have long been politicised and manipulated in Kenya by elites, from their construction during colonial contact, through to contemporary politics of ethnic nepotism and exclusion. Today, there is a widespread perception that the ruling party's tribal peers receive preferential access to state resources. In December 2007 these grievances, combined with weak political institutions, the normalisation of violence, and conflict among elites, created the foundations of the crisis (Cheeseman, 2008: 170).

The violence immediately captured the attention of the international news media. Unusually for an African news story, reports on the crisis reached the front pages of newspapers and were broadcast at the start of television and radio news bulletins around the world. Even more unusually, interest in the crisis was relatively long-lived, and it continued to receive a high level of attention throughout January and into February 2008.

The international news coverage of the crisis has been fiercely criticised by both Kenyan and international commentators. Two critiques, in particular, dominated the post-mortem analyses. First, it is claimed that coverage exaggerated the scale and severity of the violence. As one Kenyan reporter told the BBC World Service Report investigators, 'I watched the BBC and I thought this country was on fire. CNN was playing the same clip from Kibera as if it was a commercial. Part of what I saw was sensational [and created fear]' (2008: 14). The most explicit exaggerations were contained in articles that employed the term 'genocide', comparing Kenya's violence to the cataclysmic events of Rwanda in 1994; they reduced the crisis to an 'atavistic inevitability', and potentially stoked anger and fear (Somerville, 2009). The international news outlets showed little restraint in broadcasting the most explicit images, including burning houses, scared people on the move, the injured and the dead. In some cases, these images were presented without any explanation of their content, conveying the impression that the whole country was in a state of senseless anarchy.

Second, the international coverage was accused of employing tribal language that was incorrect, condescending and potentially inflammatory. Somerville notes that in the UK media the election violence was presented almost exclusively as a result of long-standing tribal hatred, with little or no reference to the political parties that were the source of much of the tension (2009: 530). The use of tribal language in reports concerned analysts who felt this framing generated misleading descriptions, gave insufficient explanations of the violence, and had pejorative and primitive connotations (Anderson, 2008; Keane, 2008; Somerville, 2009).

Local and international clash: divergent approaches to reporting

In Kenya, the local mainstream media (TV, press and radio owned by the two main media houses) adopted a very reserved approach to reporting. Concerned not to exacerbate the violence, journalists refrained from naming the different ethnic groups involved in fighting, and chose to describe clashes as occurring between different 'communities'. Speaking to the BBC World Service Trust Report Farida Karoney, a Kenyan reporter, stated her outlet's position: 'Here at KTN, when we are reporting conflict we will not refer to people by their tribe because we think that such tribal references will entrench feelings of hate' (2008: 8).[4]

This local coverage contrasts starkly with international reporters' work, and strong differences of opinion are still articulated today. Kenyan journalists argue that the international reporters demonstrated little concern for the wellbeing of Kenya or Kenyans, and were simply trying to break another story for professional gain. Kenyan journalist turned academic George Ogola, for example, writes:

It was not a desire by a section of the international media to tell the world the true story about the conflict that was slowly consuming Kenya. This was about a good story; it was about the exploitation of a people crying out for help. (2008)

Underlying this clash is a fundamental disagreement on the role of the news media during a crisis. Kenyan journalists describe an important ethical obligation to the peace process itself, and argue that the media should not produce reports that are potentially inflammatory, whether they are intended for a primarily local or international audience. This position is sometimes referred to in communications literature as 'peace journalism' or 'conflict-sensitive journalism' (Galtung, 2000), and it is regarded as being in direct competition with traditional 'hard news' (Fawcett, 2002). Many traditional foreign correspondent are exceedingly resistant to peace journalism, as it challenges their core journalistic commitment to objectivity. They argue that feelings of attachments and becoming involved in the peace process undermine the ability of journalists to objectively bear witness.

A profound split emerged within the international news bureaux of Nairobi, where Kenyan and international journalists disagreed about how the violence should be covered. Kenyan journalists tended to be more sensitive to language that framed the crisis in exclusively ethnic terms. Moreover, the Kenyan reporters felt that international journalists should be more selective and cautious with what they covered, and more reserved in the language they used.

The bureau chief at Reuters thought that his newswire did a reasonable job of avoiding the worst of the tribal language in its reports, and was fairly sensitive to the inflammatory potential of news content: 'Every meeting we had, every story we wrote, we were aware of that [trying to avoid tribal language]'. However, he believed things could have been reported in a more nuanced way and, to some extent, this reflected the fact that the Western journalists in the office dominated the editorial meetings and reporting decisions during the crisis: 'We could have done better. Afterwards when we had a big discussion that became clear' (Interview, Nairobi, 2.8.09). Time pressures meant there was little opportunity to reflect or fully discuss the issues with staff:

I couldn't fuck around – if you'll excuse me – when that was happening. I couldn't spend an hour to sit back and let's think about this and coax out people's ideas. I was like, um, a church is burning with thirty-three people inside, we need to urgently write about that. 'Is this echoes of Rwanda, isn't it echoes of Rwanda?' I mean, huge questions like that, and we were making split-second judgments on them. And there, unfortunately, those hardened correspondents here, we tended to dominate here. I wanted to make the others speak up, and they weren't. Later on, they had a lot to say, an awful lot. (Ibid)

Although Cawthorne suggests that he would have liked the Kenyan journalists to speak up, it is unclear if this would have made a big difference. It may have added nuance to some language use, but it is unlikely to have altered the general frame in which the election violence was cast. Cawthorne and the Western journalists in the Reuters office are highly intelligent, experienced professionals – most have lived and reported in east Africa for several years. These journalists were aware of the ways in which Kenya's ethnic groups have been manipulated by elites and knew about the multi-level factors that were compounding and driving the conflict. The different positions taken by Western and local journalists were not based on information asymmetry; they appeared to be based on an emotional/attachment asymmetry. The Kenyans wanted the optimal outcome for their country – for the conflict to be resolved, rather than represented at its worst in a way that might fuel fighting and resentment. This impulse directly conflicted with the hard news needs of the outlet, and it was ultimately side-lined.

Reuters was not the only divided newsroom. At the BBC, Kenyan journalist Kevin Mwachito described direct conflict between the BBC's World Service reporters and its international news team over how the election violence should be reported: 'We were careful not to say it was a Kikuyu and a Lao thing. It wasn't – people from both those groups weren't fighting, and there were a lot more groups of people involved besides.' However, he felt that the organisation's editors in the UK were not as sensitive to the issue as the correspondents based in Nairobi: 'London didn't really understand that, I don't think. They would say, "get me a Kikuyu and a Lao".' (Interview, Nairobi, 27.8.09).

In particular, a major rift emerged in the lead-up to the signing of a peace deal, which the Kenyan journalists hoped would bring the conflict to an end. The day before the deal was due to be signed, it was leaked that President Kbaki planned to hold a private meeting in State House that threatened to de-rail the peace process. Mwachito explained:

[The peace deal] was the first glimmer of hope that the fighting might end – you know, after months, and we were all so sick of the fighting. And then here's this potential meeting jeopardising the hope. And my African colleagues were very, very upset that the internationals wanted to run that story. They felt it should not be covered – you know, that the whites just wanted a story that they didn't care about this country. And if things got worse, you know, they could just jet out of there. Whereas we couldn't, it was our country.

I asked what happened when there was a rift in the newsroom: whose view prevails? Mwachito replied:

> There are channels of command and they kick in at times like that. People may have vented in private at our news editor, but at the end of the day, it's his decision. You really could tell, though, for the first time, the big gap between [local and Western reporters]. (Interview, Nairobi, 27.8.09)

In normal day-to-day reporting, Kenyan journalists in the Nairobi bureaux have a high level of involvement in decision making about the stories and angles of reporting. Kenyans run the morning news meetings, they report fairly autonomously on their own beats, and contribute to newsroom discussions. They often suggest stories that would not have been told otherwise. In the coverage of the election crisis, however, this symbiosis faltered. Despite their significant numbers, Kenyan journalists were absent from the management level of the newswires and outlets. In addition, there was a state of emergency in the newsroom and decisions were made swiftly, often without discussion or consultation; the hierarchies of management became more visible, and the Kenyan voices were side-lined. Just as crucially, the Kenyan journalists' proximity to the violence became a liability in reporting 'hard' news. As Kevin Mwato stated: 'As a Kenyan journalist, I need to say, "Was I impartial?" We wanted change' (Interview, Nairobi, 27.8.09). According to the norms of these international news organisations – and their strong commitment to objectivity – conflict-sensitive reporting was undesirable, and contrasted unfavourably with the hardened distance of the traditional foreign correspondents. At these traditional, hard-news outlets, it was the need to make profit, and the norms of the international journalistic field, that shaped and constrained reporting.

Alternative voices

Two challenges to Western-dominated reporting have arisen in recent years in the shape of Al Jazeera and Twitter. One provides more nuanced, locally-sensitive coverage of Africa, and the other is a forum for local citizens and journalists to comment on events. This section considers the ways and extent to which these media provide space for local voices to be expressed.

Al Jazeera represents an alternative to reporting told through a Western perspective. Funded by the wealthy Qatari state, Al Jazeera is insulated from the need to make profit. Moreover, it has been set up with the articulated, self-conscious goal of offering an alternative approach to news content. Its intention is to provide alternative reporting on events, including controversial and dissenting opinions, and to specifically find and report on untold and under-reported stories. In doing so, commentators note that Al Jazeera often 'portrays a concealed reality ... it gives airtime to the people who will be barred from appearing in any other network' (Biesla, 2008: 362). Journalists working at the channel echo these sentiments, and describe their desire to tell news stories from multiple perspectives, with a particular emphasis on those who have historically been marginalised (El Nawawy and Powers, 2010). Content analyses of the outlet's news indicate that, as compared with CNN and BBC, greater air time is given to issues and events in the Global South and it includes more quotes from local, non-elite sources (Figenschou, 2010; Painter, 2008).

Malcolm Webb, English-national stringer for Al Jazeera English in Uganda feels the outlet tries to specifically 'go out of their way to cover obscure places on purpose'. Webb gave the example of the Burundi elections: 'Financially, other outlets can't do this – you know, investors and readers and things, they're simply not interested in Burundi. But at Al Jaz, the attitude is: it's an election, and it's on our patch, so we do it.' Webb also felt that he had more latitude in how he shaped and framed his reporting: 'At AFP, I might have tried to present it as something quirky or headline grabbing. But at Al Jaz, it's really just, "something serious about people". And especially if they've been screwed over in some way' (Interview, Kampala, 27.8.10).

During Kenya's post-election violence, Al Jazeera English seems to have adopted a conciliatory form of journalism. Producer Andrew Simmons states that it was very important to the producers not to be provocative during the election crisis, and that this principle trumped other notions of newsworthiness:

> We tried very hard not to be inflammatory ... I was anchoring, and I would have to say to them [politicians] – during an interview – 'Look, you can't talk like that' ... I was interviewing William Ruto the night after the church burnt down. I said, 'You must condemn this atrocity' and he was just replying 'oh, the police are always committing atrocities' – I told him, and made it clear, that he was out of line saying that on television. (Interview, Nairobi, 1414.8.09)

Whereas other journalists might have turned the interview into a dramatic piece illustrating political animosity, the Al Jazeera English journalist described a pressing obligation to *de*sensationalise the statements. They were aware their news was being followed locally – AJE is available on free-to-air television in Kenya, where they have a large audience – and the journalists felt they had become important actors in the crisis, with the power to exacerbate or provide calm. In covering the election violence, AJE provided a form of peace journalism, or what El-Nawawy and Powers have described as 'Conciliatory Media': they let a variety of voices speak, did not frame issues within a traditional conflict narrative, and they represented the interest of the public in general (2010: 70).

AJE has the freedom to report in this manner for a number of reasons. The major international news wires and news outlets discussed above tend to report for an audience based in the Western world. Thus journalists working at these outlets have an implicit understanding that news needs to be framed so that Western consumers can readily understand it. Moreover, in a competitive environment, journalists are less likely to 'back off' or report more sensitively on a high-profile news story that can win them recognition and prestige. In direct contrast, AJE journalists do not have any 'home country'. They appear to pursue a more comprehensive internationalism that includes a sense of ethical obligation to the local environment where they are based and reporting from. They seem to valorise – and associate cultural capital and status with – those journalists who are able to show and share empathy with the local subjects of their reports.

Social media too has begun to alter who exactly 'speaks for Africa', and how the continent is presented to international news consumers. The power of Twitter in particular to challenge Western coverage and shape international news coverage of east Africa started to be noted in earnest in March 2012 when CNN ran a story about an isolated attempted terrorist attack on a bus in Nairobi. This was reported on the channel's news under a banner reading 'Violence in Kenya' and many observers felt that the report was sensationalised and the event taken out of context. The Kenyan 'Twitter-sphere' responded, and the hashtag #SomeonetellCNN was born. Vice President Kalonzo Musyoka, amongst many others, tweeted: 'It is extremely irresponsible for CNN to paint Kenya as a nation in chaos while we are victims of terror. #SomeonetellCNN.' These tweets expressed the strong desire of Kenyan citizens to describe events to the international community on their own terms. As @NiNanjira tweeted, '#SomeonetellCNN that Africans watch CNN too & that we will not be silent as they misrepresent us. We Will Be Heard!' The hash tags #SomeonetellCNN, became the second most trending term on Twitter that week. Eventually the east African foreign correspondent for CNN, David Mckenzie, issued an apology: 'Our reporting last night was accurate, the banner used in bulletin was not. I contacted CNN for future bulletins [to be corrected]. Apologies to all.' As more pressure mounted on Twitter, the news video was actually taken off the CNN website, with another apology from McKenzie: 'We are having offending video pulled. Again, apologies for the mistake. It was changed on air, but not online. Now it is.' In this instance the power of Twitter was made clear: it entered into, and influenced, mainstream news representations of Kenya.

During the 2013 election in Kenya, #SomeonetellCNN was resurrected and used to name and shame Western journalists that Kenyans felt were reporting sensational or inaccurate material in the lead up to the vote. The most targeted was again a CNN report, this one titled 'Kenyans armed and ready to vote' which showed a handful of men described as a 'militia', preparing for armed conflict in Kenya's Rift Valley. The piece was immediately criticised on Twitter by Kenyans who described it as staged and irresponsible (Dewey, 2013; Shiundu, 2013). Tweets redistributed rebuttals and parodies of the report from citizens and local Kenyan reporters; a *Daily Nation* piece that was widely circulated, opened with the line, 'Kenya was braced at the crossroads on Saturday amidst growing concern that the demand for clichés is outstripping supply' (Namlo, 2013).

The rise of social media represents a distinct break in historical reporting practices and, notably, the news coverage of election violence six years earlier. As media commentator Nyabola wrote in an Al Jazeera English analysis piece: 'Six years ago, in December 2007, we Kenyans were helpless and paralysed, as alarmist reports often inaccurately depicted our country as another in the litany of failed states in Africa... Now, in 2013, Kenyan presence on the internet has expanded dramatically and it is harder to get away with such overstatement' (2013).

Kenyan tweets were not restricted to the Twitter-sphere – they entered into, and became stories in mainstream international news coverage. Outlets such as the BBC, Reuters, Al Jazeera and *Washington Post* all carried stories based exclusively on tweets, foregrounding the Kenyan reaction to the international coverage and their call for unity and peace during the election. Mohammed Ademo, writing for *Columbia Journalism Review* noted:

What's new is social media's role in empowering Africans to own the narrative and protest against what they saw as stereotypical coverage of their stories ... as more Africans start to use social media, it is playing an increasingly important role in allowing them to partake in conversations about their future, and to protest unfair representations. (2013)

Or as Nyabola wrote, her previous 'experience of "voicelessness" over the construction and dissemination of my national narrative' had been, to a large extent, ameliorated by the new technology: 'What Twitter does successfully is allowing those who may not be able to claim power in the context of traditional media (with higher economic barriers to entry and with more entrenched power dynamics) to claim it in 10 characters or less ... a lot of Kenyans are determined to take control of their national narrative'(2013).

There is no doubt that Africans are appropriating the internet to represent their countries from local perspectives. Low penetration of the internet in many African countries makes this difficult (Ogunyemi, 2011: 468) but there is clearly a critical mass in Kenya that is capable of making CNN amend its reporting, and has enough participants and followers to trend Kenyan issues on Twitter's global stage.

Conclusion

From the romping pages of Evelyn Waugh's *Scoop* to the critical satire of Binyavanga Wainaina (2005, 2012), foreign correspondents in Africa have been parodied for their indulgent, ex-patriot lifestyles. Disconnected from local realities, these foreigners are seen to enjoy a parasitic relationship with the local environment, profiting from the suffering they observe. Wainaina describes foreign correspondents living in Kenya:

> Nairobi is a good place to be an international correspondent. There are regular flights to the nearest genocide, and there are green lawns, tennis courts, good fawning service. You can get pork belly, and you can hire an OK pastry chef called Elijah (surname forgotten) to work in your kitchen for $300 a month. (2012)

Wainaina's comments are consistent with a substantive postcolonial literature that draws attention to the way the image of Africa has, for centuries, been crafted and controlled by actors from outside the continent. But his comments are no longer consistent with how the majority of daily foreign news content is produced.

International news images of Africa are no longer constructed entirely – or even predominantly – by Western-born foreign correspondents; local journalists around east Africa constitute the majority of correspondents working for traditional, international news organisations. These journalists, with deep local networks and background knowledge are writing news that, in limited ways, provides an alternative and localised perspective on news events. However, these journalists are deeply embedded in international news outlets that operate on tight profit margins, and produce news for clients predominantly based in the Western world. Moreover, their work is shaped by the prevailing values of the journalistic field, with its emphasis on objectivity, and the firm notion of journalistic non-involvement. The more significant development, this chapter has suggested, is the emergence of alternative outlets and new mediums, in the guise of Al Jazeera English and Twitter. Through these media, for perhaps the first time in history, local voices are starting to construct and debate the contemporaneous image of Africa that is disseminated around the world.

Notes

1 Interviews with Andrew Cawthorne, the Nairobi Reuters Bureau Chief (2.8.09), and with John-Mark Mojon, the AFP News Editor (3.8.09).
2 It is important to note that these comparisons were particularly made in contrast to visiting or 'parachute' journalists, rather than the handful of Western correspondents who had lived and worked in the region for some time (and were often highly regarded by local journalists).
3 The symbiotic relationship between foreign correspondents and NGO representatives has been said to result in reporting that over-emphasises humanitarian frames and interpretations of crises, thereby obscuring political and historical dimensions and inadvertently reinforcing the casting of Africa in terms of development, disaster and 'humanitarian' concerns (e.g. Cooper, 2011; Mackintosh, 1996).
4 The Kenyan media were not homogenous in this approach. In particular, some vernacular radio stations were accused of allowing upset and angry callers to vent their opinions, without moderation and thus fuelling violence (Waki Report, 2008). However, in the Kenyan mainstream media – which is highly trusted by the general population (Maina, 2007) – the approach was uniformly reserved and restrained.

References

Ademo, M. (2013): 'In Kenya's election, reporting what's there, not what's assumed', *Columbia Journalism Review*, www.cjr.org/behind_the_news/coverage_of_kenyan_election.php?page=all.
Anderson, D. (2008): 'Kenya on the Brink', *Prospect Magazine* 142.
BBC World Service Trust (2008): 'The Kenyan 2007 elections and their aftermath: the role of media and communication', *BBC World Service Trust Policy Briefing #1*.
Biesla, E. (2008): 'The pivotal role of news agencies in the context of globalization: a historical approach', *Global Networks* 8(3): 347–66.

Borden, A. (2009): 'Local Heroes', in J. Owen and H. Purdey (eds), *International News Reporting* (Chichester: Wiley-Blackwell).

Bunce, M. (2010): '"This place used to be a white British boys' club"': reporting dynamics and cultural clash at an international news bureau in Nairobi', *The Round Table: The Commonwealth Journal of International Affairs* 99(114): 515–28.

Bunce, M. (2011): 'The new foreign correspondent at work: local-national "stringers" and the global news coverage of conflict in Darfur', *Reuters Report: Reuters Institute for the Study of Journalism* (Oxford University).

Bunce, M. (2013): 'Reporting from "the field": foreign correspondents and the international news coverage of east Africa', (unpublished Doctoral thesis, Oxford University).

Carroll, J. (2007): 'Foreign news coverage: the US media's undervalued asset', *Working Paper Series #1* (Joan Shorenstein Center on the Press, Politics and Public Policy, Cambridge, MA: Harvard University).

Cheeseman, N. (2008): 'The Kenyan elections of 2007: an introduction', *Journal of East African Studies* 2(2): 166–84.

Constable, P. (2007): 'No news is bad news: demise of the foreign correspondent', *The Washington Post*, 18.2.07.

Cooper, G. (2011): 'From their own correspondent?: new media and the changes in disaster coverage: lessons to be learnt', *Reuters Report: Reuters Institute for the Study of Journalism* (Oxford University).

de B'Beri, B. E. and E. Louw (2011): 'Special issue: the Afro-pessimism phenomenon', *Critical Arts* 25: 335–466.

Dewey, Caitlin (2013): 'Kenyans mock foreign media coverage on Twitter', *The Washington Post*, 4.3.13, www.washingtonpost.com/blogs/worldviews/wp/2013/03/04/kenyans-mock-foreign-media-coverage-on-twitter, accessed 17.12.14.

Dirbaba, Birhanu (2006): 'The professional orientation of journalists in Ethiopia: survey of their self-perception' (MA thesis, Addis Ababa University).

El-Nawawy, M. and S. Powers (2010): 'Al Jazeera English: a conciliatory medium in a conflict driven environment?', *Global Media and Communication* 6(1): 61–84.

Fair, J. (1993): 'War, famine, and poverty: race in the construction of Africa's media image', *Journal of Communication Inquiry* 17: 5–22.

Fawcett, L. (2002): 'Why peace journalism isn't news', *Journalism Studies* 3(2): 213–23.

Figenschou, T. U. (2010): 'A voice for the voiceless?: a quantitative content analysis of Al Jazeera English's flagship news', *Global Media and Communication* 6(1): 85–107.

Galtung, J. (2000): 'The task of peace journalism', *Ethical Perspectives* 7: 162–7.

Hamilton, J. and E. Jenner (2004): 'Foreign correspondence: evolution, not Extinction', *Neiman Reports* 58(3): 98–100.

Hasty, J. (2006): 'Performing power, composing culture: the state press in Ghana', Ethnography 7(1): 69–98.

Hawk, B. (1992): *Africa's Media Image* (New York: Praeger).

International Crisis Group (2008): 'Kenya in crisis', Africa Report No. 137.

Keane, F. (2004): 'Trapped in a time warped narrative', *Neiman Reports* 58(3).

Keane, F. (2008): 'Kenya's poor at each other's throats', BBC Online News.

Kliesch, R. E. (1991): 'The US press corps abroad rebounds: a 7th world survey of foreign correspondents', *Newspaper Research Journal* 12(1): 24–33.

Mackintosh, A. (1996): 'International aid and the media', in T. Allen, K. Hudson and J. Seaton (eds), *War, Ethnicity and the Media* (South Bank University: London).

Maina, L. (2007): *Kenya: research findings and conclusions* (African Media Development Initiative, London: BBC World Service Trust).

Mbembe, J. A. (2001): *On the Postcolony* (London: University of California Press).

Mengara, D. (ed.) (2001): *Images of Africa: stereotypes and realities* (African World Press: Trenton).

Mwesige, P. G. (2004): 'Disseminators, advocates and watchdogs: a profile of Ugandan journalists in the new millennium', *Journalism* 5(1).

Namlo, A. (2013): 'Foreign reporters armed and ready to attack Kenya', *Daily Nation* 2.3.13.

Nyabola, N. (2013): 'Kenya tweets back: #SomeonetellCNN', *Al Jazeera English*, 6.3.13.

Nyamnjoh, F. (2005): *Africa's media: democracy and the politics of belonging* (Zed Books: London).

Ogola, G. (2008): 'Kenya: "Parachute" journalists and the crisis', *Business Daily*, 18.1.08.

Ogunyemi (2011): 'Representation of Africa online: sourcing practice and frames of reference', *Journal of Black Studies* 42(3): 457–78.

Painter, J. (2008): *Counter-Hegemonic News: A case study of Al Jazeera English and TeleSUR* (Reuters Institute for the Study of Journalism, Oxford University: Oxford).

Paterson, C. (2006): 'News Agency Dominance in International News on the internet', Papers in International and Global Communication 1(6).

Ramaprasad, J. (2001): 'A profile of journalists in post-independence Tanzania', *Gazette: The International Journal for Communication* 63(6): 539–55.

Sambrook, R. (2010): *Are Foreign Correspondents Redundant?: the changing face of international news* (Challenges Series: Reuters Institute for the Study of Journalism: Oxford University).

Schudson, M. and C. Anderson (2009): 'Objectivity, professionalism, and truth seeking in journalism', in K. Wahl-Jorgensen and T. Hanitzsch (eds), *The handbook of journalism studies* (London: Routledge).

Shiundu, A. (2013): 'Online fury over CNN's story on unnamed militia group', *Daily Nation*, 1.3.13.

Shoemaker, P. and S. Reese (1996): *Mediating the Message: theories of influences on mass media content*, second edition (White Plains, NY: Longman).

Silverstone, R. (2007): *Media and Morality: on the rise of the mediapolis* (Cambridge: Polity Press).

Somerville, K. (2009): 'British media coverage of the post election violence in Kenya 2007–8', *Journal of Eastern African Studies* 3 (3): 526–42.

Spencer, G. (2005): *The Media and Peace: from Vietnam to the 'war on terror'* (Palgrave MacMillan: Basingstoke).

Wainaina, B. (2005) 'How to write about Africa', *Granta* 92.

Wainaina, B. (2012): 'How not to write about Africa in 2012: a beginners guide', *Guardian*, 3.6.12.

Waki Report (2008): 'Kenya Commission of Enquiry on the Post-election Violence', 15.10.08.

Williams, K. (2011): *International Journalism* (London: Sage).

Wu, D. and J. Hamilton (2004): 'US foreign correspondents: changes and continuity at the turn of the century', *Gazette: The International Journal for Communication Studies* 66(6): 517–32.

4

'Image management' in east Africa: Uganda, Rwanda, Kenya and their donors[1]

Jonathan Fisher

Securing the support of international actors and institutions has long been a central element of regime maintenance strategies for most African governments. Since the end of the Cold War and the withdrawal of Soviet money from Africa, Western donor states and institutions, particularly the World Bank, EU, US, UK and France, have come to enjoy almost monopolistic prominence in this regard, the recent re-entrance of China to the African diplomatic 'game' notwithstanding. Western aid and military assistance has been particularly important for regime maintenance in east Africa in recent decades – notably in Rwanda and Uganda. Access to key Western markets and industries, including tourism, has also been of critical value to less aid-dependent governments such as those in Kenya, for the same purposes.

The level and extent of Western support to these and other governments, however, has generally been contingent on the latter fitting a particular profile vis-à-vis Western interests. Commentators have consistently concluded, for example, that governments and states perceived to be geostrategically and/or economically important by donors have frequently received more generous and sustained assistance from this community than others, as have those considered to be key allies in the global security and/or development arena.

Crucially, however, the extent to which African governments meet these criteria is ultimately based on the judgement and perspective of donor institutions and officials. Governments form and modify their perceptions of other governments on the basis of various information flows, evaluations of events, and personal encounters in a highly informal and often arbitrary fashion, leading, as Jervis, Vertzberger and others have argued, to 'misperceptions' being used to shape foreign policy decisions and stances (Jervis, 1976; Vertzberger, 1990). As Dunn notes in his exploration of Congo's 'image' among Western policymakers: '[Western perceptions are based on] a gradual layering and connecting of events and meanings'; there are few guarantees, however, regarding 'which events will be selected' in this process (2004: 124–5).

This chapter will argue for the importance of considering the role of African governments themselves in this 'image management' process. Keenly aware of the crucial value of being perceived as 'an ally in the War on Terror' or a 'development success story', for example, a number of regimes, including those in Rwanda and Uganda, have proactively sought to emphasise these 'images' of themselves to donors in contrast to other, more negative ones. They have consequently, it is suggested, received sustained and enthusiastic international support from development 'partners'. Other governments, most notably those in Kenya, have been far less adept at influencing their image in Western embassies and ministries and have, as a result, experienced far more fractious relationships with the same donors. Ultimately, it is argued, those regimes which have been able to manage their international images have enjoyed greater regime security than those who have not.

The chapter will begin by examining the relationship between regime maintenance and image in African foreign relations before exploring in greater depth the space available to African governments to manage their image at the international level. The main part of the chapter will then analyse how the governments of Paul Kagame in Rwanda, Yoweri Museveni in Uganda and Daniel arap Moi and Mwai Kibaki in Kenya have engaged in this practice, to varying degrees, over the last two decades[2] under three main headings: personalisation of diplomacy; use of public relations firms; and engagement with non-governmental actors and institutions. The extent to which activity or inactivity by these governments in this regard can be used to explain levels of international support will then be assessed by way of conclusion.

In making these arguments, the chapter draws primarily on over one hundred semi-structured interviews undertaken between 2008 and 2012 (only a small number of which are cited directly) with current and former donor officials involved, or previously involved, in policy-making with regard to these four states in London, Washington DC, New York and Kampala. Interviews with Kenyan, Rwandan and Ugandan state officials were also carried out from 2009–2012, as were interviews with Western journalists and public relations firms working in or on these countries. The chapter also makes use of a variety of media sources (both Western and African), broadcasts and transcripts of speeches and interviews with both east African and Western politicians, documents submitted to the US Department of Justice by US public relations firms, historical US embassy cables leaked via *Wikileaks* since 2010 and a number of official documents released to the author by the UK Government under the Freedom of Information Act (2000) between 2009 and 2011.

Regime maintenance, 'image' and 'image management' in African foreign relations

Since independence, few African states have been governed by regimes that are not reliant, at least to some degree, on Western aid. During the Cold War era, for example, the ability of regimes from Zaire to Malawi and from Togo to Kenya to maintain power in their respective territories was contingent not so much on seeking domestic support (through elections or other means) but through accessing international aid. Since the fall of the Berlin Wall, this 'externalisation of political accountability' has become even more central to regime maintenance strategies in many African polities, as Clapham and Clark have shown (Clark, 2001; Clapham, 1996: 88–95, 201–4). Between the mid-1990s and late 2000s, for example, over half of the Ugandan and Rwandan government budgets were funded by Western donors (Campioni and Noack, 2012: 4; Tripp, 2010: 186). Likewise, a sudden suspension of aid to Kenya by donors in 1991 forced the then aid-reliant Moi regime to dismantle the country's one-party state only days after suggesting that such a process would take 'at least 200 years' (Perlez, 1991; Stokke, 1995: 47–56).

Analyses of contemporary aid allocation patterns have frequently concluded, nonetheless, that some African states and governments have received substantially more support over time than others – and rarely in proportion to the relative poverty of their respective populations ('recipient need'). Instead, donor interests – political, economic, strategic and ideological – are argued to be at the heart of such considerations, with donors offering plentiful support to governments of states perceived to be strategically or economically important to them and far less to those which do not match this profile (Harrigan and Wang, 2011; Schraeder *et al*, 1998; Whitfield and Fraser, 2010; Woods, 2005). Since the 1990s, a government's stance in relation to tackling global terrorism and successfully implementing international development goals, it is suggested, have also come to gain particular prominence within these calculations.

It is important to note, however, that no standardised, mechanistic evaluation system exists in donor institutions for officials to use in ascertaining whether or not a foreign government is, for example, a 'security ally'. Nor could there be: such judgements regarding a country's 'image' are – by their very nature – highly subjective and open to interpretation. Likewise, as Vertzberger has argued, policy-makers form judgements on issues and foreign governments in an iterative and dynamic fashion, usually in response to a highly arbitrary flow of information from a variety of sources (1990: 6–49). In 'processing' this information, the officials in question subject it to their own biases and prejudices and attempt to fit it into narratives, frameworks and historical analogies they are familiar with – a practice known as 'heuristics' amongst foreign policy analysis scholars (Dyson and Preston, 2006; Jervis, 1976; Khong, 1992; Neustadt and May, 1986).

African governments are not always simply the inert targets of this image construction process, however, as a variety of scholars have increasingly begun to show. Bayart, for example, argues that despite the 'unequal entry' of African states into global politics, African governments have not simply been the 'passive objects of a process of dependency' (2000: 219; 2009: 20). Instead, in his exploration of 'extraversion' he notes that numerous regimes, including those of Moi in Kenya, Biya in Cameroon and Bongo in Gabon, have used the 'discourse of democracy' in their interactions with Western donors as a means to extract resources and avoid aid cuts or censures in an analysis which discusses African leaders' diplomacy in terms of 'duplicity' and the use of 'make-believe' (Bayart, 2000: 225). Clapham has made a similar point in his exposition of 'subversion' as a response by some African regimes to increasingly turbulent relations with donor 'partners' in the era of political conditionality (Clapham 1996: 201–4).

More recently, Whitfield and Fraser have concluded that donor support for many regimes is based upon the 'vagaries of [how they are portrayed in] diplomatic, civil society and media representations'. Consequently, they suggest, several African governments have skillfully 'maneouevered themselves into the position of key ally of a major donor' by influencing these representations. They point specifically to the Meles regime in Ethiopia and the Kagame regime in Rwanda in this regard, arguing that both have successfully presented themselves as 'the good reformer' in their interactions with donors and, as a result, enjoyed more plentiful and uncritical support than many similar governments on the continent (2010: 40–1).

This analysis, however, paints an ambiguous picture vis-à-vis the veracity and 'African-ness' of these images. Characterising African engagement herein as 'subversion' and 'make-believe' implies, at least to some extent, a willful and instrumental misrepresentation of an objective reality on their part. In the case of Biya's democratisation adventure this may be justified. The Kagame and Meles regimes, however, have genuinely instituted many of the reforms which have won them such praise from Western donors. Likewise the Meles and Museveni regimes (see below) have undoubtedly committed considerable resources and energy into domestic and regional counter-terrorism efforts in the last two decades; they have not simply been 'pretending' to join the Global War on Terror. In all cases they have also done so for domestic, political and ideological reasons not necessarily connected to relations with donors.

Where African 'maneouevering' could be said to be a factor in these cases, therefore, is not so much through the 'invention' of these images but through the emphasis placed on them within the African-donor relationship. Where images of economic reform, domestic stability or alignment on counter-terrorism may undergird donor rationales for providing support to these regimes, for example, other equally valid images – related to corruption, regional brinkmanship and political authoritarianism – may have the opposite effect. Furthermore, these regimes' 'claims' to leadership in these areas could potentially be undermined by comparative analyses; a credible argument could be made, for example, that the Ugandan and Kenyan governments in fact possess quite similar records of cooperation with donors on counter-terrorism issues (Fisher, 2013: 1–8).

As Dunn notes, however, it is not always certain what events, issues and priorities donors will focus upon in building their image of a regime (2004: 124–5). This study will therefore emphasise how African governments have used a variety of media to 'sell' and emphasise particular images of themselves to donors – *redirecting* them from alternative, potentially more damaging ones (with the exception of Kenya). It will also explore the effects of their doing or – in Kenya's case – not doing this on domestic regime maintenance.

The interactive nature of this process also raises the question of the indigeneity of the 'images' being emphasised by these African states in their engagement with donors. Bayart's idea of extraversion, for example, posits African states accessing – and attempting to incorporate themselves into – narratives created and governed by Western donors. A similar dynamic is suggested by Whitfield and Fraser's 'maneouvering' metaphor. That donors provide support to foreign states based on perceptions of that state developed through their own conceptual lenses is arguably logical from a particular 'starting point'. As donors interact more with African officials, however, the extent to which these perceptions remain wholly Western is a more complex issue.

How far, for example, does a donor's image of a state being at the 'forefront of the Global War on Terror' remain a 'Western image' when the content of this image, in Uganda's case, becomes based, in part, on the regime's presentation of its fight against a local millenarian, rebel movement with few discernible political objectives or links to international terror networks (the Lord's Resistance Army; see Fisher, 2013:

16–19)? On the one hand this could be characterised as the Ugandan regime cynically portraying a domestic insurgency in line with Western narratives and concepts. On the other, however, it could be argued that by persuading donors to see the LRA threat as equivalent to that of Al-Qaeda or other Islamist extremist networks, the regime has successfully re-constituted, at least in part, donor understandings of the Global War on Terror itself, thereby part-Africanising a narrative clearly originating in Washington.

Exploring these wider issues of 'image authorship' is not feasible in a study of this length. They raise, however, central questions about the relationship between image management and the nature of African agency in the international system – a subject which will be returned to in the conclusion. The majority of the chapter, however, will attempt to take a more empirical approach by exploring how the governments of these three east African states have – or have not – attempted to manage their images among donors, focusing particularly on how they have – or have not – sought to 'control' the central themes in donor perceptions for regime maintenance purposes. It is first necessary, however, to contextualise the nature of donor support to these states in recent decades and how this support has been rationalised in donor minds.

Donors and regime maintenance in east Africa

The Museveni and Kagame regimes gained power with limited support beyond the African continent. In maintaining power, however, the two increasingly authoritarian governments have relied considerably on international donor assistance – particularly from the World Bank, US, UK, EU and Nordic states. Following its adoption of a World Bank Economic Recovery Programme in 1987, a year after entering office, Uganda's National Resistance Movement regime (NRM) experienced a rapid increase in donor support which involved a 63 per cent rise in international aid over eight years. This situation has continued apace into the twenty-first century; between 2003 and 2008, for example, aid flows to Uganda increased by 90 per cent (from US$991m to $1891m). Kagame's Rwandan Patriotic Front regime (RPF), taking power in the immediate aftermath of Rwanda's horrific 1994 genocide, was less swiftly embraced by donors – at least from a financial perspective (OECD, various years). This changed, however, from the mid-1990s and the country saw its aid contributions triple in less than a decade.

The degree of international support for these two governments can also be seen from other dimensions. Washington and London, for example, have been particularly generous in their provision of military assistance and training to both regimes since the early 2000s despite their armed forces' controversial interventions in Congo in recent history. Likewise, donors have been far less willing to criticise or reduce aid to Kampala or Kigali owing to democratic backsliding, human rights abuses or regional warmongering than they have with many other African administrations (Reyntjens, 2004: 206–7). Finally, some donors (particularly the UK, EU, Netherlands and Nordics) have, until very recently, been keen to support the two governments more directly in their aid contributions by moving towards the use of budget support as their preferred modality in Uganda and Rwanda. During the 2000s, for example, 40–50 per cent of UK aid to Uganda has been provided in this manner, while the figure is over 70 per cent in the case of Rwanda. This means the Museveni and Kagame regimes have become increasingly dependent on Western donors with both regimes' national budgets being 50–60 per cent funded by international actors since the 1990s (Campioni and Noack, 2012: 4; Tripp, 2010: 186).

In explaining the level, and enthusiasm, of donor support for these two governments, commentators have pointed to a number of issues. Both regimes successfully implemented IFI-recommended 'neo-liberal' economic reform packages in their early years in office leading to rapid economic recovery and sustained growth since that time. Donors have been keen, it is therefore argued, to support – and not undermine – African governments who represent some of the few 'success stories' of World Bank policies on the continent.

Second, both regimes came to power following years of turmoil and bloodshed in their respective states – the genocide in Rwanda and the dictatorial regimes of Idi Amin and Milton Obote in Uganda. Having restored, and maintained, substantial stability since gaining office, it is argued, Museveni and Kagame have consequently been embraced by donors as reliable guarantors against renewed chaos in a troubled region (Hauser, 1997: 633–64; Hayman, 2009: 592; Haynes, 2001: 183–4, 201–2). The two regimes' involvement in regional security and counter-terrorism activities – Uganda in Somalia, Rwanda in Darfur – has also, according to many scholars, earned them considerable support in Washington particularly (Beswick, 2010: 748–50; Fisher, 2012). International support for the two governments can therefore be explained by their threefold images as economic success stories, guarantors of stability and donor security allies.

The Kenyan governments of Daniel arap Moi and Mwai Kibaki, in power from 1978 to 2002 and 2002 to 2013 respectively, have not, however, enjoyed the same level of donor backing. Considered to be geostrategically important during the Cold War, Moi's Kenya rapidly lost international support after the collapse of the Soviet Union. Indeed, the corrupt and autocratic Moi regime became an early casualty of the 'political conditionality era' with major donors withholding their aid to Kenya in November 1991 and insisting that multi-party politics be restored immediately (it had been formally abolished by Moi in 1982). Though the aid-dependent Moi acquiesced rapidly, aid flows to Kenya remained faltering – aid was part-suspended in 1995 over limited 'economic and political reforms' and in 1997, 2000 and 2001 over 'corruption' (Brown, 2007: 316–17; Pinkney, 2001: 142–6). Whereas aid to Uganda and Rwanda increased from 1987 to 1999, aid to Kenya fell by 50 per cent. Donors in Kenya were also strongly opposed to moving to budget support under Moi or Kibaki (ODI, 2005: 26).

Following a brief 'honeymoon period', Kibaki's presidency has suffered the same fate – total aid to Kenya was cut by 25 per cent in 2005–6 owing to corruption concerns. From a regime maintenance perspective, however, this has been decreasingly problematic as Kenya's aid dependence has reduced in the last 15 years. Where aid represented over 16 per cent of the country's GDP in the early 1990s, for example, today it represents less than 5 per cent (compared to 15 per cent and 20 per cent in Uganda and Rwanda respectively; OECD, various years). It is crucial to note, however, that many African governments depend on Western states not only as providers of international aid but also as economic partners. Following terrorist attacks in Kenya during 2002, for example, the US and UK governments issued travel advisories encouraging their citizens to 'defer non-essential travel' to the country 'until further notice' owing to concerns regarding Kenya's competence and commitment in fighting terrorism. The effect of this action on Kenya's tourist industry (its second largest) was substantial and the sector reportedly lost around US$2m per week until the crisis was brought to a close in mid-2003 (Fisher, 2013: 11–15).

Faltering international support for the Moi and Kibaki governments has generally been explained with reference to two negative images donors have of Kenya's ruling elite. The first of these centres around the perennial involvement of leading ministers (including Kibaki himself) in high-level corruption scandals such as that involving Anglo-Leasing Finance ('Anglo-Fleecing') in 2004–5 (Wrong, 2009: 328–9). In addition, Kenya's reputation as an unreliable ally in the Global War on Terror, again, to be contrasted with those of Uganda or Rwanda, is argued to be a key reason for limited donor support in recent years (Fisher, 2013). This is despite the fact that, as I have argued elsewhere, the Kibaki administration's record in this regard is closer to that of Museveni's than many donors allow.

It is clear, therefore, that donors have viewed these four governments in line with several key images and that this has led to – in the Uganda and Rwanda cases – donors strengthening a regime's hold on power or – in the Kenya case – weakening it. With this key relationship between image and regime maintenance in mind, the remainder of this chapter will explore the extent to which the Museveni, Kagame, Moi and Kibaki regimes have attempted to manage these images in their direct and indirect engagements with donors.

Personalisation of diplomacy

A key feature of Ugandan and Rwandan image management strategies has been the personalisation and informalisation of relations with donors by Museveni and Kagame. This has been undertaken through a variety of means – particularly through providing access to donors and being willing to debate all issues openly and, seemingly, honestly. Donor officials have frequently noted how willing both Museveni and Kagame have been to meet them and give them 'their time'. Both men, for example, have been described as 'honest', 'straightforward' and 'willing to entertain other ideas' by donors and have been praised for providing 'incredible access' to local and international donor officials. Both leaders have also attempted to sustain close relationships developed in this manner by frequently 'reaching-out' to senior figures, such as former US president George W. Bush by telephone.[3]

Museveni has consolidated these personalised links through inviting key donor personnel, including former UK aid minister Lynda Chalker and former US Trade Representative Rosa Whitaker, to spend prolonged periods of time with him and his family at his farm in western Uganda. Like Kagame, although to a lesser extent, the Ugandan leader has also used humour and intellectual 'table-talk' in his meetings and 'fireside chats' with donor officials in order to further informalise and personalise the engagement (Silverstein, 2004).[4] Less of a humourist, Kagame has taken a slightly different tack by 'offering' Rwanda up as a willing guinea pig to Western developmental organisations with key links to major political figures. Rwanda became the first 'project' for former UK prime minister Tony Blair's Africa Governance Initiative in 2008, for example, and has been the focus of the UK Conservative Party's annual social action project (*Umubano*) since 2007 (Mendick, 2011).[5]

It is important to note in this regard that both leaders have purposely fostered personalised links with officials and institutions whose political perspectives are most likely to align with the positive images of Uganda and Rwanda outlined above. Both Museveni and Kagame, for example, have proactively strengthened ties with major figures in the UK's Department for International Development (DFID) – notably former ministers Clare Short and Andrew Mitchell – but not the Foreign and Commonwealth Office. Likewise, Museveni has worked hard to develop close links with White House Africanist security officials such as Susan Rice and Jendayi Frazer but less so with State Department personnel.[6] This has allowed them to emphasise the images they are most keen to highlight with those donor officials most inclined to focus on such narratives.

Beyond this, the personalisation of relations with key donor officials has allowed Museveni and Kagame to position themselves as the central sources of 'information' on their respective regimes to major policymakers in Western embassies and capitals. In proactively developing diplomatic relationships built around contact, trust, shared sympathies and 'friendship' (in the words of a former senior UK official), the two leaders have consequently been able to promote particular interpretations of their policies and activities to donors with minimal fear of being challenged or contradicted in doing so.

Conversely, neither Moi nor Kibaki, nor any leading figures in either's regime, have been willing or able to foster similarly personalised ties with donor officials. Moi's aloof personal style seemingly jarred with many donors with one describing him in hindsight as 'rather stiff and unbending with foreigners'.[7] Observers have frequently commented upon his 'unsmiling rigidness' and contrasted him unfavourably with Museveni who 'prefers a khaki safari suit … to a suit and tie, delivers riveting speeches … and rarely misses a chance to crack a joke' (*New York Times*, 1995). The former Kenyan leader's international reputation does not appear to have been helped by his antagonistic and defensive manner in personal encounters with donor officials. Moi reportedly used meetings with donors throughout the 1990s not to promote particular images of Kenya but, instead, to complain about his – and Kenya's – 'unfair' treatment at the hands of Western governments and journalists (see below).

Likewise Kibaki, whose health suffered significant setbacks following a stroke and involvement in a car crash in the early 2000s, has not been able to foster strong links with donor personnel. He adopted, according to many observers, a 'laid-back' approach to conducting Kenya's foreign policy and has been portrayed as 'comatose' by some donor officials who note that he would sometimes 'fall asleep' in bilateral meetings.[8] Kenya's relations with donors during the 2000s, therefore, were generally managed by a succession of ministers some of whom have been described by donors as 'more capable than others' and all of whom have generally been on the defensive in their engagement with donors.[9] Moreover, unlike Museveni and Kagame who have been regular visitors to 10 Downing Street and the White House over the years, neither Moi nor Kibaki have travelled very much to donor capitals during their presidencies. In constructing images of the Kenyan government, therefore, donor policy-makers have been forced to rely on other sources of information such as media reports, many of which may emphasise negative issues such as corruption rather than positive ones, such as the vibrancy of Kenyan democracy.

Use of public relations firms

Public relations – or 'lobbying' – firms have been a traditional tool employed by many governments, African and otherwise, to influence the views and policies of government officials in Washington DC, London, Brussels and elsewhere. Staffed by a variety of former administration officials with crucial informal access to the corridors of power, lobbying firms offer an important mediatory service to regimes in managing their relations with donors. Well-placed to engage with key policy-makers and distribute key 'information' on their clients' behalf, lobbying firms can be important actors within any government's image management strategy. Analysing the firms retained by Kampala, Kigali and Nairobi and the activities they have undertaken during this time is therefore a useful exercise for gaining further understanding of their approach to this issue.

During the 1990s and 2000s, lobbying firms retained by the Museveni and Kagame regimes have promoted – at their employers' behest – images of the two governments which emphasise those perspectives discussed above. Revell Communications, hired by Kampala between 1989 and 1990, focused on facilitating meetings between Museveni and US business leaders – as well as arranging for the Ugandan leader to appear on the *Financial News Network* – in order to promote Uganda as an economic success story (Revell Communications, 1990). The same is true of the Whitaker group (retained between 2003 and 2010) in their 'commercial diplomacy' work for Uganda which included organising a 2007 lunch in Washington where 'emerging market fund managers' gathered to hear Museveni speak on 'Building the Financial Infrastructure to Transform Africa'. Rosa Whitaker, the firm's CEO and former US Trade Representative, also invited her former colleague, US Treasury Secretary Hank Paulson, to this event in a letter which lauded Museveni as someone who 'works diligently to bring private investment to Uganda [and who is] a stalwart supporter of free trade and open markets' (Whitaker Group, 2008).

This is also the case for GoodWorks International, Kigali's main US lobbyist since 2005, which spent much of 2007–8 publicising a film (*Rwanda Rising*) to a variety of US audiences (including to viewers of *CNN* and all those flying internationally on *Delta Airlines*). It featured several celebrities and Kagame himself discussing Rwanda's economic success and its favourable investment climate (Goodworks International, 2007, 2008). The Museveni regime has also retained firms to promote other positive images of itself. Its hiring of Scribe Strategies via the Ugandan Defence Ministry between 2005 and 2007, for example, was specifically premised on the firm's ensuring of 'Uganda's interest under the East Africa Counter Terrorism Initiative and role in the War on Terrorism' in its engagement with administration officials and congressional legislators (Scribe Strategies, 2005). The Whitaker Group also played an important role in trying to persuade US officials in the mid-2000s that Kampala was fighting 'its own war on terrorism' in its pursuit of the LRA (Fisher, 2013: 17).

Interestingly, in Uganda's case, the regime has often sought representation from firms with a direct personal link to Museveni in a further development of its personalisation of diplomacy strategy. Since 1997, for example, Kampala has been represented in the UK by *Africa Matters Ltd*, a consultancy owned by Lynda Chalker, the UK Africa and Overseas Development Minister from 1986 to 1997 and 1989 to 1997 respectively, and a key supporter of Museveni in London from very early in the latter's presidency.[10] Similarly, Museveni's relationship with Whitaker (whose firm also hired Jendayi Frazer in 2009) predates his retention of the Whitaker Group in 2003; the former Trade Representative spent part of her Christmas vacation with Museveni's family at his farm in 2002 (Silverstein, 2004). Rather than simply hire any reputable firm, therefore, the Ugandan leader appears to have focused on working with lobbyists with a deep and personal understanding of the dynamics of Uganda's relations with key donors. While Moi and Kibaki's governments have also made use of lobbying firms in their relations with the US, these organisations' activities on Nairobi's behalf have been largely defensive. During the Moi era, Kenya's main US lobbyist – Black Manafort Stone and Kelly appears to have spent most of its time trying to convince sceptical US legislators that the regime's human rights record was not as bad as many thought. In May 1989, for example, most of the firm's activity focused on 'clarifying the human rights situation' in Kenya to officials in Washington in an attempt to avoid cuts to US aid in an 'upcoming appropriations bill' (Black *et al*, 1989). Likewise, in May 2003 the Kibaki government hired John Maina of Baraka Services purely to lobby US officials with regard to the recently-imposed travel advisory (see above; Baraka Services, 2004). Despite a clear bilateral disagreement, the firm's strategy was extremely deferential to Washington and was, again, an indication that Nairobi's engagement with donors has been mainly premised on mitigating punishments rather than image-management.

This was further confirmed in 2009 when Kibaki retained Chlopak, Leonard and Shecter (CLS) to represent Kenya in the US. The agreement with the firm acknowledged that Kenya had received much 'negative publicity' in Washington and that 'there appears to be an impression among many key policymakers ... that Kenya is "not what it used to be"'. The strategy proposed by CLS to change this, however, appears to have been based around reassuring US policy-makers that Kenya was making 'progress' in some areas (including political reform, 'healing ethnic divisions' and tackling corruption) rather than presenting a different, positive image of the country to Washington (Chlopak *et al*, 2010).

Engagement with non-governmental actors and institutions
Finally, both the Museveni and Kagame regimes have been extremely proactive in managing how prominent groups and organisations outside government portray them in donor states – both keenly aware of the influence of press reports, human rights lobbies and business communities on foreign policy-making in Western capitals. Both leaders, for example, regularly give interviews to major news networks, agencies and publications, including the BBC, ABC, CNN, Al Jazeera, *Economist*, *TIME*, in order to personally promote particular understandings of their governments' actions or policies to a Western audience. Often these leaders' officials attempt to manage the direction of questioning their presidents will face by, for example, sending 'background information kits' to the journalists in question prior to the interviews. One such 'kit', sent to a journalist on the *Financial News Network* before a 1989 interview with Museveni, included press clippings, extracts of speeches, economic statistics and a World Bank report all of which – together – portrayed Uganda as a paradigmatic African economic success story (Revell Communications, 1990). The interview itself drew heavily on this material.

Both Museveni and Kagame have also frequently spoken at think tanks, academic institutions and business associations in the UK and US in order to emphasise particular narratives on their regimes to a variety of Western audiences. Museveni, for example, has emphasised Uganda's role as a guarantor of regional stability and enemy of Islamic terrorism at the Woodrow Wilson Center and Council on Foreign Relations on a number of occasions, including in 2003 where he spoke on the topic of 'Freedom from Fear: Forging US-Africa Partnerships Against Terror' to a room packed with US journalists, academics and State Department officials (Council on Foreign Relations, 2003, 2005; Woodrow Wilson Center, 2002). Likewise, Kagame has stressed the centrality of working for 'sustainable peace and improved developmental results [in Africa]' to Rwanda's 'core ... agenda' before scholars, military personnel and Western policy-makers at a number of events in both the UK and US in the last decade (Beswick, 2010: 749).

Both leaders have also emphasised their states' economic successes during engagements with Western business leaders and economists. Museveni, for example, promoted Uganda's economic success story in a 1998 speech to economists and World Bank officials at the University of Oxford – an occasion where he also launched a 'Museveni scholarship' to sponsor African research students working on 'issues relating to African economies' (University of Oxford, 1998: 7–9). Senior Ugandan officials have also organised, via lobbying firms, lunches and breakfast meetings with major US and UK business leaders in Washington and London throughout the 1990s and 2000s where Museveni and others have spoken professorially on how to 'build the financial infrastructure to transform Africa' – with Uganda cited as a model in this regard (Channel 4, 1997; Royal Commonwealth Society, 2009; Whitaker Group, 2004). The same is true of the Rwandan government which has dispatched a number of high-level trade delegations (some headed by Kagame himself) to meet business leaders in major US cities, including Boston, San Francisco and Washington, during the 2000s (Fleishman-Hillard, 2003).

Clearly, Kampala and Kigali's engagement with Western journalists and NGOs has, at times, been of a defensive nature; democratic backsliding, intervention in Congo and accusations of human rights abuses have all featured prominently in the dialogue between these regimes and many Western media houses and NGOs. It is important to note, however, that both Museveni and Kagame have always been open to responding personally to these criticisms and have regularly spoken in defence of their regimes' actions in interviews with the BBC, CNN and France24.

Indeed, Rwandan officials have been particularly officious in tackling Western journalists, analysts and academics who have criticised Kigali's democratic record or its treatment of Hutu refugees in the immediate aftermath of the 1994 genocide. Since coming to power, the regime has routinely denied many Western NGOs and journalists access to sites where RPF-instigated violence is alleged to have taken place, excluded them from press conferences where 'information' on events has been disseminated to their less difficult colleagues and more broadly attempted to discredit the work of 'anti-Rwanda misinformation' campaigners including Human Rights Watch staff, academics and several UN panels of experts (Hayman, 2009: 131–2; Munnyaneza, 2012; Pottier, 2002: 51–5, 160–6; Reyntjens, 2004: 203–4, 2011: 26–34). In recent years, Kagame has made extensive use of Twitter to this end, as have other senior Rwandan officials including foreign minister Louise Mushikiwabo (Birrell, 2011; Pottier, 2002: 53).[11]

In the case of Kenya, however, neither Moi nor Kibaki attempted to cultivate relationships with Western media organisations. Moi, for example, did not speak to a US newspaper until June 1987 – nearly a decade into his presidency – and numerous Western journalists have commented on how difficult it has been to secure an interview with him (Harden, 1987a, 1987b; Kamau, 1999; Keane, 2002). Indeed, the former president has stated publicly that he does 'not like to give interviews or press conferences [or to] advertise [him]self' (Harden, 1987b). Kibaki too has largely avoided speaking to foreign media and has rarely submitted to even domestic press conferences. His only substantial visit to the US as president, for example – in October 2003 – involved minimal interaction with international journalists outside a 'scripted and perfunctory' press conference at the White House (Kelley, 2003b; Kelley *et al*, 2003).

In addition, where Kenyan officials have engaged with Western journalists or think tanks they have rarely attempted to advance positive images of their country or government, unlike their Ugandan or Rwandan counterparts. Instead, they have largely accepted, and worked within, the largely negative narratives used by Western policy-makers to understand successive Kenyan governments – narratives on corrupt politicians, 'tribal' politics, economic incompetence and, since 2007, ethnic violence. In a 2005 interview with the BBC, for example, information minister Raphael Tuju focused heavily on the issue of high-level corruption in Kenya and the three-year old government's putative plans to bring it under control (BBC, 2005). Similarly, in a 2009 roundtable at the Brookings Institution in Washington, a delegation of Kenyan presidential advisors, diplomats and civil servants bemoaned the myriad 'challenges' and 'obstacles' Kenya faced in its 'path to development' with the sole note of optimism being struck by one who noted that the government had 'at least' identified what these challenges were (Brookings Institution, 2009). Likewise, in a 2011 speech to policy-makers, academics and business leaders at the Washington-based Center for Strategic and International Studies, Kenyan prime minister Raila

Odinga presented the 2008 creation of a power-sharing coalition government in Kenya as a cynical tactic used by autocratic leaders to cling to power – 'a new tool for dictators' – implicitly comparing Kibaki to Zimbabwe's Robert Mugabe (CSIS, 2011).

Indeed, Kenyan officials have tended to use interviews with Western journalists or academics or speeches at policy institutes and international fora less to promote positive narratives on their government's activities and more to complain about perceived mistreatment at the hands of colleagues in Nairobi or donors. Thus in his first interview with a US journalist, Moi bemoaned that 'we [Kenya] have been taken for granted as a friend .... the US is not interested in us' (Harden, 1987a). Similarly, Kenya's foreign minister protested about his country's 'double victimisation' by Western donors at the UN in 2003 while his deputy lamented to a US academic in 2006 how 'we have tried to engage the US on the issue of Somalia without success. They have called everyone except [us] ... this kind of exclusive contact is not helpful' (Kelley, 2003a; Whitaker, 2008: 263).

Where Ugandan and Rwandan officials have used their engagement with non-governmental 'thought leaders' in the West to emphasise positive narratives on their regimes, Kenyan officials have done the opposite. Indeed, the latter have not only failed to stress favourable images of their governments in these encounters but also have seemingly substantiated more prevalent negative images held by their audiences in their choice of topics and defensive manner of interaction. This failure to 'market' particular policies or actions as part of a more positive narrative has had real implications for regime security in Nairobi. During the 1991 Gulf War, the Moi regime allowed Coalition forces to make use of its naval and air bases but did little to incorporate this into a general narrative on Kenya's reliability as a US/UK security ally in its engagement with Western media organisations; an opportunity the Museveni regime would have been highly unlikely to pass up. Months later, the US, UK and other donors suspended millions of dollars of aid to Kenya over democratisation concerns (see above), clearly having focused more on the Moi's negative reputation in this area than its – potentially – more positive one on security.

Lack of strategy or lack of need? image management and aid dependency in east Africa

Why successive Kenyan governments have been so much more uninterested in, and ineffective at, managing how they are seen by donors in comparison to their Ugandan and Rwandan counterparts is a key question arising from this analysis. While space does not allow for a thorough exploration of this important issue, it is useful to highlight a few central points in this regard which also represent areas for future study.

First, it is crucial to note that the regimes and polities of Uganda and Rwanda since 1986 and 1994 respectively have been of a very different nature to those in Kenya. Both the Museveni and Kagame regimes, for example, have grown out of – and remain governed by leading members of – highly-disciplined, personalised and centralised guerrilla movements where cohesion and unity of purpose and message have been of key importance (Ngoga, 1998: 96–102). Kenya's Moi and – particularly – Kibaki governments, however, have been formed through the uniting of disparate and often hostile coalitions of 'non-programmatic parties' which draw their support from different ethnic and regional communities (Anderson, 2005: 563–4; Mueller, 2008: 200). These differing sociologies make the formulation and implementation of coherent diplomatic strategies far more feasible in Kampala and Kigali than in Nairobi.

Moreover, the Rwandan and Ugandan regimes have relied far more on Western aid (particularly general budget support) than their Kenyan counterparts to fund their budgets and – particularly in Uganda's case – to maintain patronage networks. Kenya has not, as noted, been dependent on aid since the mid-1990s and has never received budget support. Gaining and maintaining power in contemporary Kenya has relied far more on attracting votes from particular domestic ethnic and regional constituencies and thereafter distributing the state's bounties to these groups than on securing aid flows to finance regime maintenance (*Economist*, 2007; Lind and Howell, 2010: 346–7).

Indeed, in the last two Kenyan elections winning power has partly been dependent upon attacking Western donors and their policies. In 2007, for example, presidential candidate Odinga attempted to win support from Muslim 'swing voters' in Kenya's Coast Province by criticising US policy in the region, including the rendition of some Muslims to Guantanamo Bay under the Kibaki government (BBC News website, 2007). Likewise, Uhuru Kenyatta's narrow and unexpected first round victory in the March 2013 election is believed by a range of commentators to have been secured in part through voters responding to the anti-Western sentiments at the heart of his campaign messaging (BBC News website, 2013; *Daily Nation*, 2013). Indicted for crimes against humanity in 2010 by the International Criminal Court, Kenyatta won much domestic support by attacking Western officials for seemingly attempting to warn Kenyan voters against selecting him as their next leader (*Citizen News*, 2013).

It is also notable, in this regard, how Ugandan engagement with Western donors has changed as its dependency on their aid has declined. As donor funding of the country's budget has reduced from over 50 per cent in the mid-2000s to 19 per cent in 2013 (*Daily Monitor,* 2013) so has the Museveni regime moved away from the 'pro-poor' economic and development spending priorities which won it such praise from donors in the 1990s and 2000s (Hickey, 2013: 196–202). The growing importance of Chinese state investment in Uganda, however, raises the possibility of the development of a different type of dependency for the Museveni regime and its successors. The degree to which image management strategies play into this putative future remains, of course, to be seen.

Conclusion

This chapter has highlighted the significance of an African regime's 'image' in the eyes of Western policy-makers for that regime's own security. Being perceived by donors as economic and developmental success-stories, as reliable counter-terrorism allies and as guarantors of regional stability has, it is suggested, earned Rwanda's Kagame regime and Uganda's Museveni regime extensive and sustained international support since the 1990s – support which has allowed both governments to extend and solidify their hold on power. Being perceived as corrupt, economically incompetent, politically unpredictable and unreliable in counter-terrorism policy has, however, had the reverse impact on successive Kenyan governments with both the Moi and Kibaki administrations' domestic authority being undermined by aid cuts and negative travel advisories during the same period.

In making this argument, however, the chapter has focused on the role played by these governments themselves in managing – or failing to manage – the prominence of these images in donor perceptions as part of an overall regime maintenance or security strategy. In doing so, three areas of direct and indirect interaction with donor officials have been explored – personal interaction, the use of 'lobbying' firms and engagement with Western non-governmental organisations and 'thought leaders' – and it has been concluded that while Kampala and Kigali have used all three avenues to promote particular, positive images of themselves to donors, Nairobi has not. Indeed, both the Moi and Kibaki administrations have largely confirmed the prejudices of donors in their use or non-use of such interactions.

These findings raise important questions on the nature of African agency in the international system and the role played by leaders in managing their country's relationship with Western powers. The extent to which stated Western rationales for supporting African states remain purely Western as these states' officials engage with them, interact with them and succeed in changing their content and nature is a complex but salient issue which further study on the relationship between structure, agency and Africa's place in the world might seek to address.

Notes

1 Aspects of this chapter are explored in more detail in Fisher (2012), and Fisher (2013).
2 While all have overlapped chronologically, not all of these governments have been in office during exactly the same time periods. Those of Museveni and Kagame have been in power since 1986 and 1994 respectively (Kagame as vice president until 2000) while Moi ruled between 1982 and 2002 and Kibaki from 2002 to 2013.
3 Interviews with current and former UK and US officials, October 2008 (London) and October–November 2009 (Washington DC).
4 Interviews with former UK officials, June–July 2009 (London and US officials, October–November 2009 (Washington DC).
5 Interviews with current and former UK officials, July and September 2009 (London).
6 Interviews with former UK officials, June–July 2009 (London) and former US officials, October–November 2009 (Washington DC). Museveni has, of course, maintained these links as White House officials have moved to senior positions in the State Department, as Rice and Frazer did in 1997 and 2005 respectively.
7 Interview with former UK official, July 2009 (London).
8 Interview with former UK official, May 2009 (London).
9 Interview with former UK official, March 2012 (London).
10 Interview with former UK official, July 2009 (London).
11 Kagame tweets as @PaulKagame and Mushikiwabo as @LMushikiwabo.

References

Anderson, David (2005): 'Yours in struggle for *majimbo*: nationalism and the party politics of decolonization in Kenya, 1955–64', *Journal of Contemporary History* 40(3): 547–64.
Baraka Services (2004): 'Exhibit A to registration statement', submitted to US Department of Justice, 24 February 2004.
Bayart, Jean-François (2000): 'Africa in the world: a history of extraversion', *African Affairs* 99(395): 217–67.
Bayart, Jean-François (2009): *The State in Africa*, second edition (London: Polity).

BBC (2005): Interview with Rafael Tuju, Minister of Information, Republic of Kenya on *HardTalk*, broadcast 6.7.05.

BBC News website (2007): 'Kenyan Muslims deny Sharia claims', 27.11.07.

BBC News website (2013): 'Did the ICC help Uhuru Kenyatta win Kenyan election?', 11.3.13.

Beswick, Danielle (2010): 'Peacekeeping, regime security and "African solutions to African problems": exploring motivations for Rwanda's involvement in Darfur', *Third World Quarterly* 31(5): 739–54.

Birrell, Ian (2011): 'My Twitterspat with Paul Kagame', *Guardian*, 16.5.11.

Black, Manafort, Stone and Kelly (1989): 'Supplemental Statement', submitted to US Department of Justice, 1.6.89.

Brookings Institution (2009): Presentations by Raphael Tuju, Special Advisor to the President of the Republic of Kenya, Amina Mohammed, Permanent Secretary, Ministry of Justice and National Reconciliation, Kenya, Thuita Mwangi, Permanent Secretary, Ministry of Foreign Affairs, Kenya and Sam Mwale, Principal Accounting Officer, Office of the President, Kenya at roundtable on 'Contemporary Development Challenges in Kenya', 1.10.09 (Washington DC: Brookings Institution).

Brown, Stephen (2007): 'From demiurge to midwife: changing donor roles in Kenya's democratization process', in Godwin Rapando and Shadrack Wanjala Nasong'o (eds), *Kenya: The struggle for democracy* (London: Zed Books).

Campioni, Maddalena and Patrick Noack (2012): 'Rwanda fast forward: the many perspectives that make Rwanda a unique country', in Maddalena Campioni and Patrick Noack (eds), *Rwanda Fast Forward: social, economic, military and reconciliation prospects* (London: Macmillan).

Channel 4 (UK) (1997): *The Bank, the President and the Pearl of Africa*, two-part documentary directed by Peter Chappell.

Chlopak, Leonard, Schechter and Associates (2010): 'Exhibit A to Registration Statement', submitted to US Department of Justice, 20.8.10.

Citizen News (Nairobi; 2013): 'Kenyatta, Ruto slam the West over ICC', 9.2.13.

Clapham, Christopher (1996): *Africa and the International System: the politics of state survival* (Cambridge: Cambridge University Press).

Clark, John (2001): 'Foreign policy-making in Central Africa: the imperative of regime security in a new context', in Gilbert Khadiagala and Terrence Lyons (eds), *African Foreign Policy: power and process* (Boulder, CO: Lynne Rienner).

Council on Foreign Relations (2003): 'Freedom from fear: forging US-Africa partnerships against terror', speech by Yoweri Museveni, President of the Republic of Uganda, 13.6.03 (Washington DC: Council on Foreign Relations).

Council on Foreign Relations (2005): Speech by Yoweri Museveni, President of the Republic of Uganda, 21.9.05 (Washington DC: Council on Foreign Relations).

CSIS (Center for Strategic and International Studies) (2011): 'Statesmen's

Forum – Raila Odinga, Prime Minister of Kenya', 13.4.11 (Washington DC: CSIS).

Daily Monitor (Kampala; 2013): 'Donors welcome 81% government budget funding', 14.6.13.

Daily Nation (Nairobi; 2013): 'Uhuru turned ICC indictment to his campaign advantage', 11.3.13.

Dunn, Kevin (2004): 'Narrating identity: constructing the Congo during the 1960 crisis', in Patricia Goff and Kevin Dunn (eds), *Identity and Global Politics: theoretical and empirical elaborations* (London: Macmillan).

Dyson, Stephen and Thomas Preston (2006): 'Individual characteristics of political leaders and the use of analogy in foreign policy decision making', *Political Psychology* 27(2): 265–88.

Economist (2007): 'Kenya: could the president be ousted?', 1.11.07.

Fisher, Jonathan (2012): 'Managing donor perceptions: contextualizing Uganda's 2007 intervention in Somalia', *African Affairs* 111(444): 404–23.

Fisher, Jonathan (2013): '"Some more reliable than others": image management, donor perceptions and the Global War on Terror in East African diplomacy', *Journal of Modern African Studies* 51(1): 1–31.

Fleishman-Hillard (2003): 'Exhibit A to Registration Statement', document submitted to the US Department of Justice, 22.9.03.

Goodworks International (2007): 'Supplemental Statement', submitted to the US Department of Justice, 20.11.07.

Goodworks International (2008): 'Supplemental Statement', submitted to the US Department of Justice, 14.5.08.

Harden, Blaine (1987a): 'Kenya's President Moi denies charges of rights abuses', *Washington Post*, 12.6.87.

Harden, Blaine (1987b): 'In Kenya, l'Etat C'est Moi: President's phone call gets prompt attention', *Washington Post*, 12.6.87.

Harrigan, Jane and Chengang Wang (2011): 'A new approach to the allocation of aid among developing countries: is the USA different from the rest?', *World Development* 39(8): 1281–93.

Hauser, Ellen (1997): 'Ugandan relations with Western donors in the 1990s: what impact on democratisation?', *Journal of Modern African Studies* 37(4): 621–41.

Hayman, Rachel (2009): 'From Rome to Accra via Kigali: "aid effectiveness" in Rwanda', *Development Policy Review* 27(5): 581–99.

Haynes, Jeff (2001): 'Limited democracy in Ghana and Uganda: what is most important to international actors? Stability or political freedom?', *Journal of Contemporary African Studies* 19(2): 183–204.

Hickey, Sam (2013): 'Beyond the poverty agenda? Insights from the new politics of development in Uganda', 43(3): 194–206.

Jervis, Robert (1976): *Perception and Misperception in International Politics* (Princeton, NJ: Princeton University Press).

Kamau, John (1999): 'Moi: the untold story', *New African*, 1.2.99.

Keane, Fergal (2002): 'Kenya's Big Man must answer for the catastrophe that has befallen his country', *Independent*, 28.12.02.

Kelley, Kevin (2003a): 'Kalonzo faults US on terrorism', *Daily Nation* (Nairobi), 3.10.03.

Kelley, Kevin (2003b): 'The gains from talks with Bush', *Daily Nation* (Nairobi), 12.10.03.

Kelley, Kevin, Juma Kwayera and Paul Redfern (2003): 'Kibaki's US visit: no media savvy?', *East African* (Nairobi), 13.10.03.

Khong, Yuen Foong (1992): *Analogies at War: Korea, Munich, Dien Bien Phu and the Vietnam decisions of 1965* (Princeton NJ: Princeton University Press).

Lind, Jeremy and Jude Howell (2010): 'Counter-terrorism and the politics of aid: civil society responses in Kenya', *Development and Change* 41(2): 335–53.

McNulty, Mel (1999): 'The collapse of Zaire: implosion, revolution or external sabotage?', *Journal of Modern African Studies* 37(1): 53–82.

Mendick, Robert (2011): *Daily Telegraph*, 'Tony Blair, trips to Africa and an intriguing friendship', 12.11.11.

Mueller, Susanne (2008): 'The political economy of Kenya's crisis', *Journal of Eastern African Studies* 2(2): 185–210.

Munnyaneza, James (2012): *New Times* (Kigali), 'Govt submits rebuttal to controversial UN report', 1.8.12.

Neustadt, Richard and Ernest May (1986): *Thinking in Time: The uses of history for decision makers* (New York: Free Press).

New York Times (1995): 'Uganda strongman a favourite of world leaders', 29.1.95.

Ngoga, Pascal (1998): 'Uganda: The National Resistance Army' in Christopher Clapham (ed.), *African Guerrillas* (Oxford: James Currey).

ODI (Overseas Development Institute) (2005): *Political Conditionality in Africa: an empirical study into its design, use and impact: DFID 1999–2004* (London: ODI), this report is not publicly available and was released – in redacted form – to the author under a Freedom of Information request in 2009.

OECD (Organisation for Economic Cooperation and Development) (various years): *Geographical Distribution of Financial Flows to Less Developed Countries* (Paris: OECD).

Perlez, Jane (1991): 'Kenya tightening curbs on dissident groups', *New York Times*, 23.9.91.

Pinkney, Robert (2001): *The International Politics of East Africa* (Manchester: Manchester University Press).

Pottier, Johan (2002): *Re-imagining Rwanda: conflict, survival and disinformation in the late twentieth century* (Cambridge: Cambridge University Press).

Revell Communications (1990): 'Amendment to Registration Statement', submitted to US Department of Justice, 1.1.90.

Reyntjens, Filip (April 2004): 'Rwanda: Ten Years On: From genocide to dictatorship', *African Affairs* 103(411): 177–210.

Royal Commonwealth Society (2009): Speech by Yoweri Museveni, President of the Republic of Uganda on 'Building Success: Uganda's Economic Reforms: Lessons from Africa', roundtable including presentations from Emmanuel Tumusiime-Mutebile, Governor of the Central Bank of Uganda and Joan Rwabyomere, former Ugandan High Commissioner to the UK, 9.12.09, attended by author (London: Royal Commonwealth Society).

Schraeder, Peter, Steven Hook and Bruce Taylor (1998): 'Clarifying the foreign aid puzzle: a comparison of American, Japanese, French and Swedish aid flows', *World Politics* 50(2): 294–323.

Scribe Strategies (2005): 'Supplemental Statement', submitted to US Department of Justice, 20.10.05.

Silverstein, Ken (2004): *Los Angeles Times*, 'Connections work for ex-Trade Official', 2.3.04.

Stokke, Olav (1995): 'Aid and political conditionalities: core issues and state of the art', in Olav Stokke (ed.), *Aid and Political Conditionality* (London: Frank Cass).

Tripp, Aili Mari (2010): *Museveni's Uganda: Paradoxes of Power in a Hybrid Regime* (Boulder, CO: Lynne Rienner).

University of Oxford (1998): 'CSAE/CDC Conference: Investing in Africa: does it really mean business?' 5–6 April 1998, summary of proceedings available at www.csae.ox.ac.uk/conferences/1998–CDC/CDC-CSAE-1998conference-report.PDF, accessed 1.3.13.

Vertzberger, Yaacov (1990): *The World in Their Minds: Information processing, cognition and perception in foreign policy decisionmaking* (Stanford, CA: Stanford University Press).

Whitaker, Beth Elise (2008): 'Reluctant partners: fighting terrorism and promoting democracy in Kenya', *International Studies Perspectives* 9(3): 254–71.

Whitaker Group (2004): 'Supplemental Statement', submitted to the US Department of Justice, 31.8.04.

Whitaker Group (2008): 'Supplemental Statement', submitted to the US Department of Justice, 11.4.08.

Whitfield, Lindsay and Alastair Fraser (2010): 'Negotiating aid: the structural conditions shaping the negotiating strategies of African governments', *International Negotiation* 15(3): 341–66.

Woodrow Wilson International Center for Scholars (2002): Speech by Yoweri Museveni, President of the Republic of Uganda, 14.5.02 (Washington DC: Woodrow Wilson Center).

Woods, Ngaire (2005): 'The shifting politics of foreign aid', *International Affairs* 81(2): 393–409.

Wrong, Michela (2009): *It's Our Turn to Eat: the story of a Kenyan whistle-blower* (London: Zed Books).

5

Mirrors, mimicry and the spectre of a failed state: how the government of Ethiopia deploys image

Emmanuel Fanta

In October 1984, two journalists working for the BBC, Michael Buerk and his cameraman Mohammed Amin, set out for Korem, a small village in northern Ethiopia, to report on the famine that was ravaging the area. Their report would be shown on televisions to millions of British viewers before being broadcasted throughout the globe. This historical piece of journalism sparked a massive international mobilisation to provide relief to those affected in Ethiopia, leading to the collection of millions of dollars in funding but also helping to raise the awareness of people across the globe who became concerned about the livelihood of Ethiopians threatened by hunger and war.

Buerk and Amin's report would also have a more insidious effect. With the broadcasting of images of emaciated bodies sitting seemingly motionless in a dried-out landscape, the two journalists unknowingly carved into the minds of many the image of Ethiopia as a desolated country full of suffering and hunger. Buerk had described 'a biblical famine, now, in the twentieth century' in a place that could be considered as 'the closest thing to hell on earth'. This ahistorical perception of Ethiopians (and of much of Africa) as immutable victims of the passing of time persists years after the first airing of Buerk and Amin's report (VSO, 2001; Tester, 2010).

The portrayal of famine victims as well as the discourse and imagery of development have received scholarly attention and have demonstrated how stereotypes are perpetrated and how they reinforce the image of the North as the centre of knowledge and power, and the South as un-developed, requiring intervention and change (Fair, 1993; Doty, 1996; Baaz, 2005). However, within this corpus few studies focus on how these images can be changed or acted upon by the very state and people they concern. The great majority of the work on images and perceptions of the developing world concerns the ways that these images are produced and consumed in the developed world. Ironically, many of the studies that criticise the perpetuation of negative imagery and stereotypes of the developing world, themselves fall into the trap of suggesting that these images are solely produced by Western actors and, in doing so, deny the agency of Africans to act upon these images and to participate in their formation and (re)production. The aim of this chapter is to look into this gap and try to understand how Africans are actually actively involved in the (re)production of images about themselves and how these images are in fact the result of a negotiation rather than a unilateral process.

In order to explore the different ways that images of Africa are co-constituted, this chapter uses Ethiopia as a case study and focuses on the strategies that have been used by its government to project a specific image of the country in a way that can best serve its own interest. To do so, this study recognises that perceptions by external actors are the result of a negotiation between the projection of an image, its reception and the context within which this exchange takes place. Therefore, an image is understood as having been produced by the encounter of different agents acting in a pre-defined milieu. In our case, the image of Ethiopia is the result of an interaction between Ethiopians and external actors evolving in a context already influenced by pre-existing discourses and perceptions.

There is a long history of Ethiopia negotiating with the rest of the world to project a specific image of itself (Teshale, 1996; Carnochan, 2008). This image has evolved over time because of changes at an international level, but also because of changes within Ethiopia itself, in particular the changing priorities and interests of its rulers. For example, the pan-Africanist image of Ethiopia actually originated across the Atlantic, in the Caribbean and America, and only took root in Ethiopia when the discourse on African independence at an international level became increasingly dominant, and Emperor Haile Selassie realised it would increase both his and the country's international stature and might serve as a source of legitimacy and domination.

Moving forward forty years, this chapter looks at the methods used by the Ethiopian government to affect the image of Ethiopia in a way that best serves its interest. Three major issues are explored: development, democracy and the fight against terrorism. The discourse and other speech acts of the Ethiopian government will illustrate how the image of the country is constructed both on the basis of internal policies and prevailing international discourses. In this regard, the image projected can also be seen as mimicking international meta-narratives on development, democracy and terrorism as it purposely meets the expectations of outside actors, at the same time as it challenges these international discourses and perceptions. Pre-existing perceptions and discourses can also be utilised to strengthen the Ethiopian government's hold on power, and while alternative or contradictory voices are silenced and refuted, negative imagery can be acted upon and revived as a way to legitimate certain policies and actions.

Democracy, development, anti-terrorism and the image of Ethiopia

In its image construction process, the Ethiopian government is particularly keen on placing itself alongside its international partners, and to do so it uses the same language and discourse as these partners. The repetition of the established development meta-narrative and the anti-terrorism discourse by the Ethiopian government serves its own purpose while also projecting a positive image of Ethiopia as an ally of the West (Abiye, 2011). This is particularly evident when and where the international discourse is Manichean, as in the case of the fight against terrorism. This strategy is well explained by Patrick Chabal's definition of the 'politics of the mirror', in which the North searches 'in Africa for an image of the Africa that would confirm our developmentalist assumptions about ourselves' (Chabal, 1996: 45f). Elements relating to this 'politics of the mirror' are easy to find in the discourse of Ethiopia. The phraseology used in the field of development, initially produced by the North, can be found in many different aspects of recent political, social and economic programmes and policies (Cornwall and Brock, 2005). Key terms such as 'sustainable', 'MDGs', 'participation', 'pro-poor' and 'poverty reduction' all feature abundantly in the speeches and official documents produced by the Ethiopian government. For example, the country's National Development Policy Framework aims to 'Fight and eradicate poverty through achieving broad-based and pro-poor growth' through 'medium term plans/programs such as the then Sustainable Development and Poverty Reduction Program (SDPRP) and the now Plan for Accelerated and Sustained Development to end Poverty (PASDEP), primary vehicles for overall socio-economic transformation and achieving the Millennium Development Plan (MDGs)' (MoFED, n.d.).

Both inside and outside the country, a large part of the legitimacy of the Ethiopian People Revolutionary Democratic Front (EPRDF) rests on its stated willingness to reverse the policies of previous regimes and its apparent embrace of democratisation. From early on, the EPRDF wanted to show that it was effectively committed to implementing democracy for the first time in Ethiopia (Ottaway, 1995; Joseph, 1998; Bach, 2011).

The official discourse used by the Ethiopian government still regularly highlights its 'central role in the toppling of the Derg and the liberation of Ethiopia's "nations and nationalities", commemorated in the annual Ginbot Haya (28 May) national holiday' (Hagmann and Abbink, 2011: 583). The EPRDF considers that the unbalanced representation of the different ethnic groups 'had over the centuries been one of the primary cause of [Ethiopia's] retreat from the front ranks of human civilisation' (Meles, 2010a). Federalism and democracy have thus become intertwined and are now such essential parts of the current government's credentials that they even feature in the official name of the country: Federal Democratic Republic of Ethiopia (Toggia, 2008).

The row that erupted in 2005 between the Ethiopian government and the European Union Election Observation Mission (EU-EOM) is particularly illustrative of the way in which Ethiopia is attached to defending its image as a democratising state (Abbink, 2006: 188). From the government's perspective, the 2005 elections represented the first real multi-party elections ever held in Ethiopia and the government wanted this to be recognised as such by external actors. They stressed that the unprecedented media access allowed to opposition parties, and the freedom they were granted in the electoral process, warranted recognition as 'free and fair', a qualification that the EU-EOM refused to acknowledge (Abbink, 2006: 188).

According to Tobias Hagmann and Jon Abbink, the 2005 elections fiasco also explains a shift in the image of Ethiopia: 'it is in this context of EPRDF's quest for renewed recognition against the backdrop of international condemnation of its democratic deficit that one must understand Meles Zenawi's attempt to equate his administration to a developmental state' (Hagmann and Abbink, 2011: 586). A few years earlier, one of the reasons Meles Zenawi, alongside Paul Kagame in Rwanda and Yoweri Museveni in Uganda, were being lauded as the 'new African leaders', has to do with their (apparent) embrace of the international discourse on development. In recent years, economic progress in Ethiopia has also been closely associated with the idea of Ethiopia as a development success and has been integrated into the official discourse. References to the ten years of 'double-digit growth' abound in the speeches and documents produced by government officials and other supporters of the EPRDF (MFA n.d.; MFA, 2012; Tsehaye, 2013). Ethiopia has actively placed itself in the frame of the 'African renaissance', notably by the naming of the mega-dam project being constructed on the Nile as the 'Grand Ethiopian Renaissance Dam' (Abbink, 2012).

At a more personal level, Prime Minister Meles Zenawi capitalised on his profound knowledge of development theory to become something of a 'champion' for Africa's development cause. It is as such that he was invited by Tony Blair to be part of the 'Commission for Africa', and also participated in the G8 and G20 meetings, and the World Economic Forum. The adaptability of the Ethiopian government's discourse to development 'trends' has proven successful on several occasions including in the case of climate change. The Ethiopian government was put at the forefront of developing nations after it was elected in 2009 to lead negotiations on behalf of Africa at the upcoming Conference of Parties of the United Nations Framework Convention on Climate Change, despite not yet having their own national policy on climate change. The sudden appearance of climate change in the Ethiopian government discourse coincided with the evolution of the international narrative on climate change and development towards an association with development and security (Brown, Hammill and McLeman, 2007; Detraz and Betsil, 2009).

Another topic that has shown Ethiopia's ability to re-cast itself in order to suit internationally dominant issues concerns its engagement in the fight against terrorism. Ethiopia, like many other states in the world, was quick to condemn the terrorist attacks of 9/11 and to express its support for the US fight against terrorism. But in the case of Ethiopia, the threat of terrorism and fundamental Islamism was also used to anchor the image of Ethiopia as a staunch ally of the West (Plaut, 2012). The Ethiopian government capitalised on their geopolitical and strategic importance to project an image of Ethiopia as being on the front line of the war on terror in relation to its neighbouring countries. Sudan had hosted Osama Bin Laden for several years and was led by an Islamic inspired government; Kenya had witnessed a major terrorist attack on the American embassy in Nairobi in 1998; and most importantly Somalia, where an absence of central government had allowed various Islamic groups to build a stronghold. Ethiopia itself had been threatened by a minor terrorist group, Al-Ittihad al-Islamiya, whose importance would soon be overblown to underline the view of Ethiopia as a victim of terrorism. The image of Ethiopia as a strong ally in the global fight against terrorism would be further emphasised in 2007 following the direct engagement of Ethiopian troops in Somalia to fight the Islamic Court Union (ICU) (Lefebvre, 2012).

Of mirrors and mimicry

The 'politics of the mirror' identifies the capacity of Africans to use their agency to gain favours from the West by repeating the discourse used by the latter and its expectations regarding the African continent.

However, the analysis provided by Chabal needs to be complemented in order to explain some of the tensions that arise, despite – or because of – the apparent re-appropriation of the meta-narrative. In the case of Ethiopia, several analyses of Ethiopia's relationship with its international partners have noted that despite the usage of similar discourse and an apparent agreement on broad 'development' themes, tensions still exist (Borchgrevink, 2008; Furtado and Smith, 2008; Dereje, 2011; Prizzon and Rogerson, 2013). These tensions underline the very different views that exist regarding what is understood by each of the parties when they talk about 'democracy', 'development' and even 'fighting terrorism'. The differences in these understandings are actually highlighted by the fact that the discourses are similar. The very repetition of the dominating discourse is what makes it apparent that it is *'almost the same, but not quite'* (Bhabha, 1994: 122). Therefore, the image being projected by Ethiopia suddenly becomes a way to challenge and throw into question the dominant hegemonic meta-narrative regarding development. The repetition of international discourse serves to highlight its fragilities and, in so doing, opens up a new opportunity for different meanings to emerge and to challenge fixed identities. This allows Ethiopia, while still portraying itself as being on the side of the West, to criticise and question the authority of the West. The advantage of ascribing to the development meta-narrative is thus double as it not only allows Ethiopia to gain the favours of donors but also enables it to push its own understanding on issues like development, democracy and the fight against terrorism.

Insights provided by postcolonial studies, in particular regarding the relationship between the coloniser and the colonised and the construction of their identities, help to explain how repetition as mimicry is a way to question and disrupt the power of authority and knowledge. Postcolonialism is particularly concerned by how the coloniser 'Self' ascribes a specific identity to the colonised 'Other' (Abrahamsen, 2003). Drawing on insights from Foucault, Derrida and Lacan, postcolonial scholars also highlight the fact that despite its somewhat 'subaltern' position, the colonised maintains agency in the power relationship with the coloniser and can in fact disrupt and resist this power by playing on the fragility of colonial domination. Moreover, resistance is viewed as being 'more subtle, and as part of the recovery of subaltern subject positions', thus postcolonial investigations 'have often focused on "histories from below" and everyday forms of resistance rather than revolutions, armed struggles or large-scale political opposition' (Ibid: 208).

For Homi Bhabha, occurrences of resistance permeate colonial power relations on different occasions both as discursive enunciation and as practice (Bhabha, 1994). Therefore Ethiopia's mimicking of the Western discourse on democracy, development and terrorism should also be understood by taking into account the ways in which it challenges these same discourses by exacerbating some of their flaws, and so putting their authoritative power into question. This is because 'the menace of mimicry is its double vision which in disclosing the ambivalence of colonial discourse also disrupts its authority' (Bhabha, 1994: 126). Following this line, mimicry poses a challenge to colonial authority since it addresses the colonial directly by mirroring its exercise of power and differentiation. Mimicry is in fact the Other turning to the Self and caricaturising the Self through imitation and reiteration. Postcolonial studies thus considers that the colonial can experience mimicry as a threat to its power and authority because it directly questions the differentiation between Self and Other that is a foundation of colonial domination. Mimicry offers the possibility for the colonised to turn back the gaze of the colonial, so much so that the colonial is no longer looking at the Other but is forced to look at itself as represented by the mimicking colonised (Bhabha, 1994: 127). Thus, if we return to the metaphor of the 'politics of the mirror', as identified by Chabal, by looking into the image reproduced by the (African) mirror, the West is looking for something that resembles it – or at least resembles the imagined image – but at the same time it cannot help but notice its own flaws reflected (and sometimes emphasised) by the mirror.

Using mimicry, the meta-narrative on development is easy to manipulate in order to highlight some of the problems inherent in the liberal world order that it aims for. Although they may appear hegemonic and indisputable on many occasions, discourses on democracy are still fragile and contested (Comaroff and Comaroff, 1997; Jacobs, 1999; Pieterse, 2000; Ayers, 2006). The technicalities of these discourses only partly hide their fallibility. Furthermore, it is important to note that contrary to colonial times, these discourses can no longer be enforced through physical violence. In the postcolonial context, on the other hand, the force of the discourse is based on the power/knowledge nexus.[1] The colonised resistance can therefore take the form of a reiteration of colonial discourse, for example in the form of mimicry, but one that changes the substance of the discourse itself. Bhabha illustrates the challenge to domination by telling the story of Indian Christians who, despite having adopted Christianity, still question the authority and validity of the 'English Book', the Bible (Bhabha, 1994: 145–75). It therefore appears that under the guise of adherence, the colonised puts into question the substance of the discourse and its enunciative authority. In the case of the discourses on democracy and development, their fragility and susceptibility to challenge is also enabled by the ambivalence that is inherent to both discourses. Given the fear of being seen as a (neo-) colonial imposition, the democracy and development meta-narratives highlight the need for the processes to be nationally appropriated rather than externally imposed. But in doing so it calls for the inclusion of national or local characteristics to the process and thus opens up the possibility for it to be hybridised, transformed and even disfigured.

Ethiopia has been skilfully able to use the inherent fragilities of the meta-narrative on democracy and development to resist externally-conceived understandings and push for its own vision on both issues. Thus, the type of democracy that is currently favoured by the EPRDF is in reality 'revolutionary democracy', inspired by Marxist and Leninist readings. This approach clearly differs from the liberal understanding of democracy (Abbink, 2009; Bach, 2011; Haggman and Abbink, 2011; Vaughan, 2011). Rather than a government based on representative democracy, the EPRDF insists on the role of a vanguard group to lead the country and whose legitimacy rests on its capacity to rule in favour of the masses. Therefore, revolutionary democracy can be said to have 'the trappings of multiparty democracy with parties allowed, elections held and some extent of free press media permitted, but with an unshakably dominant rule of the vanguard party, that assumed power in armed struggle and therefore cannot and will not relinquish it' (Haggman and Abbink, 2011: 582). Thus, the government in Ethiopia has been able to maintain the image and discourse of democracy while at the same time completely changing its substance. It is not so much a democracy *by* the people but rather a democracy *for* the people, or, to remain with the EPRDF terminology, for the 'masses' (Vaughan, 2011). One of the stated aims of the EPRDF is to impose a hegemonic opinion, shaped and led by the vanguard, that would become so strong as to be undisputed. The governance and power techniques used within the country actually offer very little opportunity for any form of open political debate to take place (Bach, 2011). Meanwhile, Ethiopia is able to portray itself as a democracy while at the same time criticising the Western understanding of what 'being democratic' actually means.

A similar process has been used in regard to the development agenda being put in place in Ethiopia. Encounters between the Ethiopian government and development agencies have clearly highlighted the fact that even though they might share a similar discourse on development, there is still a big difference in terms of understanding. An artificial reading of Ethiopia's discourse on development may give the impression that it fully ascribes to the models being favoured by international development and financial institutions such as the World Bank, the

International Monetary Fund and other major bilateral development agencies. However, a more in-depth look at the policies being implemented in Ethiopia and the parts of its discourse that depart from the neo-liberal understanding of development shows a very different situation. In fact, one of the main traits of Meles' approach to development has been the continuous quest for alternative models of development, especially those that emphasise a strong interventionist state. As he once stated: 'The failure of the neo-liberal paradigm in Africa is thus not a failure of implementation of the paradigm or one of lack of refinement of this or that aspect of the paradigm. It is a paradigmatic failure and can only be corrected by a shift in paradigm' (Meles, 2006: 36). The Ethiopian government rapprochement with China is not only based on economic interests but also because it offers a development alternative Ethiopia has been looking for (Clapham, 2006; Meles, 2010b; Seifudein, 2012).

Ethiopia's instrumentalisation of the discourse on the fight against terrorism also reveals how it has been re-appropriated by the Ethiopian government to serve its own needs, even outside of the framework of anti-terrorism. In doing so it offers one of the clearest examples of mimicry where the mimicry reveals all the unsightly aspects of the dominant or hegemonic discourse. Many voices in the US and in Europe have already criticised how the increasingly overarching and all-powerful nature of the war on terror could have negative consequences on civil liberties and human rights even within their own countries (Fitzpatrick 2003; Brysk and Shafir, 2007). But the Ethiopian government's use of anti-terrorist discourse to legitimate many of its violent actions further reveals the dangers that are innate to this kind of Manichean discourse. The 2009 Anti-Terrorism Proclamation has given immense power to the Ethiopian government to control and muzzle the political scene in the country (Bekele, 2010). Opposition parties that could challenge the government have been labelled as terrorist organisations and their leaders and supporters threatened with arrest. For example, given the repressive nature of the Ethiopian anti-terrorism legislation, journalists reporting on Ginbot 7, a political party that has been listed as a terrorist organisation, could be charged with promoting terrorism (HRW, 2010: 50). Under the guise of fighting terrorism, the Ethiopian government has in reality been able to further its tight grip on power while also finding a new narrative with which to legitimise persecution of opposition figures and control the media (Abiye, 2011). This reappropriation of the discourse of the fight against terrorism has thus made it difficult for Ethiopia's international partners to denounce and criticise it (Lefevbre, 2012).

Silencing alternatives and re-reading

The process of image construction is an arduous task that can easily be disturbed by the actions of external elements. Projecting any specific image includes the threat of disruption by others. Therefore one of the challenges that is part of image construction concerns the way internal alternative voices are managed and whether they are allowed to become a founding part of the constructed image or not. The choice of taking these alternate sources into account greatly depends on the added value these new storylines can offer (or not) to the main narrative. This does not mean that only the positive storylines offer benefits; much can be gained from what may seem to be negative reflections. Rather it is how these external components fit with the main meta-narrative about one-self that explains why they may or may not be accepted by the actor trying to project a specific image. In the case of Ethiopia, it is clear that differing voices are only accepted if they are in line with the way the Ethiopian government portrays itself and the country.

Alternate narratives that would go against the image of Ethiopia as a developing country that is on the road to democracy and is involved in fighting terrorism are ferociously silenced by the Ethiopian government. As mentioned earlier, the legislation that exists in regard to anti-terrorism makes it very difficult for opposition political figures to be heard. The tight control that is exercised over the media also stifles alternative voices that could disrupt the image of Ethiopia. Since 2008 the state media in Ethiopia has been instructed to work according to the concept of 'development journalism' (Skjerdal, 2011). Journalists are encouraged to set aside politically sensitive questions and focus their reporting on development projects and programmes highlighting how they are expected to serve the development of the country and benefit the general population. This media control also covers international press reporting on Ethiopia and foreign correspondents who have to subscribe to the official image in their reporting. In a remarkable feat of honesty, the expulsion of Associated Press correspondent, Anthony Mitchell, in January 2006 was justified by the spokesman for the Ministry of Foreign Affairs because the journalist 'continued to disseminate information bent on tarnishing the image of the country' (*Ethiopian Herald*, 2006). In 2012, two Swedish journalists reporting on the Ogaden National Liberation Front (ONLF) rebel group in the south-east of the country were arrested and charged with promoting terrorism. Eventually both were pardoned after having been forced to publicly recognise their faults and were even paraded on national television in a most bizarre interview where they had to praise the way they had been treated in Ethiopia.[2]

On a more mundane note, the Ethiopian government sponsored the creation in North America, of the All Ethiopian Sports Association, to offer an alternative to the Ethiopian Sports Federation (ESFNA) which was seen as a critical hotbed for opposition to the government (Nahom, 2012). The Ethiopian government is very much concerned by the voices in the diaspora which it believes contribute to the negative portrayal of Ethiopia and its government (Lyons, 2007).

Silencing alternative voices is not always possible, however. When the Ethiopian government has no control over those circulating negative stories – for example, certain foreign or international actors – a successful strategy has been to acknowledge them but offer a differing interpretation. In a process that resembles the Derridean concepts of *différance* and textual *deconstruction*, the speech acts are offered an alternate understanding through their recontextualisation and a modification of their meanings. Thus, rather than frontally attacking a particular statement, an attempt is made to subvert the binary opposition, for example good versus bad, through a process of deconstruction. The Ethiopian government is adept at deconstructing discourses that go against the image of itself by taking them apart and showcasing their self-contradiction and the tensions between rhetoric and logic they contain. This was the case in the Ethiopian government response to an appeal to development agencies and NGOs in early 2011 stating that famine was looming in parts of the country. The Prime Minister highlighted that, according to the official UN and technical definition, the situation could not be labelled a famine *per se* but should simply be considered as a drought where the local population was in need of food aid (WIC, 2011). Moreover, the confusion was explained by Meles as being motivated by both 'the need to gather as much as possible aid by institutions and non-governmental organisations working in the area of food aid' and, interestingly, by a 'political aim to exaggerate the country's need of aid, thereby mar the image of Ethiopia' (WIC, 2011). Rejecting the word 'famine' was paramount to the legitimacy of the government as it actively tried to associate it with previous regimes and to highlight its own successes against famine. This recontextualisation has enabled the Ethiopian government to reduce the extent to which the image it projects is challenged by other voices.

The Ethiopian government also uses modern communication techniques to offer rebuttals to discourses that criticise it. To push its policies and agenda in the US, Ethiopia has enlisted the help of lobby firms advocating on its behalf and ensuring it is not the target of further criticism. The Washington-registered lobbying firm, DLA Piper, was contracted by the Ethiopian government to try to block the adoption of the bill on the human rights situation in Ethiopia, H. R. 2003, presented to the US Congress in 2008 (Eviatar, 2008). The lobbying undertaken to defend Ethiopia's record attempted to disprove condemnation of Ethiopia and its government by dismissing the origin of the criticism. Human rights watchdogs have often been criticised by the Ethiopian government because of their negative assessment of the situation in Ethiopia. On one such occasion, a press release from the Ministry of Foreign Affairs considered that an article pointing out government failures could be dismissed because of 'Human Rights Watch's poor methodology, its techniques of deliberately misusing facts or misinterpreting them to suit its own claims, and of inventing elements in common with the worst of the journalistic exaggerations of the tabloid press' (MFA, 2012).

Even individuals who criticise the state face the risk of being put under a sustained barrage of character assassination. For example, following the 2005 elections, the head of the EU observation mission, Ana Gomes, who was perceived by the EPRDF to be too favourable to the opposition, was described in an open letter signed by the Prime Minister, as 'an election observer turned self-appointed colonial viceroy hell-bent on twisting the arms of the government to force it to accept her dictates' (Meles, 2005a). Such public defamation can go further, with disturbing consequences, as has been the case of the government's portrayal of Muslim protests in 2012 against government intrusion into religious affairs, including the appointment of a new head of the Supreme Council of Islamic Affairs. Unable to put an end to these protests, the government launched a smear campaign associating the protesters and their leaders with terrorist organisations and linking them with Al-Qaeda. A (pseudo-)documentary titled 'Jihadawi Harekat' (Jihadic Movement) produced by the National Intelligence and Security Services (NISS) and the Federal Police in collaboration with the Ethiopian Radio and Television Agency was even broadcast to convince the general public of the malevolent intent of the protest leaders (Allo, 2013; Qassim, 2013).

Similar techniques are used against those who criticise the development policies of the Ethiopian government. Labelling critics and opposition parties as 'traitors', 'anti-Ethiopia and anti-peace', 'destructive forces' or 'enemies of Ethiopia' has become a common practice (EPA, 2012). The discussions that have surrounded the Grand Ethiopian Renaissance Dam (GERD) illustrate how, on issues pertaining to development, critics are quickly accused of wanting to deny Ethiopia the possibility of development (Abbink, 2012). The GERD is a major infrastructure project and is seen as epitomising the country's development. Nevertheless, various international actors have questioned its environmental and social impact, as well as the effect it will have on other upstream countries. The World Bank and other international donors refused to finance the project, pushing the Ethiopian government to seek the necessary financial resources through the sale of government bonds. But in the process of doing so, the narrative on the dam has increasingly intertwined development discourse with a very nationalist one that stresses the independent nature of Ethiopia (Abbink, 2012: 135).[3] For example, speaking about critics of the GERD, Meles stated: '[They] want Africa to remain as it currently is with all its misery and poverty so that they can come and visit nature in its pristine state in the winter every so often ... I believe the position taken by such groups is not only irrational but also bordering on the criminal' (2011). The Ethiopian government is harnessing the power of the development meta-narrative whereby criticising one feature of the development policies means one can easily be accused of being anti-development altogether.

Failed state haunting

The importance of development as a cornerstone of Ethiopia's identity should not be underestimated. But it is also essential to note that development is seen as a process: the image that Ethiopia projects is in fact not focussed on what it aims to be but rather on its current status and how it has changed from the past. This is also the case concerning the democratic situation in the country. From the Ethiopian government's point of view, the country is still in the process of becoming democratic, or in the words of Meles, responding to a question on the country's stability following the 2005 elections, 'We are not out of the woods yet. We are trying to get out of it. We've made some progress. But we are not out of the woods yet' (Meles, 2005b). The Prime Minister is clearly highlighting the fragility of the state and its risk of collapse, and thus implying the need for further support for the current efforts of his government. Negative imagery associated with the Ethiopian state can be used to reinforce the EPRDF's hold on power in Ethiopia.

As noted earlier, a large part of the image the current Ethiopian government tries to project centres around its differentiation from the past government. The EPRDF's own history and image is very much based on its defeat of the *Derg* regime and the introduction of democracy (Hagmann and Abbink, 2011: 583). The trial of the *Derg* officials accused of having conducted the red terror, as well as the recent opening in the centre of Addis Ababa of a museum on the atrocities committed during the reign of Mengistu Haile Mariam, is part of this exercise of distancing from the horrors of the previous regime (Tarsitani, 2011). But it is worth noting the wording used by the government to describe the situation prior to the arrival in power of the EPRDF. For example, Meles once declared '[T]he management of [Ethiopia's] diversity has for centuries constituted a primary challenge – a challenge that has massively contributed to its *centuries long journey backwards* from the frontline of world civilisation to one of the poorest countries on earth' (emphasis mine, Meles 2010a). The references to past governments also serve to underline the progress made and remind the audience of the situation that the country once faced and could still face again. The *Derg* regime has been defeated, but some of the threats that Ethiopia faces are still considered to be very much alive. In this regard, the overarching threat that permeates Ethiopian official discourse is the one of state failure.

By re-appropriating many elements of the democracy, development and fight against terrorism meta-narratives, the Ethiopian government has shown its ability to associate itself with dominant international discourses. But it has also done so in regard to the discourse on state failure, despite the unflattering image that it conveys because as unflattering as it may be, it too offers the possibilities for the Ethiopian government to utilise and gain from it. The Foreign Affairs and National Security Policy and Strategy makes clear the risk that Ethiopia faces: 'The prospect of disintegration cannot be totally ruled out. That is why it is imperative that we expedite development and consolidate democracy' (FDRE, 2002: 23). Referring to state failure is particularly useful for the Ethiopian government as it is a concept and discourse that has come to cover a broad number of topics including development, democracy and terrorism. It is not a coincidence that these same issues are closely associated in the Foreign Affairs Policy and Strategy, or in the speeches of Ethiopian officials (Meles, 2011). The Ethiopian government is only replicating the discussions that are taking place at the international level and the discourse that is associated with state failure by such international actors as the US and the EU (Gruffydd Jones, 2013). Moreover, it plays on one of the great fears of the West, where failed states are seen as uncontrollable entities that threaten the livelihood of the developed world. For example, the EU's Security Strategy adopted in 2003 lists state failure as one of the threats that the EU needs to address to ensure its own, and the world's, security.

Chabal's description of the 'politics of the mirror' highlighted the West's quest for an image that fitted its own assumptions about itself and about Africa, thus providing a reassuring representation of the developing world. But when it comes to such issues as failed states, the image is no longer reassuring, but frightening. Expressing the threat of becoming a failed state highlights those elements that the West does not want to see or hear. As such, it can be a useful part of the process of image construction for African states. This form of strategic self-orientalisation willingly places countries such as Ethiopia in line with the greatest fears that are expressed regarding the developing world and therefore raises the need to address the looming threat of state failure. The pressure for the developed world to assist those potentially failing states proportionally increases as the menace intensifies. Ethiopia has skilfully been able to capitalise on the Derridean hauntology of the failed state. In the Ethiopian government discourse, state failure is ever-present as a menace but not as a reality, like a spectre haunting the country. The possibility for the state to fail becomes the biggest threat that would jeopardise all progress already made. As part of its representation to the outside world, preventing this threat from being realised thus becomes one of the major tasks both for Ethiopia and for external actors, and emphasises the readiness of the government to tackle this threat and ensure the stability and security of the country. This failed state menace also explains the cognitive dissonance of donor countries who provide aid to Ethiopia while knowing very well the authoritarian nature of the state and its violations of human rights. The support made available to the Ethiopian government is justified by the need to avert the unknown situation that would follow from the state's failure, whereas current threats are still perceived as manageable (Lefebvre, 2012).

Conclusion

Ethiopia's re-appropriation of the discourse on state failure is evidently linked to its image as a state engaged in a process of developing its economy, democratising and getting rid of the threat of terrorism. It also highlights the capacity of the Ethiopian government to embrace international trends and use them to build an image of Ethiopia that is in line with the expectations and representation of foreign actors, in particular donor countries and international financial institutions. This apparent acceptance of the meta-narrative on development and on the fight against terrorism should not be taken at face value. A more indepth look at the actual interpretations and usage that the Ethiopian government makes with regard to democracy and development shows that it differs significantly from the aspirations of the West. In fact, the Ethiopian position is often a critique of the dominant approach on development and democracy, while the war on terror is increasingly used as a means of political control and a way to silence the media. Nevertheless, because the Ethiopian discourse is framed in the same narrative as the hegemonic one, it is difficult to criticise it without at the same time developing a more introspective approach to internationally promoted norms. In addition, the Ethiopian government has been very skilful in constructing an image of Ethiopia as a staunch ally of the West; an ally whose downfall would present major problems in terms of security. The portrayal of Ethiopia as a country always on the brink of collapse while also being at the frontline of the war on terror has enabled the government of Ethiopia to receive the backing of important international allies.

Notes

1 Here it refers both to the understanding of postcolonial as meaning 'after colonisation' and as a post-modern and post-structural reading of the relations between Self and Other.
2 Being pardoned after publicly admitting one's fault is a common practice in Ethiopia that allows the government to force alternative voices to publicly claim their adherence to the official storyline. The process is also reminiscent of the practice of self-criticism used in the Soviet Union.
3 The nationalist discourse has also been reinforced by the geostrategic nature of the GERD and in particular Egypt's staunch opposition to the project.

References

Abbink, J. (2006): 'Discomfiture of democracy?: the 2005 election crisis in Ethiopia and its aftermath.' *African Affairs* 105(419): 173–99.
Abbink, J. (2009): 'The Ethiopian Second Republic and the fragile "social contract"', *Africa Spectrum*, 44(2): 3–28.
Abbink, J. (2012): 'Dam controversies: contested governance and developmental discourse on the Ethiopian Omo River dam', *Social Anthropology* 20(2): 125–44.
Abiye Teklemariam Mengenta (2011): 'The journalist as terrorist: an Ethiopian story', *openDemocracy*, 7.12.11, www.opendemocracy.net/abiye-teklemariam-megenta/journalist-as-terrorist-ethiopian-story, cited 15.12.12.
Abrahamsen, R. (2003): 'African studies and the postcolonial challenge', *African Affairs* 102(407): 189–210.
Allo, A. K. (2013): 'Ethiopia's "jihadi" film and its boomerang effects', *Al Jazeera*, 4.3.13, www.aljazeera.com/indepth/opinion/2013/02/2013228644 54855976.html, cited 6.3.13.
Ayers, A. J. (2006): 'Demystifying democratisation: the global constitution of (neo)liberal polities in Africa', *Third World Quarterly* 27(2): 321–38.
Baaz, M. E. (2005): *The Paternalism of Partnership: A Postcolonial Reading of Identity in Development Aid* (London and New York: Zed Books).
Bach, J-N. (2011): '*Abyotawi* democracy: neither revolutionary nor democratic, a critical review of EPRDF's conception of revolutionary democracy in post-1991 Ethiopia', *Journal of Eastern African Studies* 5(4): 641–63.

Bekele, Mehlik A. (2010): 'Counter-terrorism and the suppression of political pluralism: an examination of the Anti-terrorism Proclamation of Ethiopia' (Masters dissertation, Accra: Faculty of Law, University of Ghana).

Bhabha, H. (1994): *The Location of Culture* (Oxon: Routledge).

Borchgrevink, A. (2008): 'Limits to donor influence: Ethiopia, aid and conditionality', *Forum for Development Studies* 35(2): 195–220.

Brown, O., A. Hammill and R. McLeman (2007): 'Climate change as the new security threat: implications for Africa', *International Affairs*, 83(6): 1141–54.

Brysk, A. and G. Shafir (eds) (2007): *National Insecurity and Human Rights: democracies debate counterterrorism* (Berkeley, University of California Press).

Carnochan, W. B. (2008): *Golden Legends: images of Abyssina, Samuel Johnson to Bob Marley* (Standford, CA: Stanford University Press).

Chabal, P. (1996): 'The African crisis: context and interpretation', in R. Werbner and T. Ranger (eds), *Postcolonial Identities in Africa* (London: Zed Books): 29–54.

Clapham, C. (2006): 'Ethiopian development: the politics of emulation', *Commonwealth and Comparative Politics* 44(1): 137–50.

Comaroff, J. L. and J. Comaroff (1997): 'Postcolonial politics and discourses of democracy in southern Africa: an anthropological reflection on African political modernities', *Journal of Anthropological Research* 53(2): 123–46.

Cornwall, A. and K. Brock (2005): 'Beyond buzzwords: "poverty reduction", "participation" and "empowerment" in development policy', *Programme Paper Number 10*, UNRISD.

Dereje Feyissa (2011): 'Aid negotiation: the uneasy "partnership" between EPRDF and the donors', *Journal of Eastern African Studies* 5(4): 788–817.

Detraz, N. and M. M. Betsill (2009): 'Climate change and environmental security: for whom the discourse shifts', *International Studies Perspectives* 10(3): 303–20.

Doty, R. L. (1996): *Imperial Encounters: the politics of representation in North-South relations* (Minneapolis, MN: University of Minnesota Press).

EPA (2012): 'Editorial: Ethiopia: renewing commitment to realize Meles's vision', *Ethiopian Press Agency*, 30.8.12, http://allafrica.com/stories/201209040003.html, cited 10.3.13.

Ethiopian Herald (2006): 'IRIN and AP correspondent asked to leave', *Ethiopian Herald*, 23.1.06, http://www.afrika.no/Detailed/11310.html, cited 2.2.13.

Eviatar, D. (2008): 'DLA Piper pleads Ethiopia's case against human rights sanctions', *The American Lawyer*, 3.6.08, www.law.com/jsp/law/internatio nal/LawArticleIntl.jsp?id=1202422729631&DLA_Piper_Pleads_Ethiopias_Case_Against_Human_Rights_Sanctions&slreturn=20130325065049, cited 10.2.12.

Fair, J. E. (1993): 'War, famine and poverty: race in the construction of Africa's media image', *Journal of Communication Inquiry*, 17(2): 5–22.

FDRE (2002): *Federal Democratic Republic of Ethiopia, Foreign Affairs and*

National Security Policy and Strategy (Addis Ababa: Ministry of Information, Press and Audiovisual Department).

Fitzpatrick, J. (2003): 'Speaking law to power: the war against terrorism and human rights', *European Journal of International Law* 14(2): 241–64.

Furtado, X. and J. Smith (2008): 'Ethiopia: retaining sovereignty in the face of aid', in L. Whitfield (ed.), *The Politics of Aid: African strategies for dealing with donors* (Oxford: Oxford University Press).

Gruffydd Jones, B. (2013): '"Good governance" and "state failure": genealogies of imperial discourse', *Cambridge Review of International Affairs* 26(1): 49–70.

Hagmann, T. and J. Abbink (2011): 'Twenty years of revolutionary democratic Ethiopia, 1991 to 2011', *Journal of Eastern African Studies* 5(4): 579–95.

Human Rights Watch (HRW) (2010): *Ethiopia: 'One Hundred Ways of Putting Pressure': violations of freedom of expression and association in Ethiopia* (New York: Human Rights Watch).

Jacobs, M. (1999): 'Sustainable development as a contested concept', in A. Dobson (ed.) *Fairness and Futurity: essays on environmental sustainability and social justice* (Oxford: Oxford University Press).

Joseph, R. A. (1998): 'Oldspeak vs Newspeak', *Journal of Democracy* 9(4): 55–61.

Lefebvre, J. A. (2012): 'Choosing sides in the horn of Africa: Wikileaks, the Ethiopia imperative, and American responses to post-9/11 regional conflicts', *Diplomacy and Statecraft* 23(4): 704–27.

Lyons, T. (2007): 'Conflict-generated diasporas and transnational politics in Ethiopia', *Conflict, Security and Development* 7(4): 529–49.

Meles Zenawi (2005a): 'Letter to the Editor', *Ethiopian Herald*, 31.8.05.

Meles Zenawi (2005b): Hardtalk: interview with Ethiopian PM Meles Zenawi, BBC World Service, 4.7.05.

Meles Zenawi (2006): 'African development: dead ends and new beginnings' (unpublished Masters dissertation, Rotterdam: Erasmus University).

Meles Zenawi (2010a): Keynote address at the Fifth International Conference on Federalism, Addis Ababa, Ethiopia, 13.12.10.

Meles Zenawi (2010b): Keynote address at the Africa-China Poverty Reduction and Development Conference, Addis Ababa, Ethiopia, 1.11.10.

Meles Zenawi (2011): Address at the Hydro-power for Sustainable Development Conference, Addis Ababa, Ethiopia, 31.3.11.

MFA, Ministry of Foreign Affairs (n.d.): 'Maintaining double digit economic growth', www.mfa.gov.et/PressMore.php?pg=16, cited 3.2.13.

MFA (2012): Speech delivered on the World Economic forum, 9.5.12, www.mfa.gov.et/theMinstrMore.php?pg=28, cited 3.2.13.

MoFED, Ministry of Finance and Economic Development (n.d.): Information: National development plan, www.mofed.gov.et/English/Information/Pages/NationalDevelopmentPlan.aspx, cited 15.12.12.

Nahom Freda (2012): 'The lessons of the current Ethiopian soccer tournaments', *Awramba Times*, 9.7.12, www.awrambatimes.com/?p=1848, cited 2.2.13.

Ottaway, M. (1995): 'The Ethiopian transition: democratization or new authoritarianism?', *Northeast African Studies* 2(3): 67–87.

Patrick, S. (2007): '"Failed" states and global security: empirical questions and policy dilemmas', *International Studies Review* 9(4): 644–62.

Pieterse, J. N. (2000): 'After post-development', *Third World Quarterly* 21(2): 175–91.

Plaut, M. (2012): 'Why the West backed Ethiopia's Meles Zenawi', BBC World Service, 21.8.12, www.bbc.co.uk/news/world-africa-19332646, cited 10.3.13.

Prizzon, A. and A. Rogerson (2013): 'The age of choice: Ethiopia in the new aid landscape', *ODI Research Report* (London: Overseas Development Institute).

Qassim, F. (2013): 'Ethiopia: Jihadawi Harekat: context, objectives, and internal contradictions', *In Depth Africa*, 7.2.13, http://indepthafrica.com/ethiopia-jihadawi-harekat-context-objectives-and-internal-contradictions, cited 6.3.13.

Seifudein Adem (2012): 'China in Ethiopia: diplomacy and economics of Sino-optimism', *African Studies Review* 55(1): 143–60.

Skjerdal, T. S. (2011): 'Development journalism revived: the case of Ethiopia', *Ecquid Novi: African Journalism Studies* 32(2): 58–74.

Tarsitani, B. A. (2011): 'Linking centralised politics to custodianship of cultural heritage in Ethiopia: examples of national-level museums in Addis Ababa', *African Studies* 70(2): 302–20.

Teshale Tibebu (1996): 'Ethiopia: the "anomaly" and "paradox" of Africa', *Journal of Black Studies* 26(4): 414–30.

Tester, K. (2010): *Humanitarianism and Modern Culture* (University Park, PA: Pennsylvania State University Press).

Toggia, P. (2008): 'History writing as a state ideological project in Ethiopia', *African Identities* 6(4): 319–43.

Tsehaye Debalkew (2013): 'The glittering transformation of Ethiopia is beyond reproach', *Tigrai Online*, 31.3.13. www.tigraionline.com/articles/article130286.html, cited 5.4.13.

Vaughan, S. (2011): 'Revolutionary democratic state-building: party, state and people in the EPRDF's Ethiopia', *Journal of Eastern African Studies* 5(4): 619–40 .

VSO (2001): 'The Live Aid Legacy. The developing world through British eyes; a research report' (London: VSO Report).

WIC (2011): 'Government Food Aid System successful to prevent famine: PM Meles', *Walta Information Centre*, 17.8.11, www.ertagov.com/erta/erta-news-archive/887–government-food-aid-system-successful-to-prevent-famine-meles.html, cited 10.2.12.

6

Images of a traditional authority: the case of Ker Kwaro Acholi in northern Uganda

Clare Paine

Between 2005 and 2010 Ker Kwaro Acholi began to emerge as the revived traditional institution of the Acholi people, perceived by donors as the key to reconciliation in war-torn northern Uganda and potential agent of sustainable development more broadly. Supported by the United States Agency for International Development (USAID) and the World Bank on projects to strengthen farmer groups across Acholiland and boost local participation in community reconciliation and conflict management, it has worked with other multilateral and bilateral donors such as the United Nations and the American Embassy to promote women's rights in Acholi and to preserve Acholi cultural heritage. The success of this 'traditional authority' in attracting international attention and the endorsement of a host of bilateral and multilateral donors[1] has contributed to Ker Kwaro Acholi being today composed of a paramount chief, two deputy paramount chiefs, council of clan chiefs, prime minister, cabinet of ministers, and secretariat.

Yet despite the positive recognition received from such influential actors there is little critical analysis examining how Ker Kwaro Acholi has emerged since the turn of the twenty-first century. What has been understood about the traditional leaders associated with Ker Kwaro Acholi and the external support they have received raises concern and criticism over inventions of tradition that have accompanied the process of 'reviving' traditional leaders (Allen, 2006; 2011) and the threat that a reconstruction of chiefly authority may have on new forms of local democratisation and political inclusion in post conflict northern Uganda (Branch, 2011).

Instructively, a growing number of studies offer critiques on recent 'traditional' authority revivals across sub-Saharan Africa, with a particular interest in how discourses of international development have shaped emerging traditional institutions in their multiplicity and diversity of expressions (Englebert, 2005). Of particular relevance for my study are cases similar to Ker Kwaro Acholi that show how local actors, both claimants and advocates of traditional authority, are strategically appropriating multiple discourses, including those in development, in order to craft public images that position traditional authorities advantageously under the gaze of key stakeholders such as international development organisations (Chiweza, 2007; Kleist, 2011; Lentz, 1998; Ubink 2008; West and Kloeck-Jenson, 1999; Williams, 2010; Zeller, 2007). In post-apartheid South Africa, for example, numerous chiefs became adept at projecting 'themselves as guardians of African custom, but simultaneously as pioneers of rural development' (Kessel and Oomen, 1997: 562) and in post-conflict Mozambique, NGOs are becoming increasingly entangled with chiefs in an on-going process where the 'traditional' authority 'relies upon the NGO and its resources to construct and/or consolidate his political authority and legitimacy' (West and Kloeck-Jenson, 1999: 483). Each of these studies illustrates cases of 'traditional' authority being 'imagined' (Anderson, 1983), drawing attention to specific practices employed in the wider imagining process. In this chapter I too examine a dimension of a wider imagining process, as I shed light on the strategic crafting of images by Ker Kwaro Acholi and analyse their effects in relation to discourses of international development.

In this chapter I make three key, interrelated arguments. First, that Ker Kwaro Acholi has emerged in the context of both a renewed concern for 'the local' on the part of the international development community, and a wave of traditional authority revivals in Uganda and sub-Saharan Africa over the past two decades. This intersection has provided a fertile field of opportunity for people such as the new Paramount Chief of Acholi and his close associates, who strategically present images of the emerging Ker Kwaro Acholi that appeal to discourses within the international development community. Second, however, there is a disjuncture between the images Ker Kwaro Acholi presents of itself and how 'traditional' authority works in practice, which demands significant reinterpretation of the institution on the part of international donors. Finally, I suggest that Ker Kwaro Acholi's images and their productive effects in partnerships with donors have served to obscure inherently political agendas of Ker Kwaro Acholi's central actors; agendas which threaten to undermine attempts for peaceful reconciliation in northern Uganda.

The chapter begins by tracing the way in which Ker Kwaro Acholi presents itself as the traditional cultural authority of Acholi on the one hand and as a potential agent of sustainable development on the other, through public ceremonies, re-casting the past, aligning itself with the values of its target audience, donors, and appropriating donor rhetoric. I go on to explore the various effects of Ker Kwaro Acholi's images as they gain traction amongst donors, and draw on cases of the World Bank and USAID's engagement with Ker Kwaro Acholi that illustrate the ways in which images of Ker Kwaro Acholi reflect the preconceptions of traditional authorities and are reproduced and reinterpreted by observers. The final section of the chapter elucidates some of the underlying political agendas of Ker Kwaro Acholi, which raise concerns over continued uncritical support for the emerging 'traditional' authority.[2]

Contextualising Ker Kwaro Acholi's 'revival'

The protracted conflict in northern Uganda became widely viewed by international organisations as an inter-Acholi affair. This was in line with official government discourses that depoliticised and internalised the conflict, locating its causes 'in the "weakness" of Acholi social institutions, rather than in national or regional politics' (Bradbury, 1999: 16, 27). Ethnic mythologising of the Acholi and the fantastic emanations of the conflict produced through poor media coverage (Allen and Seaton, 1999: 4) also encouraged a view that the war in northern Uganda was too bizarre to comprehend, rendering it almost by default a humanitarian rather than a political crisis (Finnström, 2008: 116).

International development organisations were primarily concerned with humanitarian relief in the displacement camps, rehabilitation of child soldiers, and injecting funding and external support into the implementation of the traditional justice agenda, 'on the assumption that local rituals performed under the auspices of chiefs and elders would … lead to social reconciliation' (Allen and Vlassenroot, 2010: 248). Dennis Pain's report in 1997, '*The Bending of Spears': producing consensus for peace and development in Northern Uganda*, had been influential amongst NGOs, describing Acholi culture as 'unique' and resolutions to the conflict requiring a traditional Acholi-rooted response. Pain urged 'an international donor or NGO … to support the traditional authorities in establishing the reconciliation procedures to be used in resolving the conflict' (1997: 87).

Despite research following Pain's report indicating that traditional structures were 'weak and fragmented', to the extent of 'widespread disagreement' about who 'the *real* traditional leaders' actually were (Dolan, 2000), the Belgium government decided to fund a ceremony in 2000 that saw a number of clan chiefs reinstalled and a post of Paramount Chief created, with Godfrey Acana, the clan chief of the Payira lineage, elected from amongst the clan chiefs. Following Acana's sudden death in 1999, his son David Onen Acana filled the post and, catching the eye of a World Bank delegate to Uganda, was sponsored to

undertake a young leaders training programme in the US, after which
he undertook study in conflict resolution in the UK. When Paramount
Chief Acana returned from his international trips he began to transform
the loose cohort of reinstalled traditional authorities into a more organised traditional institution he called Ker Kwaro Acholi, meaning royal
kingdom of Acholi (Acana, 2011).

As more international development agencies arrived in northern
Uganda, looking for local counterparts to work with, new opportunities
opened up for 'traditional' authorities who could position themselves as
progressive and forward-looking. Ker Kwaro Acholi began to do this
by facilitating and modifying traditional cleansing ceremonies across
Acholiland (see Baines, 2005), enabling them to project ritual authority
and become visible to the small proportion of Acholi and – perhaps more
importantly – to NGOs and journalists who flocked to witness the events.
One report remarked that Ker Kwaro Acholi was able 'to stand together
as an example to local communities' and thereby strengthen their cultural leadership (Baines, 2005: 46). However, despite the involvement of
Paramount Chief Acana and a few loosely organised clan chiefs involved
in cleansing ceremonies, Ker Kwaro Acholi remained a relatively little
noticed actor, yet to catch the attention and imagination of international
development institutions seeking to embed their interventions.

Images of Ker Kwaro Acholi

The traditional cultural authority of Acholi
Two initiatives implemented by Ker Kwaro Acholi were significant in
bringing Ker Kwaro Acholi into donors' line of vision and consolidating
an image of Ker Kwaro as the traditional cultural representative of the
Acholi. The first strategic decision was to organise a public coronation
ceremony for Paramount Chief Acana and an inauguration ceremony
for the reinstalled clan chiefs. The budget for the ceremony was over 65
million Ugandan shillings (approximately US$25,000). The event was
intended to be a grand spectacle. One thousand guests were expected
to attend with great consideration paid to the 'ceremonial venue' and
surrounding area, so that its decoration 'would match the status of the
occasion' (Oketta, 2003). Ironically, a large portion of the budget was
allocated to repairing and renovating the old colonial offices where Ker
Kwaro Acholi now had an operational office. Although nothing like this
optimistic budget was raised, it illustrates Ker Kwaro Acholi's desire to
make an impressive impact.

Drawing on the powerful symbol of monarchy, and taking inspiration
from monarchies across Uganda and beyond (Oywa, 2010), money was

allocated to purchase ceremonial items, not only to set the Paramount Chief apart as the leader of the clan chiefs, but also to elevate him and position him amongst other newly-revived kings of Uganda. Royal robes, a royal carpet and a crown were purchased, with coronation shades and uniforms for guards intended to further create a sense of pomp and circumstance. Apparently a leopard skin was also bought for almost US$140 as an important symbol of clan leadership (Oketta, 2010a). In order for the images of the coronation ceremony to be widely dispersed Ker Kwaro Acholi used radio, television, print media, t-shirts, posters and banners to convey a message that the Acholi had a comparable traditional institution just like other kingdoms across Uganda and Africa.

The event took place in January 2005 with the attendance of the President of Uganda, other government officials, NGOs and members of the general public. Kings from across Uganda were invited to the following year's anniversary celebrations with fleets of cultural dancers sent to the towns of Kitgum and Pader in Acholiland and ten bulls allocated for the feast (Otto, 2006). The overall cost amounted to over 17 million Ugandan shillings, donated by individuals such as President Museveni, and institutions such as the EU-Acholi Programme, The World Bank's Northern Uganda Social Action Fund (NUSAF), World Vision and Care International (Ibid). These financial tokens of recognition illustrate an importance attached to the symbolic public display of Ker Kwaro Acholi as the Acholi traditional cultural authority. One national newspaper reported on the visual display of the ceremony, noting the 'silk blue robe decorated by golden embroidery', the 'matching headdress the enthroned Paramount Chief wore' and 'the dancers who entertained the cheering crowds, who ululated and applauded with drumming' (Wasike, Ochowun and Moro: 2005).

The same year Ker Kwaro Acholi launched its first Strategic Plan, with a second in 2009. The Strategic Plans were intended to introduce Ker Kwaro Acholi to an English speaking audience and more specifically to the development community. Kenneth Oketta, a development consultant who helped create the plan, was fully conscious of the power of the documents to project a particular image of the institution as he proudly commented to me that 'the launch of the second Strategic Plan brought so many donors, which projected our image and visibility and ... made us look not just like a footloose organisation these people used to think of, but we looked like a firm organisation with capacity' (Ibid). Referring to the second Strategic Plan, Oketta also remarked that it had come out 'properly' due to the assistance Ker Kwaro Acholi had received from USAID's Northern Uganda Transition Initiative, who had helped to 'fine tune it' (Oketta, 2010b).

In the first Strategic Plan, Ker Kwaro Acholi presents four significant, yet largely fabricated claims. These are that the revived clan chiefs form an historical alliance, known as Ker Kwaro Acholi, which comes from the Luo group and dates back to a migration into Acholiland in the fifteenth century; that today Ker Kwaro Acholi's council of clan chiefs constitutes a homogenous group hailing from lineages holding the same office in the pre-colonial period; that the traditional roles of the council of clan chiefs were and remain primarily as peacemakers and custodians of Acholi cultural practices; and finally that Ker Kwaro Acholi was weakened by the colonial regime.

Presenting Ker Kwaro Acholi's 'council of chiefs' as an alliance that dates back to the 1400s ignores and flattens the tapestry of how relations have ebbed and flowed in Acholiland over the past few centuries. While chiefdoms were headed by a royal (*kal*) clan chief, they were constituted by both the royal lineage and commoner (*lobong*) lineages through ever-shifting, complex patterns of marriage and military alliances. Drought, invasions from slave and ivory traders and colonial rulers, all provoked new military alliances and confederacies (Atkinson, 1994: 266), which have left a layered history of both cooperation and bitter hostility amongst clan chiefs and lineages across Acholiland. There is little evidence to suggest that there has ever been Acholi-wide organisation and cooperation across the area today known as Acholiland, prior to colonialism (Ibid).

The Strategic Plans emphasise that the revived clan chiefs in Acholiland are those from the pre-colonial period, and are not therefore 'chiefs of the pen' (*rwodi kalam*), appointed during the protectorate. Ker Kwaro Acholi also suggests in the Strategic Plans that reviving clan chiefs was and is straightforward because all Acholi know who their traditional clan chief is, or at least the royal lineage they are either blood related to or associated with through allegiance. The process that resulted in the 'revival' of Acholi clan chiefs is not mentioned in the Strategic Plans, but rather clan chiefs are simply described as having 'been enthroned by their various clans' with no further details given or reference to the disputes and tensions stirred in many cases by identifying and reinstalling clan chiefs. Rather, a general and simplistic picture is given of 50 'traditional leaders' organically emerging and being enthroned as a result of local desires in their clans, which suggests they hold local legitimacy. The 2009 Strategic Plan also shows that, rather than a homogenous group, Ker Kwaro Acholi in practice is constituted by both royal lineage heads (*rwodi*) and commoner lineage heads (*ludito kaka*), and indicates that at least seven 'rwodi' are heads of lineages associated, and subordinate to, a royal lineage, in contrast to the image Ker Kwaro Acholi projects of the institution.

Assigning clan chiefs to roles of peacemaking and as custodians of culture and tradition is done in conjunction with mobilising the discourse of a cultural breakdown in Acholiland that Ker Kwaro Acholi identifies as the result of colonial intervention and the recent insurgency. Clan chiefs are placed as central actors in the necessary process of 'cultural development', the neglect of which, Ker Kwaro Acholi asserts, has been the cause of a 'decline in health standards, production levels, education and unity, and rise in spread of diseases, deaths, conflicts, frustrations etc' (Ker Kwaro Acholi, 2005: 3).

Ker Kwaro Acholi also dehistoricises the Paramount Chief in its narrative, with no mention of the post being newly-created or how and why this office came into being. Instead we learn that 'the Paramount Chief of the Acholi Chiefdom come[s] from the Payira clan' and that 'each of the clans in Acholi has cultural obligations to the Paramount Chief' (Ker Kwaro Acholi, 2005: 6–7). These statements have two important implications. First, Acholi is re-inscribed as a 'chiefdom', which 'traditionalises' the boundaries that currently form the state-created Acholi sub-region and provides the Paramount Chief with a domain within which he can begin to inscribe his authority. Employing the term 'chiefdom' plays on a common misunderstanding that the Acholi existed as a coherent group of people who self-identified as Acholi prior to the colonial period, and thus the idea of an Acholi chiefdom serves to bolster the image that Ker Kwaro Acholi also existed in the distant past.

Second, the statements about the Paramount Chief imply that he always hails from Payira and the position is therefore naturally ordained and not under dispute. Payira did manage a significant degree of extra-polity functioning over nominally independent chiefdoms in the couple of centuries prior to colonialism, due to the chiefdom's size and central location in a particularly fertile part of Acholiland that was difficult to access (Atkinson, 1994: 266; Girling, 1960: 156). However, historical reference to Acholi-wide Payira authority is likely to be a reference to the central and western areas of what constitutes today's Acholiland, and not stretching to the Agago hills in the north-east, where concern for a Payira Paramount Chief is widespread (Allen, 2006: 152).

Making no distinction amongst clan chiefs enables Payira's past clan chiefs to inadvertently fall into the same category as other traditional leaders whose authority was significantly curtailed under protectorate rule. The impression given is that all clan chiefs in Acholiland suffered equally at the hands of colonial rulers, although remained resilient despite such oppression and ought to be revived today to redress this past wrong. What is not mentioned is that three clan chiefs of large chiefdoms, including Payira's Yona Odida (Paramount Chief

Acana's grandfather), were not usurped but became part of the Native Administration and might therefore be described according to Ker Kwaro Acholi's own logic as corrupt authorities which collaborated with a repressive regime. Ker Kwaro Acholi diverts attention away from such an uncomfortable and inconvenient past by elevating one of Payira's past clan chiefs from the early colonial period, Ibrahim Awich, who did resist colonial rule by famously leading the Lamogi rebellion in 1912 (Ker Kwaro Acholi, 2005: 8; see also, Anywar, 1948; Bere, 1948).

Ker Kwaro Acholi's recasting of the past, coupled with myth-making ceremonial displays of a traditional Paramount Chief, form an image of Ker Kwaro Acholi as the undisputable, age-old representative of an Acholi people with authority over Acholi culture and heritage. Clan chiefs are centrally placed within this image, and the moral impetus behind supporting Ker Kwaro Acholi's revival is rooted in a past disrupted and corrupted by colonial rule, a simplification of a complex story. Ker Kwaro Acholi's truth claims produce an attractive image and discourse of Ker Kwaro Acholi in the eyes of donors, made more attractive when coupled with an image of also being an agent of sustainable development, as I will now explore.

An agent of sustainable development

Both Strategic Plans feature a colourful photograph of Paramount Chief Acana at his coronation ceremony in 2005. He sits on a large throne-like chair, wearing a regal robe, a grand hat and meeting onlookers' gazes with a serious expression. The first half of the 2005 Strategic Plan feeds a picture of Ker Kwaro Acholi as a centuries-old institution that had been at the centre of Acholi political life until events of the last century prevented it from fulfilling its traditional roles. The rest of the shiny booklet, however, sits in contrast to this image of a traditional cultural institution, presenting it as pursuing broader development objectives in line with issues at the top of the international development agenda.

Ker Kwaro Acholi saw that its 'cultural roles' could help address the challenges that face Acholiland, such as labour productivity, poverty, HIV/AIDS and gender inequality. Evidently seeking to be active in more than a peace-building capacity, Ker Kwaro Acholi identified various activities it could facilitate, in its cultural capacity, to contribute to development in Acholiland. It laid out six Strategic Objectives:

1 Consolidating peace and reconciliation amongst the people of Acholi.
2 Mobilising the community on education, agricultural production and increasing household incomes.

3 Gender mainstreaming of cultural activities.
4 Fight against the spread of HIV/AIDS at the impact level and reduce the impact of HIV/AIDS on the community.
5 Capacity-building of the traditional institution in Acholi.
6 Documentation and communication of Acholi cultures and traditions.

This list effectively proposed that Ker Kwaro Acholi's 'cultural roles' were to mobilise people on particular issues, alter practices within 'cultural activities' that improved gender equality and practices more broadly in society related to the spread and impact of the HIV/AIDS virus, build the capacity of Ker Kwaro Acholi as well as be involved in the codification of culture and tradition.

The breakdown of activities proposed in the Strategic Plan further illustrated and reinforced an image of Ker Kwaro Acholi as an institution that could exercise influence over groups within Acholi, such as youth, clan leaders and farmer groups, and thus bring about 'development'. Under the first strategic objective, for example, Ker Kwaro Acholi proposed to 'sensitise local leaders on how to dialogue', as well as 'sensitise youth on peace building and conflict resolution' and under the second strategic objective Ker Kwaro Acholi proposed to 'organise sensitisation meetings on land matters' (Ker Kwaro Acholi, 2005: 13–14). Particularly related to youth, Ker Kwaro Acholi presented one of its roles as the 'integration of children and youth into the Acholi cultural practices and dignity' (Ibid: 12); suggesting Acholi young people had fallen 'outside' of Acholi 'cultural practices' and so had lost their dignity. The 'mission' of Ker Kwaro Acholi to 'promote, develop and preserve the culture of Acholi' is associated, therefore, with restoring a lost morality in Acholiland, particularly amongst young people.

Furthermore, Acholi 'cultural practices' are connected to material as well as moral regeneration in Acholi. Prior to the insurgency, 'cultural practices' are said by Ker Kwaro Acholi to have 'promoted economic development, good health, unity, education, and the general standard of living of the people' (Ibid: 2) but a 'steady decline in cultural development of Acholi' has resulted in 'a decline in health standards, production levels, education and unity, and [a] rise in spread of diseases, deaths, conflicts, frustrations, etc.' (Ibid: 3). Ker Kwaro Acholi does not elaborate what is meant by 'cultural practices'. The reader is offered instead a brief description of Acholi culture as comprising 'Acholi music, dance, drama, Acholi cuisines, Acholi dresses, Acholi language *Leb Lwo Kur*, and Acholi means of production' (Ibid: 2). What is made explicit is the message that 'cultural practices' promote the 'good things' that have been in decline as a result of the recent conflict (Ibid).

Although this description of Acholi culture is very restrictive, the Strategic Plan suggests elsewhere that Acholi culture, and thus identity, is in a process of fundamental change, and although the process of change may at times seem to be a project to restore and return to a 'true' Acholi identity that has been damaged over the years, the Strategic Plan also presents the process of change in Acholi culture and tradition as the taking up of 'new' values. Ker Kwaro Acholi offers a list of values that it claims have guided the institution (Ibid: 12):

- Upholding respect for human rights and dignity.
- Promoting voluntarism and self help.
- Doing much using little resources.
- Working through grassroots and community-based projects.
- Cooperating with central and local governments.
- Promoting participation and empowerment; will-power to advance together, and reciprocity.
- Transparency and accountability.
- Equity and equality, equal opportunities, equal rights for all and equality between men and women.

This list is an explicit statement that Ker Kwaro Acholi aligns itself with donor organisations which hold similar principles. Describing the principles as 'besides' Acholi culture and traditions, is an attempt by Ker Kwaro Acholi to retain its 'traditional' cultural identity, whilst also making clear, despite the evident tension, that it has signed up to a particular set of values common to discourses of international development.

In an act of 'mimicry' (Bhabha, 1994: 85–92) Ker Kwaro Acholi communicates 'we are just like you' while also emphasising that Ker Kwaro Acholi is distinctly 'other'. Setting up an Acholi/other dichotomy seems to be part of an intention by Ker Kwaro Acholi to win the institution 'membership' into the 'progressive' world of international development, ironically, by recourse to an authentic 'traditional' identity, rooted in a distinctly 'other' culture (Ferguson, 2006: 155–75).

Expectations and reinterpretation: the World Bank

The images of Ker Kwaro Acholi discussed so far were largely a product of strategic manipulation and fabrication by key players within Ker Kwaro Acholi, and were intended to give a particular impression that would resonate and appeal to donors such as the World Bank (Oketta, 2010b).

In 2005 personnel from the World Bank's NUSAF met key members of Ker Kwaro Acholi to discuss how clan chiefs could help boost local engagement in the Community Reconciliation and Conflict Management component of their Social Action Fund, which had received little local response since its launch in 2002 (World Bank, 2002a: 4 and 80–1). The broader objective of NUSAF was to 'assist Government in its efforts to tackle poverty and bring about development through participatory community efforts that utilise community value systems' (World Bank, 2002a: 30). Although the design of NUSAF was guided in part by the Ugandan government's development policies, such as the goals of the Country Assistance Strategy and Poverty Reduction Strategy Paper, it was also designed to be a move away from the top-down approach characteristic of previous World Bank programmes with a key policy change involving 'placing money and its management in the hands of the communities' (World Bank, 2002a: 2).

An assessment of community needs across northern Uganda high-lighted examples where 'traditional' or 'informal' authorities had been instrumental in mobilising communities to participate in the physical implementation of community activities and were critical for instilling values (World Bank, 2002b: 75–6). Prior to encountering Ker Kwaro Acholi, therefore, NUSAF held expectations that as a traditional author-ity in northern Uganda Ker Kwaro Acholi could potentially play a critical role in realising NUSAF's objective of strengthening community cohesion and could become 'a strong building block for ... peace build-ing' (World Bank 2002a: 75). Sharing Pain's view that the conflict was the result of an internal crisis, initiatives of peace-building by Acholi tra-ditional leaders, with support from civic organisations, was anticipated to be the 'lynch-pin for survival in the insecure areas' (Branch, 2011: 157; Office of the Prime Minister, 2002: 8).

NUSAF thus approached Ker Kwaro Acholi with a predisposition for working through locally embedded organisations; expectations derived from the behaviour of traditional leaders elsewhere; and an assumption that reconstructing the Acholi as an ethnic group was central to resolv-ing conflict. Images projected by Ker Kwaro Acholi as a traditional authority, with deep and uncontested cultural roots, unsurprisingly found fertile ground as they presented the institution in ways that repro-duced and confirmed anticipations held by NUSAF officials.

The minutes from Ker Kwaro Acholi's meeting with NUSAF conveyed Ker Kwaro Acholi's enthusiasm to act as an 'implementing agency', assigned to identify potential facilitators within communities who could generate sub-projects for NUSAF to fund, as well as identifying innovative ways traditional approaches could be used for sustainable peace and development in northern Uganda (Acana, 2005). A report the following year did not mention if these objectives were being achieved, only that Ker Kwaro Acholi was becoming stronger in its organisational integrity, 'enabling them to start influencing local government structures to deliver services to the needy and promote positive synergies between the state, civil society and the poor' (Laker and Suleiman, 2006). However, concerns of Ker Kwaro Acholi's sustainability and recognising its dependency on external funding led to advising the 'traditional' authority to continue to 'tap into various sources for funds' (Ibid).

As Ker Kwaro Acholi sought further lucrative partnerships with donors, they used NUSAF funding to purchase office furniture and equipment, began to establish a secretariat consisting of a programme manager, project officers, and a treasurer to undertake administrative duties and made a list of other 'necessary items', including a generator, fourteen tents, two hundred chairs, ten tables and thirty six office chairs (Acana, 2005), which indicates the continued importance Ker Kwaro Acholi placed upon being able to host public events where they could be on display and reproduce important images of the emerging institution. Ker Kwaro Acholi's encounter with NUSAF thus contributed to Ker Kwaro Acholi's capacity to continue to invent itself and put in place organisational and structural features that would, in the least, make it seem as if Ker Kwaro Acholi was moving towards becoming the 'traditional' authority with a measure of capacity to mobilise communities NUSAF expected at the outset.

Expectations and reinterpretation: USAID

Images of Ker Kwaro Acholi are not intended to be complete representations or even complete misrepresentations of Ker Kwaro Acholi, but are rather meant to leave space for observers to interpret and imbue the images with their own expectations and fantasies of what Ker Kwaro Acholi is and could become. As Gallagher discusses in the introduction to this book, the potency of an image according to Mbembe (2001) comes from what is absent, from its obscurity and what is left for the observer to flesh out.

By early 2010, when I visited northern Uganda, the secretariat of Ker Kwaro Acholi was staffed by two salaried project officers, an accountant and programme manager. USAID was working with Ker Kwaro Acholi on their 'Stability, Peace and Reconciliation in Northern Uganda Project' (SPRING). Ker Kwaro Acholi was one of eleven implementing partners selected to work with 314 farmer groups to address their primary production and marketing constraints, and 'help support farmers recover from conflict with dignity by addressing their reconciliation needs' (USAID, 2009b: 1). As far as Ker Kwaro Acholi was perceived by USAID, its traditional leaders were well-placed to strengthen the social contract of farmer groups, because they were thought to have a broad network and historical importance within Acholi communities (USAID, 2009a). Ker Kwaro Acholi's own historical narrative was reproduced within SPRING literature and reiterated in my interview with a senior USAID officer of the SPRING project, who repeatedly referred to Acholiland as a chiefdom and also a kingdom.

As Ker Kwaro Acholi met with SPRING to develop the project it became clear to the USAID officer that the projected images of an organisation of traditional leaders rooted in the local community and able to mobilise communities was a façade. The USAID officer made sense of this by reverting to misplaced ideas, advocated by Ker Kwaro Acholi, that the conflict had caused Ker Kwaro Acholi's disconnect from the community (USAID, 2010). As a result, one of the strategic objectives of SPRING became to 'restore and strengthen the social bonds between returning communities and local traditional leaders'.

The vision the USAID officer had for Ker Kwaro Acholi was that it would become 'not so much an authority structure' but rather an 'organising structure' for communicating 'consistent messages throughout the kingdom' and for acting as 'an anchor' for SPRING to work through (2010). USAID anticipated that Ker Kwaro Acholi could assist in 'finding the chiefs in the village' so that the latter could influence the behaviour of farmer groups in their commitment to cooperation and non-violent dispute resolution (2009a). However, it became evident that, contrary to the images Ker Kwaro Acholi projects of being a traditional institution of traditional leaders, there was a disconnect between Ker Kwaro Acholi and various levels of traditional leadership. In response, and on the assumption Ker Kwaro Acholi ought to become 'the institutional focal point' across Acholiland, SPRING made the strengthening of communication between Ker Kwaro Acholi and all levels of traditional leadership one of its objectives.

Partnering with Ker Kwaro Acholi highlighted the disjuncture between the image and practice of Ker Kwaro Acholi as an effective agent of development, although the USAID officer said they had anticipated there would be challenges with the institution (2010). The two project officers working at Ker Kwaro Acholi at the time also recalled in interviews the ineffectiveness of Ker Kwaro Acholi. Frustrated, one said that Ker Kwaro Acholi had not implemented a project in three months and found the programme coordinator, who was brother to Paramount Chief Acana, regularly demanding money for personal use.

This officer saw his experience of working with Ker Kwaro Acholi as tarnishing his professional profile (Project Officer A, 2010: April). The other project officer had similar experiences to share and spoke of Ker Kwaro Acholi's ineffectiveness on the gender-based violence project she had been employed to work on in partnership with UNIFEM (Project Officer B, 2010: April). She was asked to 'cook up activities' and fake receipts by the programme coordinator and prime minister to account for money that had been creamed from donor funds. Both project officers also complained of a bias towards those in Ker Kwaro Acholi who were from the Payira clan: 'They look at us as if we are thieves ... as if we are not part of them' (Ibid).

The USAID officer was also aware of Ker Kwaro Acholi's 'corruption challenges' and poor leadership and whilst acknowledging these as bad practice, she interestingly cited it as evidence of Ker Kwaro Acholi's credentials as an authentically traditional institution. They have 'inherited [a] way of working', she explained, because Ker Kwaro Acholi was not 'starting from complete scratch' (2010: April). The USAID officer's response to the problems she encountered with Ker Kwaro Acholi in practice, including Ker Kwaro Acholi's failure to live up to the core values listed in its 2009 Strategic Plan,[3] was to excuse them as 'an inherited way of working', and to regard Ker Kwaro Acholi as a 'start up NGO' (Ibid), a 'learning institution' (see Howes and Sattar, 1992) on a progressive path towards becoming an effective agent of development.

The USAID officer considered Ker Kwaro Acholi's core values to be something that the institution was aspiring to, rather than its actual current principles. The stated core values also became evidence for the USAID officer that Ker Kwaro Acholi was 'not going to be anchored on the past' but that 'the institution could possibly become a very important [and] useful institution ... that it's looking at its relevance in the present and future contexts; that they are striving for these to be the core values tells me that' (Ibid). She went on to suggest that Ker Kwaro Acholi would improve and benefit from adopting 'other structures of civil society organisations' and through a pragmatic lens turned Ker Kwaro Acholi's 'failure' to reflect its images into productive failures that fuelled further reasons for USAID to continue to partner the 'traditional' authority in order to assist it with becoming more like a development NGO (Ibid).

The tension in being a traditional authority transforming into an NGO agency that is also a traditional authority was not lost on the USAID officer, but this was described as 'part of the growing pains of the organisation ... because it is expected to function like an NGO but it's also expected to be its own governance structure' (Ibid). In her opinion, Ker Kwaro Acholi would develop a more effective governance structure, with improved response in the community, if it shifted more towards becoming an NGO, which seemed to amount to Ker Kwaro Acholi adopting a range of policies and administrative structures and processes. 'Ker Kwaro Acholi needs to do a little work to make it clear that they are not the authority over these chiefs, but rather an administrative body to support the chiefs.' With administration as the goal of Ker Kwaro Acholi, the USAID officer thought the institution 'would go quite far' and saw for herself a role in pushing that forward (Ibid).

These two case studies draw on two significant donor engagements with Ker Kwaro Acholi and allow for an exploration of how Ker Kwaro Acholi's images shaped the encounters. Both NUSAF and SPRING approached Ker Kwaro Acholi in a way commonly found amongst international organisations, as a 'readily available local counterpart[s] with a substantial measure of authority and capacity to mobilise' (Englebert, 2005). They expected, at least initially, that Ker Kwaro Acholi could act as a mediator between donors and the rural population, whether to promote participation in NUSAF sub-projects or by becoming an institutional focal point that could anchor SPRING programmes. In the first case we saw an example of Ker Kwaro Acholi's projected images resonating and meeting the expectations of NUSAF officers, which resulted in a partnership that brought Ker Kwaro Acholi financial capital that was used on the one hand to facilitate further moments where it could display tradition and on the other to furnish offices and thereby begin to look like the agent of development it professed to being. SPRING's encounter with Ker Kwaro Acholi illustrates that in a case where images of Ker Kwaro Acholi did not fully match the institution in practice, images were reinterpreted in ways that served to support a continued partnership between Ker Kwaro Acholi and USAID. Images of Ker Kwaro Acholi were reinterpreted as the aspirations of a weakened traditional authority seeking relevance and importance by placing itself at the centre of post-conflict reconstruction in northern Uganda.

Conclusion

Zoe Marriage has described NGOs and donors in southern Sudan as playing a certain game where both buy into a fantasy that denies 'reality' to enable the continuation of assistance (2006: 186–205). 'Denying reality allows new elements to be created through fantasy ... and can be seen in the way NGOs exaggerate their impact, flatter donors, and simplify or gloss difficulties' (Ibid: 187). In a situation where NGO staff are aware of a difficult and complicated situation but are faced with 'uncertainty over what to do and freedom to make extraordinary claims tempts them to deny, omitting parts that are too big – they both know, and do not know' (Ibid). The senior USAID officer's response to encountering the ineffectiveness of Ker Kwaro Acholi to communicate with traditional leaders and live up to the core values stated in its Strategic Plans, was to reinterpret Ker Kwaro Acholi's image as a well-placed agent of development as a goal that the institution was aspiring towards, rather than a reflection of the institution in the present. Whether the USAID officer believed this or not, there was an evident compulsion to work with Ker Kwaro Acholi as a government-recognised 'traditional' authority in Acholiland and to make 'improvements' to the institution, that indicate that the officer was choosing simultaneously to 'know and not know'. West and Kloeck-Jenson have noted that pressures of time upon NGOs or donors provide a compulsion 'to simply work with the "recognised" local "traditional authority" without actually investigating upon what that authority is based and whether local communities and categories of people therein perceive that authority to be legitimate' (1999: 482–3). NUSAF's application of studies on traditional authorities elsewhere to Ker Kwaro Acholi might here be seen as a case in point.

   An Acholi elder, Rosalba Oywa, has worked closely with Ker Kwaro Acholi and was a central advocate for the revival of Acholi traditional leaders in the late 1990s. Oywa shared concerns in our interview over the subliminal agendas of Payira dominance and kingdom-making being pursued by central actors within Ker Kwaro Acholi (2010: April). Her views support the argument that images of Ker Kwaro Acholi do not accurately reflect the 'traditional' authority in practice and the afore-mentioned agendas. Oywa remarked with frustration and anger:

> When we talk about Ker Kwaro, they always want us to believe we are talking about chiefdoms [but] I know there is a real distinction between the two, Ker Kwaro Acholi is a mobile structure which came from nowhere, it is more borrowing things from Buganda, from the Kingdoms and trying to make them here and it is another way of centralising people as if we want to become a kingdom. (Ibid)

Ker Kwaro Acholi's images, which reflect donor expectations and enable donor reinterpretation through their ambiguity, not only obscure a more complex reality, but mask inherently political agendas at the centre of Ker Kwaro Acholi. Tensions within Ker Kwaro Acholi, particularly over the paramount chief post and Payira dominance more broadly, threaten crucial peace-building efforts in northern Uganda that Ker Kwaro Acholi professes a commitment to. While there may be Acholi who do not want to miss out on the financial investment and potential political capital that comes from mimicking Buganda in a process of monarchisation and kingdom-making (Bradbury, 1999: 19), if this endeavour contin-ues to contribute significantly to disproportionate benefits amongst clans this may also inflame inter-clan tensions. Oywa saw the local National Resistance Movement politician's interest for Payira holding the Paramount Chief post as 'very dangerous' and as putting Acana 'at risk' because it was 'drawing hatred from all other clans' (2010: April). Ker Kwaro Acholi's continued co-optation by the state is likely to lead to the institution remaining wedded to discourses that depoliticise past con-flict and unhelpfully locate its causes and solutions internally. In addi-tion, if Ker Kwaro Acholi remains closely dependent upon donors then, as Branch has flagged, the 'traditional' authority may become part of a project of reconstruction in Acholiland that 'is equivalent to discipline and coercion and', as I have also argued, 'may set the stage for future conflict' (2011: 178). If donors such as the World Bank and USAID want to ensure they contribute to peace-building and sustainable development in northern Uganda it is time, at least as a crucial first step, to encounter images of Ker Kwaro Acholi with a more critical gaze.

Notes

1 Such as the UK's Department for International Development (DfID), the Danish Ministry of Foreign Affairs (DANIDA), the Belgium Government, Ireland's Department for Foreign Affairs and Trade (Irish Aid), Norwegian Refugee Council, World Vision, Oxfam and Caritas.
2 Insights offered in this chapter draw on six months fieldwork in northern Uganda in 2010 and archival research at Gulu District Council offices, Entebbe archives and Rhodes House at the University of Oxford.
3 The core values stated are: upholds respect for human rights and dignity; trans-parency and accountability; equality and equity; commitment and dedication; open to learning; innovative and inclusive (Ker Kwaro Acholi, 2009: 3).

References

Acana, David Onen (2005): *Report on Consultation Meeting for Traditional Leaders of Acholi and NUSAF* (Gulu: Gulu District Archives), 5.11.05.
Acana, David Onen (2011): Interview, Birmingham, UK, 20.6.11.
Acana, David Onen (2012): Email correspondence, 1.2.12.
Agence France-Presse (2003): 'War in Northern Uganda world's worst forgotten crisis', *Reliefweb*, 11.11.03.
Allen, Tim (2006): *Trial Justice: the International Criminal Court and the Lord's Resistance Army* (London: Zed Books).
Allen, Tim and Jean Seaton (eds) (1999): *The Media of Conflict: War reporting and representations of ethnic violence* (London: Zed Books).

Allen, Tim and Koen Vlassenroot (eds) (2010): *The Lord's Resistance Army: myth and reality* (London: Zed Books).

Anderson, Benedict (1983): *Imagined Communities: reflections on the origin and spread of nationalism* (London: Verso).

Anywar, Reuben (1948): 'The life of Rwot Ibrahim Awich', *Uganda Journal* 12(1): 72–81.

Atkinson, Ronald (1994): *The Roots of Ethnicity. the origins of the acholi in uganda before 1800* (Philadelphia: University of Pennsylvania Press).

Baines, Erin (2005): *Roco Wat I Acholi, Restoring Relationships in Acholi-Land: traditional approaches to justice and reintegration* (Vancouver: University of British Columbia).

Bere, R. M. (1947): 'An outline of Acholi history', *Uganda Journal* 11(1): 1–8.

Bere, R. M. (1948): 'Awich: a biographical note and a chapter of Acholi history', *Uganda Journal* 10(2): 76–8.

Bhabha, Homi (1994): *The Location of Culture* (London and New York: Routledge).

Bradbury, Mark (1999): *An Overview of Initiatives for Peace in Acholi, Northern Uganda* (Cambridge: Collaborative for Development Action).

Branch, Adam (2010): 'The roots of LRA violence', in Tim Allen and Koen Vlassenroot (eds), *The Lord's Resistance Army: myth and reality* (London: Zed Books).

Branch, Adam (2011): *Displacing Human Rights: war and intervention in Northern Uganda* (Oxford: Oxford University Press).

Buur, Lars and Helene Maria Kyed (eds) (2007): *State Recognition and Democratization in Sub-Saharan Africa: a new dawn for traditional authorities?* (Basingstoke: Palgrave Macmillan).

Chiweza, Asiyati Lorraine (2007): 'The ambivalent role of chiefs: rural decentralization initiatives in Malawi', in Buur and Kyed (eds), *State Recognition and Democratization in Sub-Saharan Africa: a new dawn for traditional authorities?* (Basingstoke: Palgrave Macmillan).

Crazzolara, Joseph Pasquale (1937/1938): 'The Lwoo People', *Uganda Journal* 5(1): 1–21.

Dolan, Chris (2000): 'Key research findings: an introduction to the conference', in *Background Papers Presented to the Conference on 'Peace Research and the Reconciliation Agenda', Gulu, Northern Uganda, September 1999*, (Cope Working Papers, London: ACORD).

Dolan, Chris (2009): *Social Torture: the case of Northern Uganda, 1986–2006* (Oxford: Berghahn Books).

Englebert, Pierre (2002): 'Born again Buganda and the limits of traditional resurgence in Africa', *Journal of Modern African Studies* 40(3): 345–68.

Englebert, Pierre (2005): 'Back to the future?: resurgent indigenous structures and the reconfiguration of power in Africa', in Olufemi Vaughan (ed.), *Tradition and Politics: indigenous political structures in Africa*, (Trenton, NJ: Africa World Press): 33–62.

Ferguson, James (2006): *Global Shadows: Africa in the neoliberal world order* (Durham, NC: Duke University Press).

Finnström, Sverker (2008): *Living with Bad Surroundings* (Durham: Duke University Press).

Finnström, Sverker (2010): 'An African hell of colonial imagination?: the Lord's Resistance Army in Uganda, another story', in T. Allen and K. Vlassenroot (eds), *The Lord's Resistance Army: myth and reality* (London: Zed Books).

Gertzel, Cheryl (1974): *Party and Locality in Northern Uganda, 1945–1962* (London: Athlone Press).

Girling, F. K. (1960): *The Acholi of Uganda* (London: HMSO).

Gray, Sir John Milner (1951): 'Acholi History, 1860–1901: Part I', *Uganda Journal* 15(2): 121–43.

Howes, Mick and M. G. Sattar (1992): 'Bigger and better? Scaling-up strategies pursued by BRAC 1972–1991', in Michael Edwards and David Hulme (eds), *Making a Difference: NGOs and development in a changing world* (London: Earthscan).

Ker Kwaro Acholi (2005): *Strategic Plan 2005–2007* (Gulu: Ker Kwaro Acholi).

Ker Kwaro Acholi (2006): *Proposed Government Structure Concept Paper* (Gulu: Gulu District Archives, CR1059/2).

Ker Kwaro Acholi (2009): *Strategic Plan 2009–2014* (Gulu: Ker Kwaro Acholi).

Kessel, Ineka van and Barbara Oomen (1997): 'One chief, one vote: The revival of traditional authorities in post-apartheid South Africa', *African Affairs* 96 (385), 561-85.

Kleist, Nauja (2011): 'Modern chiefs, tradition, development and return among traditional authorities in Ghana,' *African Affairs* 110(441), 629–47.

Laker, Chris and Namara Suleiman (2006): *The Northern Uganda Social Action Fund: community reconciliation and conflict management empower commu nities in a post-conflict setting* (Washington DC: The World Bank).

Lentz, Carola (1998): 'The chief, the mine captain and the politician: legitimating power in Northern Ghana', *Africa* 68(1), 46–67.

Leys, Colin (1967): *Politicians and Policies: an essay on politics in Acholi, Uganda 1962–65* (Nairobi: East African Publishing House).

Mamdani, Mahmood (1996): *Citizen and Subject: contemporary Africa and the legacy of late colonialism* (Princeton: Princeton University Press).

Marriage, Zoe (2006): *Not Breaking the Rules, Not Playing the Game: international assistance to countries at war* (London: Hurst and Co.).

Mbembe, Achille (2001): *On the Postcolony* (Berkeley: University of California Press).

Museveni, Yoweri (1997): *Sowing the Mustard Seed: the struggle for freedom and democracy in Uganda* (London: Macmillan Education).

Nsibambi, Apolo R. (1995): 'The restoration of traditional rulers', in H. B. Hansen and M. Twaddle (eds), *From Chaos to Order: the politics of constitution making in Uganda,* (London: James Currey).

Office of the Prime Minister (2002): *Community Reconciliation and Conflict Management Handbook* (Kampala: Northern Uganda Social Action Fund).

Okema, Santo (2010): Interviews, Gulu, Uganda, 8.3.10 and 6.4.10.

Oketta, Kenneth (2003): *Budget for Coronation of the Paramount Chief of Acholi – Rwot David Onen Acana II – and Inauguration of the Council of Acholi Traditional Chiefs* (Gulu: Gulu District Archive).

Oketta, Kenneth (2010a): Interview, Kampala, Uganda, 12.4.10.

Oketta, Kenneth (2010b): Interview, Gulu, Uganda, 19.6.10.

Olupot, M. and C. Ocowan (2010): 'Museveni gives Acholi chiefs houses', *New Vision*, 17.11.10.

Otto, J. A. A. (2006): *Letter from James A.A. Otto, Chairman of the Finance Sub-Committee to the Organising Committee of the First Anniversay Celebrations, 27 February* (Gulu: Gulu District Archive).

Oywa, Rosalba (2010): Interview, Gulu, Uganda, 20.4.10.

Pain, Dennis (1997): *'The Bending of Spears': Producing Consensus for Peace and Development in Northern Uganda* (London: International Alert, in partnership with Kacoke Madit).

Project Officer A, Ker Kwaro Acholi (2010): Interviews, Gulu, Uganda, 6–10.4.10.

Project Officer B, Ker Kwaro Acholi (2010): Interviews, Gulu, Uganda, 7.4.10.

Ubink, Janine M. (2008): *Traditional Authorities in Africa: resurgence in an era of democratisation* (Amsterdam: Amsterdam University Press).

USAID (2009a) *Tender Announcements: Strengthening the Social Contract for Farmer Groups in the Acholi Sub-Region,* 29.5.09.

USAID (2009b): *Stability, Peace and Reconciliation in Northern Uganda Project (SPRING) Implementation Partners Information Packet* (unpublished).

USAID Officer, Programme Director SPRING (2010): Interview, USAID offices, Gulu, Uganda, 21.4.10.

Wasike, A., C. Ochowun, and J. Moro (2005): 'Acana, Acholi's hereditary leader', *New Vision,* 16.1.05.

West, H. G. and S. Kloeck-Jenson (1999): 'Betwixt and between: "traditional authority" and democratic decentralization in post-war Mozambique', *African Affairs* 98:455–84.

Williams, J. M. (2010): *Chieftancy, the State, and Democracy: political legitimacy in post-apartheid South Africa* (Bloomington, IN: Indiana University Press).

World Bank (2000): *Northern Uganda Reconstruction Project: Performance Audit Report* (Washington DC: World Bank).

World Bank (2002a): *Project Appraisal Document on a Proposed Credit in the Amount of Sdr 80.1 Million (US$ 100 Million Equivalent) to the Republic of Uganda for a Northern Uganda Social Action Fund* (Washington DC: World Bank).

World Bank (2002b): *Social Funds: Assessing effectiveness* (Washington DC: World Bank).

Zeller, Wolfgang (2007): '"Now we are a town": chiefs, investors and the state in Zambia's Western Province', in Lars Buur and Helene Maria Kyed (eds), *State Recognition and Democratization in Sub-Saharan Africa: a new dawn for traditional authorities?* (Basingstoke: Palgrave Macmillan).

7

The war of images in the Ivoirian post-electoral crisis: the role of news and online blogs in constructing political personas

Anne Schumann[1]

The Ivoirian Crisis of 2002–7 was accompanied by a media war which has been so virulent that observers have at times labelled Ivoirian media as 'hate media' (Witcher, 2006). The vigorous public debate has also taken place on relatively new platforms outside established information channels, such as popular music (Schumann, 2013) and open-air public discussion sites called *parlements* and *agoras* (Bahi, 2003). As Dina Ligaga observes with reference to Kenya, the 'internet provides alternative routes of expression of popular culture, bringing to the fore aspects of social and political lives and ideas that would otherwise have remained hidden from public discourse' (2012: 1). During the Ivoirian post-electoral crisis of 2010–11, internet discussion sites became a focal point of the political debate and the place where it was writ-large. This is partly due to relatively dense internet connectivity throughout Abidjan, a large Ivoirian diaspora community and a concerted effort by the pro-Gbagbo camp *La Majorité présidentielle* (LMP) to obtain a strong internet presence through online campaigning (Moncrieff, 2012).

In an attempt to stay in power despite electoral defeat, the LMP accused international news media of partiality towards the newly elected president Ouattara of the coalition *Rassemblement des houphouétistes pour la démocratie et la paix* (RHDP), and as part of a plot by the international community, led by the former colonial power France, to install Ouattara as a puppet. Websites and blogs linked to the LMP proliferated, interpreting the Ivoirian post-electoral crisis in an anti-colonialist idiom and portraying Gbagbo as the last guardian of national sovereignty. This corresponded well with the idiom of a second, genuine independence which was part of the *camp présidentiel's* (Gbagbo and the elite surrounding him) strategy throughout the Ivoirian Crisis of 2002–7 of pitching national sovereignty and *souverainisme* against France and the international community to block outside attempts at peace broker-age unfavourable to his regime (Piccolino, 2012).

During the 2010 elections (and especially during the second round of these elections) Ouattara was repeatedly presented as the candidate with strong (read neo-colonial) ties to France, an image reinforced through his long-standing strong personal connections with the then French president, Nicolas Sarkozy (Boisbouvier, 2012). Indeed, much of the post-electoral crisis simply brought the key issues and tropes of the Ivoirian Crisis of 2002–7 back to the fore. However, the extent of the use of the internet as a battleground for internal and international perceptions of the crisis was new. In this chapter, I particularly focus on the websites and blogs linked to the LMP as platforms for alternative readings of the Ivoirian post-electoral crisis.

The creation of images by both Gbagbo and Ouattara during the post-electoral crisis played out to a large extent in international terms, as each was partly characterised by his supposed relationship to France. The debates around each candidate's relationship with France and the international community as a whole became both substantive and exis-tential reference points in the creation of images directed to appeal to domestic audiences. These images were circulated in an international medium, yet they were primarily aimed at Ivoirian (local and diaspora) audiences. The internet became a site where counter-narratives to main-stream Western news and alternative images of the crisis and its pro-tagonists were created and circulated, and the internet has also provided a platform in which opposing readings of the Ivoirian post-electoral crisis could emerge.

In the websites and blogs linked to the LMP, international pres-sure was transformed into a political opportunity. By casting Laurent Gbagbo as the victim of French neo-colonial aggression, these web-sites attempted to turn him into a symbol of African resistance. In this manner, blogs and websites functioned as a site where the image of Gbagbo as portrayed by international media, and indeed the interpre-tation of the entire post-electoral crisis, could be challenged by those Ivoirian actors aligned with the LMP.

Of course, these websites did not exist in isolation. This chapter will therefore consider the broader struggle over the 'truth' in the Ivoirian post-electoral crisis, as well as the conflicting representations, narra-tives and counter-narratives of the crisis of which this 'war of images' is one part. It will also set out to establish what that part was, and its significance to the election and the violence that followed it. To set this discussion in context, a brief historical overview of the restrictions of media freedom as well as access to information is in order.

Media in Côte d'Ivoire

During the first thirty years of independence under president Félix Houphouët-Boigny and single party rule by the Democratic Party of Côte d'Ivoire (*Parti Démocratique de la Côte d'Ivoire*, PDCI), the press, notably the daily newspaper *Fraternité Matin* and the weeklies *Fraternité Hebdo* and *Ivoire Dimanche* as well as the publicly-owned radio and television authority, *Radiodiffusion-Télévision Ivoirienne* (RTI) were mouthpieces of the government. Political pluralism was reinstated in 1990 due to mounting internal and external pressure and in 1991 several new laws established the legal framework for the print media and defined the juridical status of journalists.[2] Law 91–1033 was the first law to guarantee the freedom of the press in Côte d'Ivoire, authorising the publication of privately-owned, independent publications (Gnonzion, 2011: 302). However, the exercise of this freedom was limited from the outset through the institution of 'violations of press norms' within this very law (Ibid: 305). Also 'offences against the chief of state' rendered these advances in press freedom ineffective and throughout the 1990s there were instances of publications being suppressed and journalists being punished through fines, beatings or imprisonment. Under Houphouët-Boigny's successor Henri Konan Bédié, Côte d'Ivoire gained the deplorable record as the second most repressive nation in Africa (after Sudan) with regards to attempts against freedom of the press (Ibid: 307).

As Lori-Anne Théroux-Bénoni has noted, newspapers created after 1990 were seldom thought of as economic enterprises, but rather had the goal of 'occupy[ing] a space', in other words, 'to manifest the existence of a particular political current, to defend oneself politically, to express discontent while facing a given situation' (2009: 6). Many of the main newspapers were associated with political parties from this time period and throughout the Ivoirian Crisis of 2002–7 and the post-electoral crisis of 2010–11.

The attempted coup d'état-cum-rebellion of 2002 led to further restrictions on Côte d'Ivoire's media. The rebellion spread when army mutineers took over the towns of Bouake and Korhogo and announced the formation of an insurgent group, the Côte d'Ivoire Patriotic Movement (*Mouvement patriotique de Côte d'Ivoire*, MPCI). The rebellion, which initially comprised numerous sub-groups, soon became known as the New Forces (*Forces Nouvelles*, FN). This was the beginning of the crisis that was to split the country in two for five years. During this crisis, media freedom deteriorated considerably, as Gnonzion points out: 'in the area of the rebellion, freedom of the press was practically eliminated, but freedoms were equally restricted in the area of governmental control' (2011: 308). Only three days after the failed coup d'état, the rebellion's leaders released the first number of their *Journal Officiel* (later, new titles such as *Liberté* and *Tam-Tam* appeared). They also took over the public audio-visual media from which they disseminated propaganda; in the rebel-occupied north, the RTI was re-named *Télé-mutins*, and then *Notre Patrie* (Reporters Sans Frontières, 2005: 6).

The government-controlled southern part of the country became the site of repeated threats against journalists and editorial offices of publications associated with the opposition. For example, the offices of *Le Patriote* and *Le Liberal* (with eight printing presses) were burned during the crisis of 2002–7, as well as the studios of *Radio Nostalgie*. Several journalists were killed during this period, including Gonzeu Toué, correspondent of the Ivoirian Press Agency, Antoine Massé, journalist with the *Courrier d'Abidjan* and Jean Hélène, a correspondent with *Radio France International*. The Canadian journalist Guy-André Kieffer disappeared and was never found (Gnonzion, 2011: 309).

The Ivoirian presidential election of 2010

During the Ivoirian Crisis of 2002–7 and the run-up to the 2010 elections, the newspaper *Notre Voie* was associated with the Ivoirian Popular Front (*Front populaire ivoirien*, FPI) and Gbagbo, *Le Patriote* with the Rally of Republicans (*Rassemblement des Républicains*, RDR) and Ouattara, *Le Nouveau Réveil* with the PDCI and Bédié. Each of these newspapers has been singled out by Reporters Without Borders for not respecting 'the basic rules of journalistic ethics and professional conduct' (2010). In the context of the 2010 presidential election, partisan newspapers contributed to polarisation and to the expectation of victory in each camp through reports on the leadership of their candidates in the polls before results were officially announced (or as in the case of *Le Mandat*, before the election had even taken place). The headline of *Le Mandat* (no.380 dated 19 October 2010) ran: 'Bédié, the great favourite.' The newspaper *Notre Voie* (no. 3723 dated 3 November 2010) ran the headline: 'Gbagbo is leading the ball' while the newspaper *Le Patriote* (no. 3313 of the same day) stated 'ADO, President: It's almost done.' Each side also published the election results before they were officially announced online. The first round of the presidential election took place on 31 October 2010, in which Gbagbo came first, albeit without enough to win outright, on

38 per cent, to Ouattara's 32 per cent. When it turned out that Gbagbo and Ouattara would be facing each other and that Bédié was out of the presidential race, the following day the newspaper *Le Nouveau Réveil* (no. 2664 dated 4 November 2010) ran the following headline: 'They stole his victory! Bédié contests the results. No second round without recounting!' However, Bédié's request for a re-count was denied.

The run-off ballot between Gbagbo and Ouattara took place on 28 November 2010. On 2 December 2010, a member of the Independent Election Commission (CEI) declared that Ouattara had won with 54.1 per cent of the vote compared with 45.9 per cent for Gbagbo. However, on 3 December 2010, the Constitutional Council rejected the results, cancelling the vote in seven northern departments where, it was claimed, a number of irregularities had compromised the election results, and declared Gbagbo the winner. Using the CEI's results for these areas, the votes received by Ouattara and Gbagbo in these departments were subtracted and then summed up as follows: 'Laurent Gbagbo won the election with 51.45 per cent of the vote to Ouattara's 48.55 per cent'. The following day, 4 December 2010, the court swore in Gbagbo as President (Bassett, 2011: 478).Ouattara organised a separate swearing-in ceremony for himself at the *Hôtel du Golf*, which had functioned a key base of the New Forces rebellion in Abidjan since the Ouagadougou (peace) Agreement of 2007. The UN endorsed Ouattara as the winner of the elections and as the new president of Côte d'Ivoire, and the African Union, the West African ECOWAS bloc, the US, the EU and others followed suit. However, by 'placing himself under the protective wing of the international community, and continually appealing for outside mediation, ADO [Ouattara] reinforced the caricature created of him as the "overseas candidate", weak and indecisive' (Banégas, 2011: 462). Additionally, by using the *Hôtel du Golf* as interim headquarters for his government, Ouattara reinforced the caricature created of him as the sponsor of the rebellion.

As the post-electoral crisis of 2010–11 intensified, the media became a target yet again. In early February 2011, the leadership of the National Press Council (CNP) was dismissed and replaced with journalists who were members of the FPI or known supporters of Gbagbo. The United Nations radio station ONUCI FM had its broadcasting permit cancelled and the French TV channels TV5 and France 24 were suspended (Reporters Without Borders, 10 February 2011). The climate for the media remained tense and in March 2011 nine pro-RHDP (that is, pro-Ouattara) newspapers suspended publication for the duration of a week (six issues) to protest against threats and harassment. Ouattara supporters launched an armed attack on the RTI's main transmission centre in Abobo on the night of 26 February 2011, and in early March there were reports of attacks on news kiosks and newspaper vendors by Ouattara supporters, in which copies of those pro-Gbagbo newspapers which continued to publish were torn up (Reporters Without Borders, 8 March 2011).

Evidently, as noted by Reporters Without Borders, an all-out battle for news and information was fought in parallel to the military clashes (Reporters Without Borders, 6 April 2011). Control of the state broadcaster RTI, 'a real propaganda machine and vehicle for "hate campaigns"' (Banégas, 2011: 459), reinforced the LMP political-administrative hegemony. 'RTI drummed home its one-way messages, calling for popular resistance against Ouattara and his foreign backers, and played a significant role in consolidating the regime and stoking up violence' (Ibid: 459).The RTI soon became a target of fighting, and the struggle over control of the RTI between the pro-Gbagbo army *Forces de défense et de sécurité* (FDS) and the pro-Ouattara *Forces républic-aines de Côte d'Ivoire* (FRCI) damaged the premises and equipment. The RTI also became the target of airstrikes by the UN and French peacekeeping forces, with the objective of destroying the RTI anten-nae. Reporters Without Borders strongly cautioned against strikes on media structures as military targets, noting that despite the dissemina-tion of propaganda, the RTI remained a civilian building (Reporters Without Borders, 6 April 2011). By April 2011, most journalists were unable to venture outside due to the airstrikes and curfews, and many received anonymous death threats which prompted some to go into hiding (Reporters Without Borders, 6 April 2011). Due to the intensity of the fighting, newspaper publication ceased in early April 2011. On 11 April 2011 pro-Ouattara forces captured and arrested Gbagbo from a bunker in the presidential palace. Pro-Gbagbo newspaper offices were then occupied by pro-Ouattara forces, and for one month after Laurent Gbagbo's fall, newspapers loyal to the deposed leader failed to reappear (Reporters Without Borders, 10 May 2011).

This brief sketch provides a glimpse into the environment of restrictions to media freedom, as well as restrictions of access to infor-mation. This created a context of unreliable, biased newspaper and audio-visual media coverage, with concerted attempts by the govern-ment to restrict access to information. Simultaneously, opposing sides of the conflict increasingly developed opposing narratives of what was actually happening. Indeed, radically different understandings of the crisis point not to alternative political programmes, but to different conceptions of the state and citizenship, different accounts of national history, and different visions of national sovereignty (Schumann, 2011). According to one reading of the crisis, Ouattara had won the elections, and Gbagbo was illegitimately clinging on to power, becoming ever more brutally repressive. By annulling the votes of departments in the north and the centre of the country, electors from these regions were denied full civic participation and delegated to second class citizenship. According to Miran-Guyon, the cancellation of these votes was in line with Gbagbo's ethno-nationalist vision: only members of indigenous ethnic groups from the south of Côte d'Ivoire were deemed 'true' citizens (and the doubts over Ouattara's heritage was just one case in point; see Miran-Guyon 2011, and Foreign Policy online 'Open Letter: Ivory Coast, the war against civilians'). Gbagbo's call for a re-count of the votes was seen as a strategy to gain time and consolidate power, and was denied. According to this interpretation of the post-electoral crisis, the French and UN-led intervention was about peacekeepers protecting the civilian population and re-establishing democracy (Schumann, 2011).

Many of Gbagbo's supporters adopted a different narrative: they claimed that the election was rigged in favour of Ouattara by the former rebels, who controlled the central and northern departments, and that Ouattara first tried to come to power by fomenting rebellion since 2002 and, when this failed, by rigging the 2010 elections. According to their narrative of the crisis, Ouattara lost the elections, and has since refused a recount of the ballot. Instead, he called on rebels and the former colonial power France to launch an assault on the main city of Abidjan. According to this reading, France was using its military weight to help resolve an electoral dispute in its favour by installing Ouattara as a president who will serve French interests (Ibid). While France denies direct involvement in the arrest of Gbagbo, the French/UN air strikes laid the groundwork by destroying much of the heavy weaponry of the Gbagbo regime. The fact that these airstrikes have taken place during the battle for Abidjan and have shifted the balance in power in favour of the pro-Ouattara fighters has given rise to the view among the Gbagbo-supporting population that this was a political intervention, rather than a humanitarian one (Ibid).

Opposing interpretations of the post-electoral crisis coalesced into opposing 'truths'. The common saying *'c'est ça qui est la vérité'* – a *Nouchi* (Ivoirian street slang) idiom roughly translating to 'that's the truth' points to exactly this issue: an intense dispute as to what the truth really was, as well as to what was at stake in this crisis, while rumours and conspiracy theories flourished. Opposing political sides had merged into opposing accounts of reality. In the context of pro-Gbagbo websites, the narrative often boiled down to depicting Ouattara as a French neo-colonial puppet, and a Gbagbo as an anti-colonial hero.[3] Accordingly, the imagined relationship with the former colonial power France, and the international community at large, became a central idiom in the construction of the images of the opposing protagonists of the Ivoirian post-electoral crisis.

The internet, as an international medium and as a site in which the circulation of information is less easily restricted, also became a platform for debate and exchange of information among the diaspora and those residing in Côte d'Ivoire. In this context of opposing narratives and counter-narratives, of half-truths, untruths and counter-truths, of a long history of politically partial news reporting, and of rigorous government efforts to restrict access to information, the internet became an important platform for debate and exchange of information throughout the elections and the ensuing crisis. Partisans of Gbagbo depicted international and French news agencies in particular as biased towards the rebellion during the Ivoirian crisis and towards Ouattara during the post-electoral crisis. Their expressions soon found their way into *Nouchi* slang: an idiom for telling untruths to take advantage of a given situation was 'spinning AFPs' (Agence France Presse), *'filer les AFP'*. RFI (Radio France International) was renamed 'Radio Intentional Fraud' (*'Radio Fraude Intentionnel'*). As Karin Barber points out, 'more usually ... people's disillusion and resentment is expressed in a more subterranean manner, in the form of jokes, catchphrases, and anecdotes that circulate with great rapidity and undergo many phases of elaboration while they are in vogue' (1987: 5).

Given the relatively low percentage of regular internet users in Abidjan (and in Côte d'Ivoire generally), it is interesting that the internet remained relevant and influential throughout and following the post-electoral crisis of 2010–11 (see also Musangi, 2009).[4] Online activity was a means for Ivoirians (and large numbers from the Ivoirian diaspora) to try to access information about developments of the post-electoral crisis. Members of the elite turned to social media to organise volunteer solidarity groups, getting humanitarian aid and medical attention to the (internally displaced) civilian population caught in the crisis.[5]

Online activity was also a means by which untruths were spread. In *Nouchi* parlance, it became ever more difficult to distinguish *'info'* from *'intox'* (intoxication; untruth), as photo-shopped images of either Gbagbo or Ouattara under arrest flourished, as well as images from Rwanda and Nigeria depicting atrocities allegedly committed in Côte d'Ivoire alongside genuine images of atrocities committed by pro-Gbagbo and pro-Ouattara forces. The online debates were usually 'highly polemical, centred on insulting the leading Ivoirian players, with little regard for facts or credibility of sources' (Moncrieff, 2012: 31). The internet soon developed into a site for a 'war of images'.

A case in point is a demonstration by women protesters in the neighbourhood of Abobo on 3 March 2011, in which the women were shot by national army tanks, leaving seven dead. A video of this event circulated on YouTube[6] and was soon disseminated by partisans of Ouattara to illustrate the brutality of the Gbagbo regime. Another video was disseminated by partisans of Gbagbo seeking to demonstrate that these women did not actually die, and that the original video was a montage made by supporters of Ouattara to discredit the Gbagbo regime.[7] As Mike McGovern put it, 'there is in Côte d'Ivoire today a sort of palpable satisfaction taken in each subsequent abuse, whether by the French or by the "enemy" on the opposite side of the *zone de confiance*. This *volonté d'avoir des charniers* (will to have mass graves) as it was once described to me, simultaneously disqualifies the enemy as a serious political interlocutor and justifies retaliation by the victims' (McGovern, 2011: 22). A struggle over the international reputation of each opposing side is also evident. Patrick Achi, government spokesman for Ouattara, published several editorials in the British newspaper the *Guardian*, calling for international intervention as the crisis continued to escalate.

Beyond a struggle of representation to the outside world, the internet became a platform where conflicting views of the crisis where circulated among Ivoirians in Côte d'Ivoire and abroad. It was also a place where the powerful and the antagonists of the Ivoirian post-electoral crisis could be ridiculed.

'Multimatum' (see figure 7.1) refers to the multiple ultimatums made to Gbagbo to hand over the presidency issued by Ouattara, his government and the international community. Note the 'sponsorship' of the UN, the EU, the US and the African Union (AU), all of which backed Ouattara's win. The second image (figure 7.2) includes the text: 'Laurent Gbagbo, master baker. Until 31 December 2010 get the best rolls and multiply the quality tenfold.' This refers to the French expression *'rouler dans la farine'* (literally, to roll in baking flour) which translates to 'to con': Gbagbo was depicted as the master baker by Ouattara's supporters, as according to their view he tried to con the international community into accepting a re-count of the ballot. The diplomatic and financial measures employed by the international community to make Gbagbo back down were proving ineffective (Banégas, 2011: 458). Note the line at the bottom of the image: these

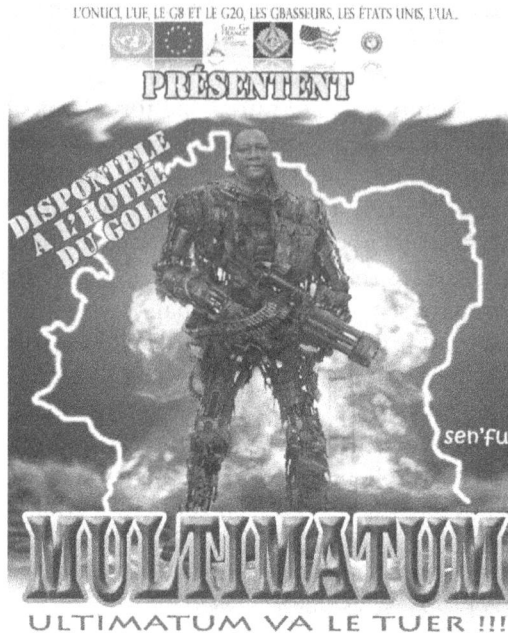

7.1 *Multimatum: ultimatum va le tuer!!!*

'rolls' are available at the Economic Community of West African States (ECOWAS; French: *Communauté économique des États de l'Afrique de l'Ouest*, CEDEAO), West African Monetary Union (*Union monétaire ouest-africaine*, UMOA), the UN, France, US, EU and AU (all those countries and multilateral organisations whose pressure Gbagbo consistently ignored).

In the context of an intensifying and violent post-electoral crisis, neither online discussions nor offline news coverage followed the high ideals of rational debate or even deliberative democracy (see also Dahlgren, 2005: 156). Online exchanges often exhibited little tolerance toward those who hold opposing views, and ethnic stereotypes and insults became a common feature as the conflict intensified. Simultaneously, 'magical signs' that peace would be imminent circulated, most common among these were photos of hearts that appeared in cooking pots of palm-nut stew (*sauce graine*). The television station RTI also aired reports on the hearts that appeared in cooking pots of palm-nut stew as traditional media such as television started exhibiting some of the spurious and irrational stories usually confined to the internet.

Uncertainty and lack of access to information fed into the production and circulation of rumours. Certain groups deliberately produced an

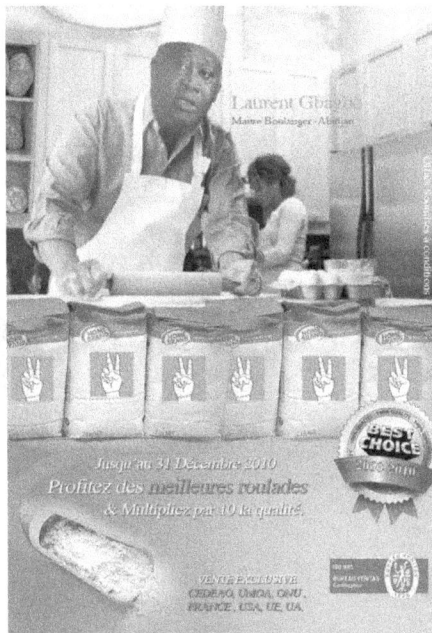

7.2 *Laurent Gbagbo: Maitre Boulanger-Abidjan*

image of mystery to avoid detection, but also to instil fear, such as the Invisible Commando of the neighbourhood Abobo (*Commando invisible*), an armed group which acted in support of Ouattara but was not officially affiliated with his forces, and which became feared for committing human right abuses (Amnesty International, 2011). Before the capture and arrest of Laurent Gbagbo, Ouattara's forces became implicated in large-scale massacres and human rights abuses (notably in western Côte d'Ivoire, such as in the town Duékoué, see Amnesty International, 2011 and Human Rights Watch, 2011) and several cartoons were circulated on pro-Gbagbo sites depicting Ouattara marching over dead bodies on his way to the presidential chair (Chappatte, 'Ouattara's Tarnished Victory', dated 7 April 2011). One cartoon also takes up the narrative of Ouattara as a puppet of France, again making the international dimension a reference point in its imagery. It is presented as a book published by TCI Press Publishers. The TCI (*Télévision Côte d'Ivoire*) was set up by the Ouattara government as a parallel pirate TV station in early 2011 from the provisional headquarters at the *Hôtel du Golf*, as the RTI turned into a propaganda outlet for the Gbagbo government. However the TCI has also been cautioned by Reporters Without Borders for continuing to broadcast campaign slogans and

7.3 Roland Polman, Caric-Actu, 2011.

songs that Ouattara used when he was a candidate, and for failing to act
as a public service medium and address all Ivoirians (Reporters Without
Borders, 10 May 2011). Certainly, the war of images remained primarily directed at the Ivoirian population.

Ouattara was officially sworn in on 6 May and inaugurated in a large
ceremony on 21 May, while Gbagbo was held in prison in northern
Côte d'Ivoire, before being transferred to the International Criminal
Court (ICC) in The Hague on 30 November 2011. Polman, an Ivoirian
cartoonist, also depicts the presidential chair as positioned on dead
bodies in front of a torn Ivoirian flag (a situation that according to the
depiction in this cartoon doesn't change whether Gbagbo or Ouattara
occupies it) as the post-electoral crisis cost an estimated three thousand
lives in Côte d'Ivoire (figure 7.3).

The day after Gbagbo's capture and arrest by the pro-Ouattara
forces FRCI with military support from France and the UN, the Swiss
cartoonist Chappatte depicted Ivoirians as having two presidents again,
this time Ouattara and Sarkozy. This cartoon was widely circulated
on pro-Gbagbo websites, again taking up the theme of Ouattara as a
French puppet: 'Here we are with 2 presidents again … Ouattara and
Sarkozy.' As this cartoon reveals, the central role played by France in
Gbagbo's arrest did not escape outside observers. However, in Côte

7.4 Chappatte, 'Ivory Coast', 2011.

d'Ivoire, sympathisers of Gbagbo saw it as proof that Ouattara was the 'overseas candidate'.

During the time of Gbagbo's arrest in northern Côte d'Ivoire, before his transfer to the ICC, pro-Gbagbo bloggers, such as Claudus Kouadio, stayed active, offering a contrasting narrative. Gbagbo was presented, not as a former head of state about to appear on trial before the ICC for crimes against humanity, but as the hero of anti-colonial struggle against imperialist France with a vision for all of Africa. One of Kouadio's blog posts, from 1 June 2011, reviews the book *Laurent Gbagbo: one man, one vision (Laurent Gbagbo: un home, une vision)* (Kouadio, 2011a). This blog rehashes the idiom of a second, genuine independence which was part of the *camp présidentiel's* (Gbagbo and the elite surrounding him) strategy throughout the Ivoirian Crisis of 2002–7 of pitching national sovereignty and *souverainisme* against France and the international community to block outside attempts at peace brokerage unfavourable to his regime (Piccolino, 2012). The same blogger uplifted the ideas of Laurent Gbagbo to an ideology bearing its own distinct name, *Gbagboïsme* (Kouadio, 2011b).

There is considerable overlap between online and offline publications: the book reviewed by blogger Claudus Kouadio online, of course, has first and foremost an offline existence. As Margolis and Resnick succinctly note, 'there is an extensive political life on the Net, but it is mostly an extension of political life off the Net' (cited in Dahlgren, 2005: 154). Indeed, different media repeatedly coalesced in the struggle over representation: the cover of the pro-Gbagbo newspaper *Le Nouveau Courrier* dated 9 February 2012 featured the cover of a book by Gregory Protché entitled *On a gagné les élections mais on a perdu la guerre* (English: we have won the elections, but we have lost the war), which then widely circulated online via blogs supportive of Gbagbo. This book ran the sub-title 'Ivoirian Crisis: here is the new truth-book'. Again, the struggle over different narratives of 'truth' is evident.

Finally, the website *Pensées Noires* which dedicates itself to 'reflection and freedom of expression' was founded by the Ivoirian author Jean-David N'Da and is edited by members of the Ivoirian diaspora in New York. This website posted the article *'J'ai entendu parler de Lumumba mais J'ai vu Gbagbo'* (English: I heard talk about Lumumba, but I saw Gbagbo) by Marjolaine Goué in June 2011, which was subsequently massively re-posted on Facebook, again depicting Laurent Gbagbo as a hero of the anti-colonial struggle (Goué, 2011).

Jean-David N'Da's own book entitled *Médias colons et mondialisation: le cas de la Côte d'Ivoire* (2013) (English: colonial media and globalisation: the case of Côte d'Ivoire) has been advertised on the author's website with the following text:

> The media lynching of Côte d'Ivoire executed by the French media system for more than a decade is a success. The international public, culturally predisposed to get drunk off the lies of its leaders, has quickly been won over. At the same time, the socio-political history of a heavily indebted poor country in Sub-Saharan Africa has been carefully rewritten with the objective that Ivoirians kowtow and agree. This work explains without prevarication the racist geo-strategy that stands behind the assault of colonial media and reveals the hypocrisy of greedy, predatory and impoverishing globalization that underlies it. The dangerous game of Ivoirian political actors is clearly revealed. The only alternative: taking individual and collective consciousness and plan a concrete response and the complete break with the dominant order. (www.jeandavidnda.com)

As Franklin and Love note, 'what is considered worth knowing about the world is defined and controlled by the west. And the media in all its globalised forms can be seen as an agent in this enterprise .... The west's explanations for events in Africa become common-sensical' (Franklin and Love, 1998: 547). Thus, pro-Gbagbo websites have attempted to challenge the 'common-sensical' narrative of the Ivoirian post-electoral crisis of Western media. As evident from N'Da's book, the struggle over the representation of Côte d'Ivoire's history and politics in Western media has been regarded as a central part of the anti-colonial struggle for the actors aligned with Gbagbo and the LMP, again referring to the idea of a second, genuine independence which has become a recurring motif in their imagery. Clearly the internet has provided a platform for alternative readings of the Ivoirian post-electoral crisis; however, some would argue that 'the multiplication of opportunities to express and to self-represent does *not* translate to greater visibility or recognition' (Goode, 2010: 532, original emphasis) and the narrative of Gbagbo as the real winner of the elections, or as an icon of the anti-colonial struggle has been shunned in mainstream Western media.

Conclusions

Internet discussion sites have become a focal point of the political debate in Côte d'Ivoire (along with other new platforms such as popular music and open-air discussion spaces). In a context of severe restrictions of media freedom and limited trust of official news sources, including international news, the internet has become a site of struggle over rumours, truth and falsehood, and a site of struggle over opposing narratives of the Ivoirian post-electoral crisis. Websites and blogs linked to the LMP proliferated, casting the Ivoirian post-electoral crisis in an anti-colonialist idiom and attempting to discredit Ouattara as a puppet forcibly installed to serve French geopolitical and economic interests. The imagined relationship with the former colonial power France, and the international community at large, became a central idiom in the construction of the images of the opposing protagonists of the Ivoirian post-electoral crisis. These images were circulated in an international medium, yet they were primarily aimed at Ivoirian (local and diaspora) audiences. The internet became a site where counter-narratives to mainstream Western news and alternative images of the crisis and its protagonists were created and circulated, and the internet has also provided a platform in which opposing readings of the Ivoirian post-electoral crisis could emerge.

In the context of pro-Gbagbo websites, the narrative was often reduced to depicting Ouattara as a French neo-colonial puppet, and Gbagbo as an anti-colonial hero. Portraying Gbagbo as the last guardian of national sovereignty and the post-electoral crisis as yet another stage in Côte d'Ivoire's 'second war of independence', these internet discussion sites transformed international pressure into a political opportunity. Indeed, the struggle over the image of Laurent Gbagbo and competing narratives of the Ivoirian post-electoral crisis were presented as part of a larger struggle for a second independence and against the 'assault of colonial media' (N'Da, 2013). Blogs and websites functioned as a site where the image of Laurent Gbagbo as portrayed by international media, and indeed the interpretation of the entire post-electoral crisis, could be challenged by those Ivoirian actors aligned with the LMP. Indeed, in these websites (as well as other media), the very act of challenging the portrayal of the Ivoirian post-electoral crisis as depicted on international news media became an integral part of the stance against Western hegemony.

However, as mentioned earlier, during the Ivoirian post-electoral crisis, 'the multiplication of opportunities to express and to self-represent [did] *not* translate to greater visibility or recognition' for the LMP (Goode, 2010: 532, original emphasis). The heavy reliance on the internet by the actors aligned with the LMP can indeed be read as a sign of their weak position after losing international credibility as multilateral organizations including the UN, EU, ECOWAS, African Union and almost all foreign governments (notably the US, France and Nigeria) endorsed Ouattara as the winner of the elections. Additionally, most of Gbagbo's international allies did not claim that he won the elections, merely that it was unclear (e.g. Mbeki, 2011). The internet thus became the last readily available platform where the LMP could promulgate their readings of the post-electoral crisis.

The virulent online diatribes do not reflect the opinions of the majority, and the portrayal of Laurent Gbagbo as a hero in the struggle for a 'second independence' clearly has an instrumental dimension. However, the wish to break with the practices of *Françafrique* and to redefine the old postcolonial relationship has become a common register which has also been adopted by individuals who were not Gbagbo sympathisers (see Schumann, 2013) and should therefore not be easily dismissed.

Notes

1 I am indebted to John James for his insightful comments on a draft of this chapter. The research upon which this chapter is based was supported by the Andrew W. Mellon Foundation and the Wits SPARC Fund.
2 Laws no. 91-1033 and 91-1034 respectively; see Gnonzion 2011, 302.
3 Websites (most of which are not officially affiliated with the FPI, LMP or LG; the connection is often deliberately blurred) include: abidjandirect.net, abidjanici.net, directscoop.net, eburnienews.net, infoscotedivoire.net, ivoire-business.net, ivoireverite.com, ivoirien.net, monsaphir.com, penseesnoires. info, souverainete-africaine.com, telediaspora.net. Blogs include: african-liberty.ivoire-blog.com, claudus.ivoire-blog.com, cotedivoire-lavraie.over-

blog.fr, infosivoire.centerblog.net, ivoireverite.wordpress.com, kouamouo. ivoire-blog.com, re.ivoire-blog.com. 'Official' pro-Gbagbo websites include: votonsgbagbo.net, lgconnect.net, lgvictoire.over-blog.org, gbagbo.ci, laurent-gbagbo-president.com, jevotegbagbo.blogspot.com, revuedepressecigbagbo. over-blog.com, gbagbovictorieux.centerblog.net.

4 Internet usage, especially via mobile phones, is increasing rapidly.

5 Solidarity groups organised online include the Facebook groups *Chaine de solidarité des déplacés d'Abobo* (Solidarity chain for the displaced population of Abobo), *SOS Médecins Conseils* (SOS Medical advice), *Facebookeur du Cœur* (Facebooker with heart), the ICT NGO Akendewa, as well as the Twitter hashtags #CIV2010 and #CIVSOCIAL. For more information on these remarkable initiatives, see the documentary *L'Autre Côte d'Ivoire* by Honoré Essoh, Kpata Films Production, 2014.

6 www.youtube.com/watch?v=JKCKDOdx6Jc&bpctr=1362234432

7 www.youtube.com/watch?v=dc-82bYEFd0

References

Amnesty International (2011): '"They looked at his identity card and shot him dead": six months of post-electoral violence in Côte d'Ivoire', Report Afr 31/002/2011 English, www.amnesty.org/en/library/info/AFR31/002/2011, cited 6.3.13.

Bahi Aghi (2003): 'La Sorbonne d'Abidjan: rêve de démocratie ou naissance d'un espace public?', *Revue africaine de sociologie* 7(1): 52–72.

Banégas, Richard (2011): 'Post-election crisis in Côte d'Ivoire: the *gbonhi* war', *African Affairs* 110(440): 457–68.

Barber, Karin (1987): 'Popular arts in Africa', *African Studies Review* 30(3): 1–78.

Bassett, Thomas J. (2011): 'Winning coalition, sore loser: Côte d'Ivoire's 2010 presidential elections', *African Affairs* 110(440): 469–79.

Boisbouvier, Christophe (2012): 'Côte d'Ivoire – France: Ouattara et Sarkozy, comme les doigts de la main', *Jeune Afrique* online 26.1.12, www.jeuneafrique.com/Article/JA2663p016.xml0, cited 6.3.13.

Chappatte, Patrick (2011): Cartoon: 'Ivory Coast', *International Herald Tribune*, 12.4.11.

Chappatte, Patrick (2011): Cartoon: 'Ouattara's Tarnished Victory', *International Herald Tribune*, 6.4.11.

Dahlgren, Peter (2005): 'The internet, public spheres, and political communication: dispersion and deliberation', *Political Communication* 22(2): 147–62.

Essoh, Honoré (2014): *L'Autre Côte d'Ivoire*. Kpata Films Productions, 15.1.14, www.youtube.com/watch?v=02o2DXlBHjs

Foreign Policy online (2011): Open Letter: 'Ivory Coast, the war against civilians', 31.1.11, www.foreignpolicy.com/articles/2011/01/31/open_letter_ivory_coast_the_war_against_civilians, cited 6.3.13.

Images of Africa

Franklin, Anita and Roy Love (1998): 'Whose news?: control of the media in Africa', *Review of African Political Economy* 78: 545–50.

Goode, Luke (2010): 'Cultural citizenship online: the internet and digital culture', *Citizenship Studies* 14(5): 527–42.

Gnonzion, Célestin (2011): 'The struggle for media freedom in Côte d'Ivoire', *African Communication Research* 4(2): 302–11.

Goué, Marjolaine (2011): 'J'ai entendu parler de Lumumba mais j'ai vu Gbagbo', *Pensées Noires*, 18.6.11, www.penseesnoires.info/2011/06/18/j%E2%80%99ai-entendu-parler-de-lumumba-mais-jai-vu-gbagbo, cited 6.3.13.

Human Rights Watch (2011): *Côte d'Ivoire: 'Ils les ont tués comme si de rien n'était'. Le besoin de justice pour les crimes post-électoraux en Côte d'Ivoire*, www.hrw.org/sites/default/files/reports/cdi1011frwebwcover.pdf, cited 6.3.13.

Kouadio, Claudus (2011a): 'Laurent Gbagbo: un homme, une vision', Claudus. ivoire-blog.com, 1.6.11, http://claudus.ivoire-blog.com/archive/2010/06/01/laurent-gbagbo-un-homme-une-vision.html, cited 6.3.13.

Kouadio, Claudus (2011b): 'C'est quoi le Gbagboïsme?', Claudus.ivoire-blog. com, 9.10.11, http://claudus.ivoire-blog.com/archive/2011/10/09/c-est-quoi-le-gbagboisme1.html, cited 6.3.13.

Ligaga, Dina (2012): '"Virtual expressions": alternative online spaces and the staging of Kenyan popular cultures', *Research in African Literatures* 43(4): 1–16.

Mbeki, Thabo (2011): 'What the world got wrong in Côte d'Ivoire' *Foreign Policy* 29.4.11, www.foreignpolicy.com/articles/2011/04/29/what_the_world_got_wrong_in_Côte_d_ivoire, cited 26.4.14.

McGovern, Mike (2011): *Making war in Côte d'Ivoire* (Chicago: University of Chicago Press).

Miran-Guyon, Marie (2011): 'Cyclone post-électoral : la production de la violence en Côte d'Ivoire', *Journal des anthropologues* 124–125: 373–80.

Moncrieff, Richard (2012): *French Relations with Sub-Saharan Africa Under President Sarkozy*, South African Institute of International Relations Occasional Paper 107.

Musangi, Jennifer (2009): '"Only a few cases of skirmishes here and there": interrogating the "truth" of an election in the Kenyan blogosphere', *Africa Insight* 39(1): 86–96.

N'Da, Jean-David (2013): *Médias colons et mondialisation: le cas de la Côte d'Ivoire* (Paris: L'Harmattan).

Piccolino, Giulia (2012): 'David against Goliath in Côte d'Ivoire?: Laurent Gbagbo's war against global governance', *African Affairs* 111 (442): 1–23.

Polman, Roland (2011): 'ADO prend le pouvoir par la force' in *L'actu 2011 en dessins de presse* (Abidjan : Caric-Actu).

Protché, Gregory (2012): *On a gagné les élections mais on a perdu la guerre : les raisons de ne pas marcher à la victoire de Ouattara* (Paris: Editions Le Gri-Gri).

Reporters Sans Frontières (2005): *Côte d'Ivoire: Il est temps de 'désarmer les esprits, les plumes et les micros'*, http://fr.rsf.org/cote-d-ivoire-il-est-temps-de-desarmer-les-27–05–2005,13933.html, cited 6.3.13.

Reporters Without Borders (2010): 'Assessment of media's coverage of campaign for presidential election second round', 27 November, http://en.rsf.org/cote-d-ivoire-assessment-of-media-s-coverage-of-27–11–2010,38913.html, cited 6.3.13.

Reporters Without Borders (2011): 'Media freedom set back 20 years', 10 February, http://en.rsf.org/cote-d-ivoire-media-freedom-set-back-20–years-10–02–2011,39531.html, cited 6.3.13.

Reporters Without Borders (2011): 'Nine newspapers resume publishing after week-long protest against harassment', 8 March, http://en.rsf.org/cote-d-ivoire-amid-continuing-political-deadlock-01–03–2011,39652.html, cited 6.3.13.

Reporters Without Borders (2011): 'Violence, terror and lack of information – initial evaluation of battle for Abidjan's impact on media', 6 April, http://en.rsf.org/cote-d-ivoire-violence-terror-and-lack-of-06–04–2011,39969.html, cited 6.3.13.

Reporters Without Borders (2011): 'Press in turmoil after Gbagbo fall', 10 May, http://en.rsf.org/cote-d-ivoire-press-in-turmoil-after-gbagbo-fall-10–05–2011, 40263.html, cited 6.3.13.

Schumann, Anne (2011): 'Ivory Coast: the agonies of reconciliation', *Guardian Online, Comment is Free*, 8.5.11, www.guardian.co.uk/commentisfree/2011/may/08/ivory-coast-agonies-reconciliation, cited 6.3.13.

Schumann, Anne (2013): 'Songs of a new era: popular music and political expression in the Ivoirian Crisis', *African Affairs* 112(448): 440–59.

Théroux-Bénoni, Lori-Anne (2009):'Manufacturing conflict?: an ethnographic study of the news community in Abidjan, Côte d'Ivoire' (PhD dissertation, University of Toronto).

Witcher, Pureterrah (2006): 'Hate media: gagging Côte d'Ivoire's peace process', *UN Chronicle* 3.

8

Negotiating narratives of human rights abuses: image management in conflicts in the eastern Democratic Republic of Congo

Georgina Holmes

While there is recognition that non-state armed groups operating in Africa attempt to manage their reputation internationally, the reasons for their engagement with the international community and the approaches taken by these groups deserves more attention. Over the last decade, the new media environment and Web 2.0 technologies have provided armed groups in the east of Congo such as the Forces Démocratiques de Libération du Rwanda (FDLR), former-National Congress for the Defence of the People (CNDP) and Movement 23 (M23) with increased access to a range of audiences, allowing them to engage with members of the international community directly and with greater speed. Web 2.0 technologies serve to amplify the voices of non-state armed groups at the international level. Yet, these actors are required to work within the discursive power structures that define African subjects within the international system, as well as negotiate narratives about conflict and insecurity in Africa produced externally by states, intergovernmental organisations and human rights interest groups. This chapter considers the image management strategy of one armed group operating at the sub-state level: the Forces Démocratiques de Libération du Rwanda (FDLR), which has been active in the region for nearly two decades and has operated via an international network. The chapter explores how image management is a relational process, comprising a series of discursive exchanges between external actors and African non-state armed groups. It reveals how over a period of eight years, the FDLR presented itself as a 'morally proper' political subject and aimed to influence international political decision-making on the type of intervention required in the east of Congo, thereby ensuring the FDLR's survival. This was achieved discursively by appropriating externally created 'strategic narratives' about human insecurity and human rights abuses, including rape and sexual violence in the east of Congo and then, through the appropriation of these narratives, by weakening the legitimacy of FDLR enemies.

There is a broad consensus in academia and international policy that armed groups use public relations (PR) to present themselves as legitimate actors in times of conflict or political unrest, although no universal definition of what constitutes an armed group exists, nor is there agreement on how to assess whether an armed group's motives for using violence can be regarded as 'legitimate'. Therefore, analysis of how an armed group attempts to manage its external image must consider the group's history and political origins, as well as the context within which knowledge about the group's use of violence is produced, both locally and internationally. It also requires one to identify the external actors from whom the group is seeking legitimation, and why – and how the tactics of the group change in response to external perceptions of them.

This chapter first explores notions of legitimacy in relation to the behaviour of armed groups in the international system, before discussing the concept of 'strategic narratives' – an emerging body of research located at the intersection of international relations theory and political communication that seeks to understand how actors use narratives strategically during times of major change within the international system. Here, the concept is discussed in relation to the level of interest powerful states have in 'other people's wars', notably on the African continent. This part of the chapter also considers the challenges and opportunities African actors are afforded by Web 2.0 technologies, as their ability to operate discursively within the same grids of knowledge as external actors strengthens. Finally, the chapter analyses the FDLR's political discourse and explores how African actors, engaged in processes of extraversion, mobilise externally produced strategic narratives about human rights abuses and insecurity in order to establish external legitimacy. A total of 121 FDLR press releases and communiqués published on the FDLR website between January 2001 and March 2009 are examined using critical discourse analysis. Trends and patterns within the press releases are mapped to establish meanings across texts, and are then analysed in relation to the historical and political context of the FDLR's knowledge production. The chapter offers some concluding remarks on the way in which armed groups engaged in African conflicts – recognising that power resides in the discursive realm of international relations – are able to capitalise on the lack of clarity within the international community on what constitutes a legitimate armed group.

Legitimacy and armed groups in Africa

The term 'armed group' describes a diversity of actors, ranging from terrorists to freedom fighters. Non-state armed groups (NSAGs) may be defined as 'social organisations with an identifiable internal structure or chain of command which use force to challenge the authority', usually a nation state (Hoffman, 1998: 43). Shultz *et al* determine that NSAGs combine politico-military strategy with a revolutionary ideology in order to redefine society and challenge the authority of the state (2004: 16–17). Podder notes that NSAGs may offer an alternative leadership in the face of an inefficient, weak or authoritarian government, but they may also be predatory, abusive instigators of human insecurity and disruptive to peace (2013: 19). Sivakumaran argues that armed opposition groups 'possess an organised military force and an authority' responsible for 'committing acts above the level of banditry' (2006: 392). This distinction separates NSAGs that use violence strategically to achieve legitimate political aims from groups that operate as a brute force, using violence as a means to exert dominance over subjects (citizens) within their immediate locale. Since armed groups differ in terms of their size, motives, 'structure, leadership, command capabilities, mode of operations, resources and support base', it is not possible to adopt a 'one size fits all' approach to engaging with them in order to achieve peace (Podder, 2013: 17). Determining whether an armed group's purpose, motives and behaviours are legitimate is also challenging, with much resting on the degree to which an armed group is perceived to be legitimate – and by whom.

Within the academy, contemporary definitions of legitimacy emphasise the importance of belief or opinion, where it is thought that 'people hold the belief that if existing institutions are appropriate or morally proper, then those institutions are legitimate' (Dogan, 1992: 116). The correlation between legitimacy and public support is considered particularly important in democracies, where authority is granted by the people. Steffek takes the Weberian view that 'all enduring structures of domination' require 'some feeling or belief on the part of the ruled-over' that prevailing 'norms or commands are binding', and that, to 'follow a command because it is considered binding is essentially a moral choice' (2003: 254). As Weber's concept of domination incorporates many types of social relationships, Steffek concedes that people are embedded within 'overlapping relationships, concerning different aspects of their lives', reminding us that perceptions of what constitutes a legitimate group or institution can vary from public to public, rule to rule and can change dramatically over the course of time. At the level of the international, it cannot be assumed that international organisations are automatically endowed with the ability to make decisions on behalf of the people' (Casses in Steffek, 2003: 251). Therefore, states and global institutions develop 'good justifications', promoting the self-image of 'rational actor' which, if accepted and their actions believed to be 'morally proper', enable them to acquire legitimacy and support from other international actors and publics (Steffek, 2003: 250–1). The question of which norms and principles are accepted and obeyed, however, pervades international legitimacy debates between both International Relations theorists and international lawyers. Franck considers how in the international system, which is dependent on voluntary compliance, rather than coercion, international law affords so much legitimacy. For Franck, legitimacy here refers to 'that quality of a rule which derives from a perception on the part of those to whom it is addressed that it has come into being in accordance with the right process' (1988: 706). Recognising that legitimacy based on identity alone is not enough, both Franck and Steffek point to the importance of discourse (for Franck, the textual determinacy of a rule, for Steffek, inter-subjective communication) in enabling legitimacy. Legitimacy is 'created through a process of communication', where decision-makers communicate reasons for their decisions to publics (the rule addressees)', often via the media (Steffek, 2003: 258). Weber himself inferred the importance of 'rational communication' where, as Steffek notes, 'communicability of reasons is an indispensable precondition for many processes of social rationalisation, such as legalisation, bureaucratisation and ethical universalism'. Communication tools provide the mechanisms that enable individuals and groups to 'exchange their views and communicatively to agree on strategies of action' (Ibid, 2003: 262). In this sense, according to Steffek, legitimacy 'can only be generated through a public discourse', while 'any challenge to already existing legitimacy must enter the public domain first' (2003: 265).

The idea that legitimation is constructed around accepted norms and principles, rather than on the democratic polis model alone, has also been applied to recent debates on the legitimacy of armed groups. Hazan has shown how at the local level, armed groups that are part of wider social movements in Nigeria and Sierra Leone leverage popular support as a means to legitimise their violent campaigns against the state (Hazan, 2009: 281). Bangerter reveals that internal legitimacy among foot soldiers and leaderships is often maintained through a series of rules and codes such as a code of conduct, or codes of warfare, which may draw on 'moral, religious, and/or traditional codes' (Bangerter, 2011: 370). At the international level, external perceptions determining whether an armed group is legitimate (based on the group's aims, objectives and behaviours) tend to be assessed according to two norms or principles, although, as the discussion below suggests, these in themselves do not explain fully why in reality one actor in the international system would support an armed group while another actor would not. The first concerns the environment within which the armed group operates: does the state or states in question support a democratic process and is the armed group genuinely calling for democracy? Here, as Hazan's analysis suggests, the armed group's behaviour may be justified because it is engaged in a political struggle on behalf of citizens who oppose an authoritarian state. This explains why in the early 1990s, the Rwandan Patriotic Front (RPF) was afforded legitimacy internationally as a rebel group in opposition to the authoritarian MRND government in Rwanda which was eventually responsible for genocide in 1994.

The second relates to the extent to which the armed group complies with the rules of international humanitarian law (IHL), in particular the Geneva Conventions and the Additional Protocols that bind armed groups involved in internal conflicts. Bangerter distinguishes between armed groups who 'genuinely respect IHL and those who do not' and observes a correlation whereby increased respect for IHL signifies greater external recognition. She notes that a NSAG's acceptance of the rules of IHL depends on the decisions a group makes, rather than on the type of group it is (Bangerter, 2011: 355). However, in both cases, NSAGs may use IHL as a PR exercise, or as 'lawfare' in order to present a legitimate self-image to external stakeholders, although there is no certainty that members of the NSAG understand IHL or interpret it correctly. Despite this, research indicates that in the past ten years the rules of IHL are increasingly discussed within armed groups and by their leaders (Bangerter, 2011: 354). The interest in IHL among NSAGs is due in part to the attention they receive once they commit acts above the level of banditry, which forces them 'onto the international plane', affording them an 'international legal personality' (Sivakumaran, 2006: 390). Yet paradoxically, having secured an international legal personality, NSAGs are required to manage their image in order to acquire legitimacy and support from external actors. This poses a series of challenges for the leaders of African NSAGs since, as postcolonial theorist V.Y. Mudimbe has conceded, Africans are required to operate from within the same grids of knowledge that constitute the dominant discourses historically produced and controlled by the 'West', which in turn influence contemporary external ('Western') perceptions of the African subject and African war (Holmes, 2014: 62).

This part of the chapter has considered how legitimacy is constructed discursively by actors operating within the international system. We now turn to examine the concept of 'strategic narratives' before examining how, through the mobilisation of these narratives, the FDLR was able to construct its identity through discourse, directly targeting more powerful actors and diaspora groups in order to garner external support and legitimacy.

Strategic narratives

An emerging body of research located at the intersection of international relations and political communications studies is considering how great powers and other (state) actors use narratives strategically during times of major change within the international system. Roselle first observed that great powers develop strategic narratives to explain war, both leading up to, during and after conflict. These narratives target both domestic and international audiences, and are often employed by great powers to present the outcome of war in successful terms, even when in reality the war has been lost (see Roselle, 2006). Antoniades *et al* consider how all states 'seek to mobilise narratives' in an effort to 'influence and shape the behaviour of third parties' within the international system (Antoniades *et. al*, 2010: 1). A narrative is considered 'strategic' because it combines the interests and goals of an actor to 'suggest medium- and long-term goals or desirable end-states, and how to get there, based on representations of the situation' (Antoniades *et al*, 2010: 6). Strategic narratives are a 'tool for political actors to change the discursive environment in which they operate, manage expectations, and extend their influence'. Through the use of strategic narratives, states aim to define themselves (to establish legitimacy) and the system in which they operate, re-establishing the past, present and future to articulate a future (international) order and their position within that order (Ibid: 3). Strategic narratives serve to establish a chronology of events and actions, while providing frameworks and language to describe them. Central to all public relations strategies, they are often termed 'key messages' by public relations professionals or 'lines to take' by policymakers and diplomats. When used in a consistent manner, strategic narratives help to create and manage the image of a state. As part of this image management (or reputation management) technique, strategic narratives provide politicians and civil servants with 'rules' for how to behave when articulating foreign policy initiatives to both domestic and foreign audiences or when responding to political crises.

This research has examined the use of strategic narratives by great powers in order to justify intervention or engagement in, as Susan Curruthers has termed it 'our wars' (i.e. wars where US, European or 'Western' troops are directly engaged in fighting).[1] However, there is also a requirement to consider how powerful states use narratives strategically during 'other people's wars' and 'other people's human insecurity', for example, on the African continent. Here, strategic narratives provide states, collective global actors such as the EU and international institutions such as the UN with rules and frameworks for explaining decisions on whether or not to intervene during a crisis; the level and type of intervention, should intervention be deemed appropriate, and to describe intervention in the post-conflict phase. However, states and international political institutions are not the only actors producing strategic narratives about human insecurity in 'other people's wars'. International human rights organisations such as Amnesty International and Human Rights Watch (HRW) and interest groups such as the US based group ENOUGH play an important role, creating new narratives which they use in their global campaigns to expose perpetrators and lobby political leaders into action. Human rights organisations share an end-goal of eradicating human rights abuses and political inequalities, but, like states, use narratives strategically to extend their own influence and manage external expectations. As norm entrepreneurs, they are particularly good at producing narratives which disrupt the status quo in order to bring to the world's attention new problems (new norms) that need to be addressed. While reports produced follow certain rules and incorporate specific criteria and terminology, including 'references to appropriate human rights standards' to ensure impartiality, human rights organisations use various tactics to shock publics and governments out of denial when atrocities take place (Cohen, 1996: 518–9).[2] For example, between 2000 and 2012, Amnesty International and HRW published in English some seventy five reports, briefings and open letters detailing the extent of the human insecurity in the DRC. These reports catalogued crimes against humanity and provided testimonies by witnesses and victims. Of these reports, nine specifically drew attention to the problem of rape, and sexual and gender-based violence (SGBV) and the impact these crimes were having on women and children in order to push political leaders into acknowledging that the problem of rape was not just the by-product of war.[3]

The strategic narratives contained within these reports have a moralising function: they help to define a global 'moral subject', separating perpetrators and actors who ignore instances of human rights violation from actors (states, international organisations and publics) who call for intervention to take place. They show how perpetrators of human rights abuses exist outside of the imagined 'international order' and aim to convince states that their own goals (to change the international order and their position within it) cannot be realised unless perpetrators are caught and convicted. Shock tactics used by international human rights organisations are also adopted by other global actors, such as the first UN Special Representative on Sexual Violence in Conflict, Margot Wallström of Sweden, when she announced in August 2010 that the DRC was the 'rape capital of the world'. Wallström's statement was qualified by a Thompson Reuters Foundation report published in June 2011, which prompted international media and human rights organisations to circulate a second narrative, announcing that the Congo was the 'world's most dangerous place for women' (Anderson, 2011).

Despite the value that strategic narratives offer to human rights campaigners and political actors, the very nature of the narrative form is disruptive. Strategic narratives are not fixed or controlled by one set of actors; rather they are 'talk-in-interaction' embedded in 'larger social processes' (De Fina and Georgakopoulou, 2008: 379). States aim to change the perceptions and behaviour of other actors (Antoniades *et al*, 2010: 8), and human rights organisations aim to change the behaviour of states and global institutions. Both sets of strategic narrative are 'shaped by previous thought and action' and 'cannot be disassociated from an engagement with surrounding discourse activity' (De Fina and Georgakopoulou, 2008: 381). Requiring agency, strategic narratives are re-interpreted through the narrator's perspective, and through processes of negotiation and selection new or alternative narratives are produced in accordance with another actor's end-goals (Patterson and Monroe, 1998: 315). While this dynamic has always existed, the new media environment has significantly altered the discursive environment in which actors operate in the international system. Since the early 2000s there has been a rise of interactive media and 'new forms of public participation and conversation' (Antoniades *et al*, 2010: 7). Interactive websites, blogs, micro-blogs, online videos, podcasts and new communications technologies enable governments and international political institutions to broaden the scope of their public diplomacy efforts. Human rights organisations are also able to reach and engage with wider publics more cost-effectively via new media communications channels. The documentation produced by these organisations no longer 'flows only within a closed circuit of other human rights organisations, governments or intergovernmental bodies' (Cohen, 1996: 518). Conversely, the new media environment and the 'noise' it generates, 'makes the process of projecting strategic narratives an increasingly difficult one' (Antoniades *et al*, 2010: 3). As discussed below, the increase in availability and access to Web 2.0 technologies have thus provided non-state and substate actors, such as the FDLR, with new tools to reach out to real or imagined communities (see Archetti: 2013).

The FDLR

The political and historical context within which the Forces Démocratiques de Libération du Rwanda was required to establish external support and legitimacy in the early 2000s is complex. Both Rwanda and the Congolese governments came to power under circumstances of mixed legitimacy. The rebel group the Rwandan Patriotic Front (RPF) took control of Rwanda in July 1994 following victory in a civil war against the authoritarian Hutu extremist regime, while simultaneously ending the genocide. Although responsible for war crimes, the new government was accepted as legitimate by the international community. However, the RPF government's reputation was damaged when in 1996 the Rwanda Patriotic Army attacked the Hutu refugee camp, Kibeho, killing thousands of Hutu and forcing hundreds to flee further into Zaire. Increasingly throughout the 2000s, President Paul Kagame's control over freedom of speech and efforts to restrict the democratic process was also met with external criticism. In the DRC, Joseph Kabila had come to power in an instance of hereditary succession following the death of his father Laurent-Désiré Kabila in 2001. Under Kabila II's leadership, the Congolese government's commitment to democracy was also questionable, although for different reasons. Leading up to the 2006 presidential elections there were reports of high levels of corruption, as well as state-sanctioned human rights violations against political opposition groups and human rights activists.

In the late 1990s, international actors perceived the non-state armed group that was to eventually become the FDLR as a brute force and a legacy of the 1994 genocidal regime. Both its leaders and foot soldiers were understood to be former officers of the Rwandan ex-Forces Armées Rwandaises (FAR) and Hutu extremist Interahamwe. This negative image was exacerbated by evidence gathered by the UN and the Rwandan government that the ex-FAR and its supporters were staging attacks and planning incursions into the north-west of Rwanda. Such behaviour confirmed that the ex-FAR, as members of a former authoritarian regime, aimed to invade Rwanda and reclaim power and as a consequence the group was not regarded as possessing legitimate political motives. In the attempt to change this negative image and distance itself from the legacy of the 1994 genocide in Rwanda, the ex-FAR renamed itself the Armée pour la Libération du Rwanda (ALiR), later morphing into the Forces Démocratiques de Libération du Rwanda (FDLR) in 2000. By this point, the group was considered less of a threat to the stronger Rwanda Patriotic Army, but the FDLR itself was now responsible for crimes against humanity on the ground in the DRC and had therefore already acquired an international legal personality that was separate from the legal personalities acquired by those members who were responsible for genocide in 1994. The FDLR therefore abandoned military attacks on Rwanda in favour of obtaining ideological support for their political cause and in 2000 established two wings – one military, one political.

Its military wing, with headquarters located in the Walikale region of the DRC, operated alongside a number of smaller breakaway groups such as the Rasta and Soki and other NSAGs including PARECO. The military wing also fought alongside units from the Congolese Forces Armées de la République Démocratique du Congo (FARDC) in opposition to the Rwandan backed National Congress for the Defense of People (CNDP), led by Laurent Nkunda (Omaar, 2008: 8). The collapse of the Zairian state in 1997, the rise of informal economies in the eastern DRC and the continual shifting of allegiances between NSAGs, combined with the geography of the region, made it difficult for observers to obtain accurate facts and figures about who exactly was accountable for crimes against humanity. However, according to reports by several human rights organisations and the UN, the FDLR had a predatory economic behaviour and was responsible for some of the worst human rights abuses. By the end of 2008, the military wing comprised some 6500 to 7000 fighters (Crisis Group Africa Report, 2009: 7). At this time, US-based campaign group ENOUGH called for the neutralisation of the FDLR, describing the group in a briefing published online as an abusive instigator of human insecurity:

> The FDLR are a source of harassment, violence, destruction, and rape in eastern Congo. Their presence is the raison d'être for some Congolese rebel groups, including Laurent Nkunda's National Congress for the Defense of People, or CNDP, who purport to protect their communities from the FDLR threat but are also guilty of atrocities. The FDLR also potentially threaten Rwanda and thus are a major impediment to peace and security in the Great Lakes region more broadly. (2012: 2–3)

The FDLR's political wing was located abroad. Its leaders, commander of the military wing and president, Sylvestre Mudacumura and Chairman Ignace Murwanashyaka were based in Germany and the US. Spokesman Callixte Mbarushimana was in Paris, while some nineteen cells existed across Europe, North America and Africa including in the US and Canada, Belgium, Norway, the Netherlands and France. None of the leadership, with the exception of Mbarushimana, were suspected of genocide, which helped to further distance the political wing from the 1994 genocide. There were also cells in Spain, Italy, Switzerland, Sweden and the UK. In Africa, the FDLR was present in Zambia, Malawi and

Mozambique and had representatives in Kenya and Tanzania (Omaar, 2008: 24). The FDLR actively communicated to communities both in the Great Lakes region and internationally via its website www.fdlr.org. Combining efforts to secure local support in the Great Lakes region with diplomatic efforts to engage members of the international community, the FDLR also aimed to develop a political support base in the global diaspora. The significance of reaching out to the diaspora should not be underestimated, since these groups were in a position to lobby politicians and diplomats, while ensuring good relations with NGOs and churches.

Throughout the two Congo wars (1997 to 2003) and towards the end of the 2000s, the FDLR was also required to challenge international public perceptions about conflict and instability in the DRC more generally, which was largely influenced by international media reports. These reports played on the familiar stereotypes about primitive, tribal African conflicts perpetuated by savage, barbaric 'irrational' African men. They remind us of the structural conditions formed out of colonial discourse which the FDLR, as all African actors, are required to compete against when constituting and constructing new identities. Militias in the DRC were depicted as an a-political, a-historical homogenous mob; rape and SGBV were not considered to be a weapon of war, or a product of the breakdown of society, but an example of the primitive nature of the hypersexual African man. Hyperbolic statements reiterated colonial imaginings about fever, madness and violence in Congo. In contrast, media reports on perpetrators of the 1994 genocide focused on the International Criminal Tribunal for Rwanda (ICTR) and on cases where suspects were extradited to either Rwanda or Tanzania, where the ICTR was located. This helped to reinforce a geographical and political divide between conflict in the DRC and post-genocide Rwanda. At the same time, international institutions such as the UN, EU and the UN Mission in Congo (MONUC) were enjoying increased public visibility and were thus able to influence public discourse on events in the DRC, as, to a lesser extent, were other NSAGs such as the CNDP. This and international media reporting on conflict in the east of Congo presented the FDLR's political wing with the dual challenge of competing against the dominant 'Western' discourses that shaped international (policy and public) perceptions about African subjects and conflict in Africa, and the dominant discourse on the 1994 Rwandan genocide, which incorporated the image of the FDLR as génocidaires.

As part of a 'common plan',[4] Mbarushimana agreed with Mudacumura and Murwanashyaka to devise an international media campaign, publishing press releases, communiqués, historical narratives and situation reports to provide background information which journalists could refer to before interviewing them (ICC, 2011: para. 302, 133). The plan was not designed to mobilise FDLR troops on the ground and only concerned 'the relationship of the FDLR with the media and the external world' (Ibid: para 207, 131). According to the Prosecution at the International Criminal Court (ICC) at a pre-trial session in December 2011, the political wing set out

> a diplomatic strategy of insisting on the necessity of a pacific solution, arguing that the war imposed on the population in the region is useless, and stat[ing] that the FDLR military strategy should be directed at defending itself from the attacks of the Rwandan-Congolese coalition. (Ibid: para. 302, 133)

In the early years of their campaign, the FDLR focused on targeting world leaders, raising their profile and garnering support for their political goals. On 25 July 2001 the FDLR published a letter to US President George W. Bush, copying in world leaders including the Pope John-Paul II, the President of the World Bank, the Managing Director of the International Monetary Fund and President Paul Kagame, calling for an 'inter-Rwandan dialogue' and threatening to launch an armed struggle (2001a).

Distancing themselves from the 1994 genocide, the FDLR political wing presented themselves to the international community as 'freedom fighters' and a 'liberation movement' (2008a). They claimed to have a 'democratically elected leadership' (2007b) and were inclusive of 'all ethnic groups' (2001b). However, they were also able to capitalise on the Rwandan government's tight control over freedom of speech and restriction of political space. They saw themselves as the only true opposition to Kagame's RPF and 'the voice of the voiceless, survivors of various tragedies experienced by Rwanda since 1 October 1990', when civil war between the Habyarimana regime and the RPF commenced (2008c). Their stated goals were to 'liberate Rwanda, plead in favour of the oppressed and excluded' and 'open a new era of peace' (Omaar, 2008: 54). According to their statute, the FDLR were a political military group seeking to 'reconquer and defend the national sovereignty' of Rwanda' (FDLR in ICC, 2011: 6). In contrast to the actions of ALiR, the political wing of the FDLR also claimed they did 'not want war against the Rwandan government or a foreign country'. Instead, they wished to 'bring together the Rwandan government, the opposition and civil society to draw up a new social contract that will put an end to wars against other countries, ethnic conflicts, discrimination, oppression, injustice and violations of human rights' (FDLR, 2001b).

Presenting themselves as an NSAG with legitimate political aims, supporting the democratic process and fighting for freedom of speech for an oppressed population, the FDLR's political wing argued that they had a right to use self-defence to protect their men and 'protect the civil populations that are with them (2007d). As part of their image management strategy, the political wing aimed to present the FDLR as a rational actor rather than a brute force, asserting that the group was bound by international humanitarian law, repeatedly claiming to recognise and act in accordance with the Rome Statute. They also claimed to be a cohesive group, whose soldiers abided by military rules and regulations. To demonstrate this, the political wing frequently condemned foot soldiers who were accused of committing crimes against humanity under IHL. For example they announced in a press release published on 31 August 2007 that they had excluded three for 'bad conduct' and for committing 'high treason' (FDLR, 2007c).

Having established itself through its discourse as a rational actor, when reports from the DRC described the military wing as an irrational brute force, the FDLR was faced with the challenge of maintaining its image as both a 'morally proper' political subject and legitimate political opposition to the Rwandan government on an ongoing basis. As a non-state armed group, the FDLR was clearly in a weak position discursively, in spite of the political wing's presence in US and Europe. The Rwandan government refused to consider the FDLR a legitimate NSAG and would not agree to their involvement in regional peace negotiations. To counter this, the FDLR tried to engage in, and influence, debates circulating internationally on the type of intervention required in the region in order to bring about peace.

Bayart's theory of extraversion helps to describe the discursive strategies the FDLR adopted in the 2000s. Bayart maintains that, in addition to the resources available in their own societies, African actors adopt strategies of extraversion by 'mobilising resources derived from their (possibly unequal) relationship with the external environment' (1993: 21). Through these strategies of appropriation and mobilisation, African actors 'compensate for their difficulties in the autonomisation of their power and in intensifying the exploitation of their dependents'. (Ibid: 21) Resources of extraversion may include cultural resources (mastery of 'Western' knowledge and 'Western' systems of knowledge production), economic (participation in global trade) and technical resources (mastery and adaption of technologies) (Ibid: 74). Since African NSAGs, like African governments, are required to operate within the same grids of knowledge (the same international political discourse) as the actors from whom they seek legitimacy and support, their approach to creating and sustaining an external self-image comprises a series of discursive exchanges. In mastering 'Western' systems of knowledge production, the FDLR adopted through the process of extraversion many of the discursive techniques that governments and international institutions use to establish legitimacy and support for the decisions made during times of war from other actors in the international system – notably through the appropriation (and negotiation) of strategic narratives.

Negotiating narratives of human rights abuses

At a pre-trial session in December 2011, the Prosecution at the ICC contended that Mbarushimana was 'the linchpin, the man who could transform crimes committed in the Kivus into political leverage for the FDLR in Rwanda' (ICC, 2011: para.67, 180). In the process of transforming crimes committed in the eastern DRC into political capital, the FDLR accessed and mobilised strategic narratives about human security and human rights abuses produced by the UN and human rights organisations to achieve a number of aims.

First, to sustain the image of a 'rational actor', the political wing employed strategic narratives to prove that the FDLR did not perpetrate human rights abuses, but rather, as a morally proper political subject, operated legitimately within the same imagined global order identified in NGO and UN discourses. When in the late 2000s, Amnesty International, HRW, ENOUGH and Women*for*Women International became increasingly vocal about the issue of SGBV, narratives concerning the mass raping of Congolese women featured more frequently in FDLR discourse. In a press release published on 26 July 2007, the political wing defined opposition NSAGs in the east of Congo as irrational brute forces, stating that the CNDP under Nkunda, along with 'partner groups' the Rasta, Mudundu 40 and Col 106, 'committed barbarian acts, killing civil populations', 'massively raping women, burning villages and causing massive displacements of populations'. These 'troops commit such horrific acts in order to put them on the FDLR' (2007f). Later in August that year, the FDLR presented themselves as liberators of women, 'condemn[ing] once again the acts of kidnapping women and young girls' by the 'criminal groups operating in the DRC', and 'inform[ing] the public that they have recently liberated three women that had been kidnapped by the "Rastas" group' (2007h).

Second, through processes of extraversion, the FDLR appropriated the same rhetoric and impartial style of discourse used by human rights organisations and the UN in order to create a voice of authority, often using declarative sentences – 'the FDLR urge', 'the FDLR declare', 'the FDLR denounce' – while writing recommendations and calling for the international community to act, which further served to construct

the image of a legitimate, morally correct political subject (see FDLR
2001c; 2003a). They repeatedly asked members of the international
community, including the UN, the EU, the African Union and Rwandan
and Congolese citizens to be 'vigilant' and to monitor the situation on
the ground. This appeal draws on wider recognition that the international community failed to adequately monitor Rwandan politics in the
lead up to the 1994 genocide. Where reports, news articles and press
releases published by the UN, MONUC, HRW and journalists claimed
that the FDLR were responsible for committing atrocities, the FDLR
leadership's discourse attempted to discredit their information. This is
particularly noticeable in 2007 and 2008, as human rights organisations put more pressure on the UN and member states to neutralise the
FDLR. In July 2007 they published an open letter to HRW wherein they
'refute and condemn the defamatory and false information contained in
the report ... entitled "DR Congo: Peace Accord Fails to End Killings
of Civilians"', demanding that the organisation 'publicly apologises
for this unfair and unacceptable slander' (2007f). In August that year,
when accused of attacking the village of Nyakakoma and taking villagers hostage, they 'invite MONUC to measure the consequences of
spreading unproven information and urge the UN mission to refrain
from publishing information with fallacious character aimed only at
provoking and stirring ethnic hatred in a region where the climate is
already tense' (2007i). In June 2008, they called on MONUC to 'stop
accusing the FDLR without prior investigation', claimed to 'unreservedly
condemn attacks against the displaced Congolese camp of Kinyandoni in
Rutshuru territory', before 'urg[ing] the United Nations to set up without
delay an inquiry commission in order to determine the identity of the
perpetrators of these heinous crimes and bring them to justice' (2008g).
Here, the FDLR denial tactics are reminiscent of the approaches used by
nation states accused of committing human rights violations (see Cohen,
1996). At times, the FDLR also published press releases in an attempt
to influence international public perceptions when UN and Congolese
government officials or leaders of other NSAGS spoke to international
journalists. For example, in August 2008 they accused the UN of taking
part in a 'media war' (2008g) and when on 23 October 2007 a CNDP
spokesperson was interviewed by the BBC, the FDLR claimed his allega-
tions against the FDLR were 'fanciful and unfounded' (2007j).

Third, the political wing aimed to weaken the legitimacy of the
Rwandan government – already called into question by critics of the
administration. To influence external perceptions, the FDLR identified
the Rwandan government as a fascist regime, holding authoritarian control over its citizens whom the FDLR aimed to liberate. By weakening

the RPF government's legitimacy, the FDLR would stand more chance of being perceived as a legitimate political opposition party worthy of being included in peace negotiations, and ultimately able to return to Rwanda as a political party. The FDLR's commitment to the democratic process is emphasised further in their statements of support for the 2006 presidential elections in the DRC. In a press release published on 26 October 2006, the leadership state that they 'welcome the maturity of the Congolese people and their leadership who have realized that legitimate power is not given by deadly weapons but by the people through free and fair elections' (FDLR, 2006). To reinforce the negative image of Kagame, the political wing argued that all human rights abuses in eastern DRC were committed by Rwanda's proxy armed groups and that insecurity in the Great Lakes region was symptomatic of the 'Rwanda problem' (2007e). In 2002, the FDLR posted on their website a letter sent by the HRW Director, Kenneth Roth to the US Permanent Representative to the UN, John Negroponte. The letter referred to crimes committed by the Rwandan Patriotic Army, allowing the FDLR to draw on evidence provided in a report published by the UN Commission of Experts. In so doing, the FDLR aimed to expose how Kagame's regime was 'the only destabilizing factor of the African Great Lakes region' (2007d). This tactic continued throughout the 2000s. For example in 2008 the FDLR denied association with the armed group SOKI, which human rights organisations and the UN had accused them of, arguing that SOKI was 'a group of criminals working for the Kigali regime'. Instead, SOKI had 'no connection with the FDLR and was guilty of several serious violations of human rights in this region aimed at besmirching the good reputation that the FDLR enjoy with the local population' (2008b). On 7 April 2008 the FDLR 'condemn[ed] the ongoing preparations of new massacres of innocent populations by the Kigali regime' before stating that they had 'reliable information that agents of the Rwandese Patriotic Front … claiming to be members of the FDLR' were 'distributing within Rwanda fake FDLR membership cards in order to later legitimise already planned massacres of civilians using the media's argument of hunting FDLR infiltrators' (2008d).

The FDLR's political wing also appropriated strategic narratives in an attempt to influence political institutions and nation states at key decision-making moments, with the aim of persuading these actors to change their intervention strategy in the region. On 11 November 2001, they appealed to UN Secretary General Kofi Annan regarding Phase III of MONUC, expressing concern at plans to disarm 'freedom fighters', and urging the UN to 'take into account [their] legitimate aspirations aimed at bringing durable solutions and peaceful settlement of the crises in Rwanda and the Great Lakes region' (2001d). When African leaders were

due to meet in New York on 14 May 2008 to discuss the renewed security crisis in the eastern DRC, which led to the breakdown of the Amani
Peace agreement later that year, the FDLR published a four-page com-
muniqué detailing their 'call' on African leaders 'for a real a lasting peace
in Rwanda and in the Great Lakes Region'. The publication provides
an FDLR-friendly interpretation of the history of conflicts in the region,
along with a series of demands, most of which are directed at prosecuting
Kagame for crimes against humanity and war crimes (2008g).

In analysing the political discourse over an eight-year period, it
becomes apparent that the FDLR changed its approach in accordance to
changing external perceptions. For most of the 2000s, the FDLR were
tolerated by the international community, in spite of awareness that
they were operating as a brute force in the DRC. However, in 2008 and
2009 as international attention turned towards neutralising the FDLR
and the net was closing in on the leadership based in Europe and the
US, the armed group's press releases contained more defensive rhetoric.
When chief media spokesman Callixte Mbarushimana was arrested
in July 2008 in Germany, President Ignace Murwanashyaka issued a
declaration, wherein he claimed that the arrest of Mbarushimana was
part of 'continuing attempts to intimidate the leadership of the FDLR'.
Mbarushimana had been 'subjected' to 'judicial harassment' 'at the insti-
gation of the Kagame regime', but since 2001 had 'started experienc-
ing the ill-motivated ostracism campaigns which were and are tailored
against all Intellectual Hutus' (2008i). During this period, the FDLR
leadership were particularly critical of both international and local
media, condemning reports issued by the UN-sponsored Radio Okapi,
AFP, French broadsheet *Libération* and the BBC and urging 'the media
to avoid publishing information not verified on the ground' (2008j).

Later in 2008, once Kabila and Kagame had agreed to integrate armed
groups such as the CNDP into the Congolese government army (the
FARDC) and undertake the joint operation, Umoja Wetu, to disband the
FDLR, the FDLR leadership published an open letter to Special Envoy of
the UN Secretary General to the African Great Lakes Region, Olusegun
Obasanjo, copying in a host of political leaders and international civil
servants including UN Secretary General Ban Ki Moon, the Chairperson
of the African Union Commission Jean Ping, heads of state in the Great
Lakes region of Africa, former President of Tanzania and Special Envoy
of the African Union in the DRC, Benjamin Mkapa, and Alan Doss, then
Special Representative of the Secretary General of the UN in the DRC.
In the letter, dated 4 December 2008, Murwanashyaka claims the FDLR
are 'peace-loving actors' and sets out once more the political goals of the
FDLR, arguing that 'the problem of [the FDLR's] presence in eastern

DRC cannot be solved militarily'. He threatens that 'any attempt to start a war to neutralise the FDLR may unnecessarily increase the suffering of innocent civilians and increase further instability in the region' (2008k). Murwanashyaka then puts forth a series of recommendations; first 'to the international community' and then 'to the Kigali regime', again adopting rhetoric reminiscent of international policy documents and reports produced by human rights organisations (2008k). He appeals to the international community to 'recognise that the FDLR are not "negative forces"' and to 'push the Kigali regime to engage without delay in direct and frank talks with its opposition' (2008k).

In a statement published on 8 December 2008, Murwanashyaka heightened his threat, stating that 'any solution based on the desire to destroy militarily the FDLR is not only counterproductive but also extremely dangerous because it could plunge an entire region into a fraticidal, dreadful and long war, and whose consequences are immeasurable' (2008l). That same day, Lieutenant-Colonel Edmond Ngarambe 'bombarded the media with phone calls, arguing that it was vital to appoint an international mediator to resolve the dispute with the Kigali regime' (Crisis Group Africa Report, 2009: 4). One week later, the FDLR reacted to a final report published by the Panel of Experts on the DRC which implicated all armed groups, including the CNDP, FARDC soldiers and the FDLR in committing human rights abuses and partaking in the illegal trade of natural resources. Here, the FDLR leadership argued more forcibly that the group did not perpetuate instability in the east of Congo, claiming that 'accusations formulated in the report that the FDLR might be exploiting the mineral resources of the DRC are false and groundless', before indicating that they were 'surprised to note that the UN experts based their accusations mainly on statements made by deserters from the FDLR'. They called instead for the UN Security Council to 'lift without delay the unjust sanctions against their leadership' (2008l), utilising once more narratives about SGBV to deny 'committ[ing] sexual violence' during this renewed period of fighting (2009e).

From late December 2008 until early March 2009, as the joint Rwandan-Congolese government mission to disband the FDLR picked up pace, the FDLR leadership chose to address its network of supporters, rather than engage directly with the international community. It seems at this stage, the FDLR had recognised that the international community regarded them first and foremost as a brute force in the DRC, rather than a legitimate NSAG fighting to return to Rwanda. The challenge therefore was to maintain legitimacy and support from the diaspora. Above all, the political wing tried to instil fear and anger in both local populations and members of the diaspora, condemning

Rwandan security forces for allegedly capturing members of the FDLR
in Rwanda and calling for 'all ethnicities to remain vigilant' (2008m).
In January 2009, Murwanashyaka referred to Umoja Wetu as 'a new
war' and called on all FDLR to remain united. (2009a). On 5 February
2009, the FDLR leadership released a situation report wherein they
claimed that 'the coalition RPA/FARDC is in the process of committing
serious violations of human rights (torture, theft, rape, massacres), not
only against the Rwandan Hutu refugee population but also against
the Congolese people that the coalition accuse of sympathising with the
FDLR' (2009b). Continuing to employ the language of war, in February
2009, the FDLR accused the Congolese authorities of 'kidnapping'
FDLR (2009c), and warned that FDLR who are rehabilitated back in
Rwanda are sent to 'nazi-style' concentration camps as 'prisoners of
war'. (FDLR, 2009d). Here, they urged their 'brave freedom fighters' to
'remain united', 'determined to ensure the protection of civilian populations', while 'continu[ing] to demonstrate their discipline in order to
face the challenges imposed by their enemy' (Ibid).

Conclusion

This chapter has considered how image management and image creation
are relational processes comprising a series of discursive exchanges
between external actors and African non-state armed groups. Through
processes of extraversion, the FDLR was able to mobilise strategic narratives created by external actors in order to position the group as a
rational, 'morally proper' political subject operating in accordance with
international humanitarian law. Recognising that power resides in the
discursive realm of international relations, the FDLR's political wing
aimed to transform the negative image it had acquired at the end of the
1990s as a brute force and the legacy of a genocidal regime, into a more
positive – if nuanced – image of a NSAG with legitimate political goals,
when in reality the military wing of the FDLR continued to operate as
a brute force in eastern DRC, attacking civilians indiscriminately and
often for economic gain. To many observers and critics the NSAG was
considered 'an obstacle to the Congolese state's efforts to re-establish
authority, a barrier to the transparent exploitation of the DRC's natural
riches and an obstacle to regional economic integration' (Crisis Group
Africa Report, 2009: 16). However, the FDLR's media and diplomatic
campaign was successful to a degree. Their claim to represent genuine
political opposition to Kagame led to debates about the extent to which
the group was strategically using violence to sustain a 'brutal insurgency'
in the eastern DRC. This in itself says much about the international

community's acceptance of high levels of violence in Africa that would not necessarily be tolerated elsewhere. The view held in Congolese political circles seemed to suggest that ministers, politicians and civil society perceived the FDLR to be a legitimate NSAG when in 2007 they signed a petition calling for an inter-Rwandan dialogue (Stearns, 2009a). Internationally, it seems the FDLR leveraged legitimacy from those states that had the capacity to arrest the political wing. Former coordinator of the UN Group of Experts on the Congo Jason Stearns notes that, in the early 2000s, when the UN had approached 'the US, France and other countries about FDLR operatives, they all said that they respected free speech and that these people had themselves not done anything illegal', while efforts by Germany to arrest Ignace Murwanashyaka were hindered by the 'limited laws against being a member of foreign rebel group, especially one that does not impinge on the host state' (Stearns, 2009b).

In spite of external perceptions of the FDLR, one can only speculate on whether Rwandan citizens, in particular those calling for a broader political base, regarded the FDLR as a legitimate political opposition, since the group was considered to be connected to the 1994 genocide (Ibid). Indeed, in spite of the political lobbying of human rights organisations and the UN, and much to the embarrassment of MONUC, those nation states with the power to arrest members of the FDLR political wing only took action after Kabila and Kagame had made their secret deal, itself an illegitimate act in the eyes of the international community. On 3 March 2009, ten days after the end of the joint Congolese-Rwanda mission, the US, Belgium, France and the UK provided the UN Security Council with a list of four senior members of the FDLR, including Callixte Mbarushimana. Under Resolution 1857 (2008) these four faced a travel ban and assets freeze. The US also imposed sanctions on the four on American territory, in addition to General Sylvestre Mudacumura; added the FDLR to their 2009 terrorist list and blocked the FDLR website (Crisis Group Africa Report, 2009: 10). In the US Country Terrorism Report 2008, published in April 2009 – one month after this sea-change in policy – the FDLR is described as 'potential terrorists' to Rwanda (US Country Report on Terrorism 2008, 2009: 18) and the presence of 'former soldiers and supporters of the regime that orchestrated the 1994 Rwanda genocide' in the military ranks is emphasised (Ibid: 18).

Considered at the time by Crisis Group Africa as symbolic, these acts nonetheless demonstrated for the first time a collective agreement among states with influence that the FDLR was a criminal group. Nevertheless, over a period of eight years prior to these events, the political wing was able to create and project an image of itself as a legitimate non-state armed group, despite the evidence and contextual information provided in UN situation reports and civil society documentation. This raises a number of questions, not least about how NSAGs should be engaged in peace processes, but also concerning the length of time it takes, and the events that occur, before consensus can be reached on the political status of an NSAG in relation to the impact their violence – whether strategic or brutal – is having on innocent civilians. Collective agreement on what constitutes a terrorist group in the context of violence in Africa is not just required at the international level. Indeed, at the point when the FDLR political wing was most active, member states of the African Union were yet to legislate new counterterrorism language, to be used first and foremost in legislation to 'combat money laundering and other financial crimes' (US Country Terrorism Report 2009, 2010: 15). According to the US Country Terrorism Report 2009, this process was being delayed because 'some AU members states maintained that Africa's colonial legacy made it difficult to accept a definition of terrorism that excluded an exception for 'freedom fighters', in spite of the AU's record for condemning terrorism attacks (Ibid).

Notes

1 For a discussion on the distinction between 'our wars' and 'other people's wars', see Susan Curruthers, 2011.
2 See Cohen, 2001, for a comprehensive analysis of the techniques NGOs and human rights organisations use.
3 Search conducted on Amnesty International and HRW websites in June 2013. These figures do not include reports published in French.
4 The term 'common plan' is used by the ICC and refers to a situation where two or more people agree to partake in a criminal activity (ICC, 2011: X).

References

Anderson, Lisa (2011): 'Analysis: Poll highlights hidden but deadly dangers for women', Thompson Reuters Foundation, 15.6.11, www.trust.org/item/?map=analysis-poll-highlights-hidden-but-deadly-dangers-for-women, cited 23.4.13.
Antoniades, Andreas, Ben O'Loughlin and Alister Miskimmon (2010): 'Great power politics and strategic narratives', Working Paper Number 7, University of Sussex, www.sussex.ac.uk/webteam/gateway/file.php?name=cgpe-wp07–antoniades-miskimmon-oloughlin.pdf&site=359, cited 15.4.13.
Archetti, Cristina (2013): 'Narrative wars: understanding terrorism in the era of global interconnectedness', in A. Miskimmon, B. O'Loughlin and L. Roselle (eds), *Forging the World: strategic narratives and international relations* (Ann Arbor: University of Michigan Press).
Bangerter, Olivia (2011): 'Reasons why armed groups choose to respect international humanitarian law or not', *International Review of the Red Cross* 93: 882.

Bayart, Jean-François (1993): *The State in Africa: the politics of the belly* (London: Longman).

Carruthers, Susan (2011): *The Media at War* (Basingstoke: Palgrave Macmillan).

Cohen, Stanley (1996): 'Government responses to human rights reports: claims, denials, and counterclaims', *Human Rights Quarterly* 18(3): 517–43.

Cohen, Stanley (2001): *States of Denial: knowing about atrocities and suffering* (Cambridge: Polity).

Crisis Group Africa Report, (2009): 'Congo: a comprehensive strategy to disarm the FDLR', Report No. 151, www.crisisgroup.org/en/regions/africa/central-africa/dr-congo/151–congo-a-comprehensive-strategy-to-disarm-the-fdlr.aspx, cited 8.7.13.

De Fina, Anna and Alexandra Georgakopoulou (2008) 'Analysing narratives as practices', *Qualitative Research* 8: 379–87.

Dogan, Mattei (1992): 'Conceptions of Legitimacy' in M. E. Hawkesworth and Maurice Kogan (eds), *Encyclopedia of Government and Politics, Volume 1* (London: Routledge).

ENOUGH (2012) 'Armed groups in Eastern Congo', www.enoughproject.org/conflicts/eastern_congo/armed-groups.

FDLR (2001a): *Press release*, 25.7.01.

FDLR (2001b): *Press release*, 15.8.01.

FDLR (2001c): *Press release*, 28.7.01.

FDLR (2001d): *Press release*, 11.11.01.

FDLR (2003a): *Press release*, n.d.

FDLR (2006): *Press release*, 27.10.06.

FDLR (2007a): *Press release*, 21.11.07.

FDLR (2007b): *Press release*, 27.9.07.

FDLR (2007c): *Press release*, 29.5.07.

FDLR (2007d): *Press release*, 13.9.07.

FDLR (2007e): *Press release*, 27.9.07.

FDLR (2007f): *Press release*, 26.7.07.

FDLR (2007g): *Press release*, 13.8.07.

FDLR (2007h): *Press release*, 24.8.07.

FDLR (2007i): *Press release*, 27.8.07.

FDLR (2007j): *Press release*, 23.10.07.

FDLR (2008a): *Press release*, 20.5.08.

FDLR (2008b): *Press release*, 24.6.08.

FDLR (2008c): *Press release*, 4.12.08.

FDLR (2008d): *Press release*, 7.4.08.

FDLR (2008e): *Press release*, 5.6.08.

FDLR (2008f): *Press release*, 28.7.08.

FDLR (2008g): *Press release*, 4.8.08.

FDLR (2008h): *Press release*, 14.5.08.

FDLR (2008i): *Press release*, 10.7.08.

FDLR (2008j): *Press release*, 26.8.08.

FDLR (2008k): *Press release*, 4.12.08.

FDLR (2008l): *Press release*, 8.12.08.

FDLR (2008m): *Press release*, 30.12.08.

FDLR (2009a): *Press release*, 14.1.09.

FDLR (2009b): *Press release*, 5.2.09.

FDLR (2009c): *Press release*, 11.2.09.

FDLR (2009d): *Press release*, 20.2.09.

FDLR (2009e): *Press release*, 5.3.09.

Franck, Thomas M. (1988): 'Legitimacy in the international system', *The American Journal of International Law* 82(4): 705–59.

Hazan, Jennifer M. (2009): 'From social movement to armed group: a case study from Nigeria', *Contemporary Security Policy* 30(2): 281–300.

Hoffman, Bruce (1998): *Inside Terrorism* (New York: Columbia Press).

Holmes, Georgina (2014): *Women and War in Rwanda: gender, media and the representation of genocide* (London: IB. Tauris).

Human Rights Watch (2009): 'You will be punished: attacks on civilians in Eastern Congo', www.hrw.org/reports/2009/12/13/you-will-be-punished, cited 23.4.10.

International Criminal Court (ICC) Pre-Trial Chamber (2011): 'Situation in the Democratic Republic of Congo in the case of the prosecutor V. Callixte Mbarushimana', Public redacted version, www.icc-cpi.int/iccdocs/doc/doc1286409.pdf, cited 5.1.12.

Miskimmon, Alister, Ben O'Loughlin and Laura Roselle (2012): 'Forging the world: strategic narratives and International Relations', http://newpolcom. rhul.ac.uk / storage / Forging % 20the % 20World % 20Working % 20Paper%20 2012.pdf

Miskimmon, Alister, Ben O'Loughlin and Laura Roselle (eds) (2013): *Forging the World: strategic narratives and International Relations* (Ann Arbor: University of Michigan Press).

Miskimmon, Alister, Ben O'Loughlin and Laura Roselle (2013): *Strategic Narratives: communication power and the New World Order* (London and New York: Routledge).

Omaar, Rakiya (2008): 'The Leadership of Rwandan Armed Groups Abroad with a Focus on the FDLR and RUD/Urunana' (London: Africa Rights).

Patterson, Molly and Kristen Renwick Monroe (1998): 'Narrative in Political Science', *Annual Review of Political Science* 1: 315–31.

Podder, Sukanya (2013): 'Non-state armed groups and stability: reconsidering legitimacy and inclusion', *Contemporary Security Policy* 34(1): 16–39.

Roselle, Laura (2006): *Media and the Politics of Failure: great powers, communications failures and military defeats* (London and New York: Palgrave Macmillan).

Schultz, Richard, Douglas Farah and Itamara Lochard (2004): *Armed Groups: a tier-one priority* (Colorado Springs, Colorado: INSS, USAF Academy).

Sivakumaran, Sandesh (2006): 'Binding armed opposition groups', *The International and Comparative Law Quarterly* 55(2): 369–94.

Stearns, Jason (2009a): 'Dealing with the FDLR: the art of the possible', 5.12.09, http://congosiasa.blogspot.co.uk / 2009 / 12 / dealing - with - fdlr - art - of - possible. html, cited 9.7.13.

Stearns, Jason (2009b) 'Ignace in handcuffs', 18.11.09, http://congosiasa.blogspot. co.uk/2009/11/ignace-in-handcuffs.html, cited 9.7.12.

Stearns, Jason (2012): 'UN Group of experts interview (Part II)', 9.2.12., http:// congosiasa.blogspot.co.uk/2012/02/un-group-of-experts-interview-part-ii.html, cited 14.2.12.

Steffek, Jens (2003): 'The Legitimation of International Governance: A Discourse Approach', *E Journal of International Relations* June, 9(2): 249–75.

United States Department of State (2009): 'Country Reports on Terrorism 2008', http:// www.state.gov/documents/organization/122599.pdf, cited 10.4.12.

United States Department of State (2010): 'Country Reports on Terrorism 2009', http:// www.state.gov/r/pa/prs/ps/2010/08/145737.htm, cited 10.4.12.

9

Re-imagining Ethiopia: from campaign imagery to contemporary art

Wanja Kimani

From early colonial ethnography to charity advertising, Africa has been perceived as a suffering and distant 'other' with imperial campaign traditions reducing the depiction of a continent to famine, corruption and sensationalised violence, collectively framing viewers and the viewed as 'us' and 'them'. Ethiopia in particular came to embody this view as in 1984–5 it was thrust under the pitying eyes of the world by the Live Aid campaign. A resulting backlash against these flat and disempowering images saw many in Ethiopia – particularly among political elites – calling for more assertive depictions of the country, which stressed its claim to be the birthplace of humanity, and its rejection of colonialism. Some of these have trodden dangerously close to nationalistic and overly grandiose depictions of the country, airbrushing the problems and ambiguities that many of its people confront daily.

This chapter explores the delicate path between these two extremes that is navigated by a growing number of artists working in Ethiopia, part of a lively art scene centred on the capital, Addis Ababa. These individuals attempt to capture and project far more nuanced and thoughtful images of the country and the people who live there, exploring difficult questions about history, culture, tradition and the country's relationship with the wider world, but doing so in ways that try to enter into the life-world of those they are depicting instead of turning them into artefacts for external consumption.

With increasing cultural programming in the country and a growing interest in contemporary African art, it is an opportune time to examine the successes and challenges faced by local initiatives such as the Addis Foto Fest and the work of practicing visual artists. In four parts, this chapter explores the creation of images of Ethiopia from the collection of African artefacts and the images of Live Aid, to modern productions of photography and art.

Collecting cultures: from 'primitive' artefacts to starving children

From visual abstraction to sculpture to architecture, African art influenced the course of twentieth century art in Europe. Artists including Pablo Picasso and Paul Gauguin were influenced by so-called 'primitive' forms, which surpassed familiar frameworks and delved into the mystical and religious, presenting artists in Europe with a greater freedom of expression. In the early twentieth century, opportunities to travel increased and sought-after African art and artefacts found their way into private collections in the West in a process Olabisi Silva identifies as 'cultural colonialism' (Silva, 1997: 16). This system of collecting can be likened to that of an empire, which in theory is a collection of countries where governors are collectors and the governed are collected (Elsner and Cardinal, 1994: 2). Cultural objects were collected as a result of their aesthetic virtue, and as a result they were often classified with limited cultural context. These decontextualised objects – prized solely for their beauty – led to a paternalistic approach to the classification of art from the continent, which propagated an idea of Africa as one homogenous country. On one hand, objects of interest were well-preserved for future generations, whilst on the other hand there was a distinct drain that left a cultural vacuum.

In the 1950s and 1960s, a number of young Ethiopian artists had the opportunity to study art abroad. Their experiences, coupled with travelling exhibitions in Europe and America, raised an awareness of Ethiopian art. These students included the renowned artists Skunder Boghossian (1937–2003) and Gebre Kristos Desta (1932–1981) who influenced the face of modern art in Ethiopia. Despite this, scholars still struggled to assign Ethiopian art within their recognised categories and opted to reduce it to folk art or omit the works entirely (Leroy, 1964: 6). The Western value system that they used to assign works restricted the dissemination of knowledge and histories. Complex cultures were reduced to artefacts, which carried minimal context.

A similarly paternalistic approach saw the image of Ethiopia married to famine during the Live Aid campaign in 1985, when the country was reduced to photographs of hungry, snotty and fly-ridden children, with the broader historical, political and social contexts omitted from the depiction. Such images effectively stripped Ethiopians to the position of artefacts.

The 1984–5 famine in Ethiopia affected millions of people in what are today's Ethiopia and Eritrea, sparking international sympathy that led to one of the largest ever charitable fundraising initiatives, said to have launched the modern era of aid (Gill, 2011). The number of deaths has been disputed for a number of reasons including inaccurate census figures for affected areas and the role of counter-insurgency methods of the Ethiopian government against people in rural areas (Africa Watch 1991: 21). The economic structure in Ethiopia is highly centralised, with the government owning all the land and leasing it to citizens and more recently to foreign investors. Although famines in Ethiopia are not a recent phenomenon, this controversial land tenure policy combined with a suppression of civil and economic rights is believed to be a major contributory factor to persistent famine (Kifle, 2009). The policy is criticised for hampering private investment and leaving farmers dependent on subsistence agriculture and vulnerable to crop failure when rain fails to fall.

The Live Aid campaign was spearheaded by the Band Aid Charitable Trust, which was a British charity set up in 1985 'to help relieve hunger and poverty in Ethiopia and the surrounding countries' (Band Aid Charitable Trust, 2011). Televised campaign imagery, celebrity endorsement and Live Aid concerts organised by Bob Geldof and Midge Ure 'raised the international profile and successfully raised much-needed money that provided food, shelter, medical supplies and water equipment to famine victims' (Geldof, 1991: 4). A double concert, Live Aid, staged in London and Philadelphia on 13 July 1985 was televised globally and attracted an audience of 1.9 billion that felt empowered by their role in changing the world (Jones, 2005). However, concerns over whether the funded programmes actually benefited those people worst affected and the transferability of skills and knowledge learnt brought to question the sustainability of the campaign (Jenden 1991: 7). In particular, one legacy of the campaign was the portrait of famine that had been painted to provoke sympathy and encourage financial giving. This contributed to aligning an image of Ethiopia with images of emaciated children in the minds of international audiences.

Twenty years later, the 2005 British campaign Make Poverty History signalled another heroic ambition to stamp out global poverty. Despite efforts early on to distance the campaign from the familiar imagery of emaciated African children and famine landscapes, the campaign followed the imperial nature of campaign traditions and Africanised poverty (Harrison, 2010: 392). Musicians Bob Geldof and Bono, mistakenly seen by the public to represent the campaign (Ibid: 403), staged ten concerts internationally and gathered public support, which replicated the empowerment and exhilaration felt during the 1985 concerts. Bono claimed to be advocating for Africans who he believed 'have no voice at all.... They haven't asked me to represent them. It's cheeky but I hope they're glad I do and in God's order of things they're most important' (quoted in O'Neill, 2005). As a musician, Bono is apparently removed from the political sphere, but with a large fan base, he maintains access to public support, key individuals and institutions granted from his philanthropic interventions. In his biography of Bono, Browne states that 'for nearly three decades as a public figure, Bono has been ... amplifying elite discourses, advocating ineffective solutions, patronising the poor and kissing the arses of the rich and powerful' (Browne, quoted in Monbiot, 2013).

The Make Poverty History campaign was a coalition of campaign agencies with different aims and agendas. By nature, campaigns are framed in order to generate imagery and moral appeals to drive their ambitions. William Gamsom identifies three distinct frames that campaigns fall into, including the injustice frame, which aims to correct mistakes of the past; the agency frame, which presents the campaign as feasible and realistic; and the identity frame (1995: 91). This final distinction, the identity frame, constructs a 'we' and 'them' and is integral to the depiction of famine and Ethiopia in both Live Aid and Make Poverty History campaigns. Although the separate NGOs and aid agencies may have independently produced their own more 'involved' images, the campaign maintained a collective image of poverty, which produced an abstract and hollow view of poverty synonymous with Ethiopia (Harrison 2010: 397). Stereotypical images are justified when they produce the required emotions or move people to give their money or time to the respective cause. The resulting effects are temporarily disturbing and cease to exist when one averts one's eyes (Sealy, 2008: 27). Charitable organisations and aid agencies fall prey to this form of visual exploitation as a result of objectives such as maximising donations for the given cause.

By failing to question the underlying issues, the image that is projected is uninformed and the solutions remain unidentified and therefore, unattainable. Poverty is not the sole concern in Ethiopia, but is connected to unmet basic needs, which are considered central to 'unlocking the potential of people to deal with their own problems, to hold the authorities to account and to harness their resources in the most effective way' (Bekele, 2008). The legacy of such campaigns, however noble the initial intention, places an unshakable stamp on the individuals and nations featured in the images. The meanings within images get lost when visual exploitation is fostered and promoted. Like the disembodied African art in foreign collections, the aid industry creates and projects decontextualised images, reducing Ethiopia's people to artefacts. These images portray people stuck in an unchanging past, summed up by Michael Beurke's 'Biblical famine' analogy.

It is possible, even as an outsider, to create richer and better contextualised images. In order to do so, Mikhail Bakhtin suggests that one must be able to locate oneself outside of one's own understanding and question the culture one wishes to understand. In this way, 'a dialogic encounter of two cultures does not result in mixing or merging ... each retains its own unity and *open* totality, but they are mutually enriched' (1986: 7). In such a case, the image would not necessarily need to provoke sympathy, but rather engage on a level that questions the viewer's own humanity and encourages a relationship between the viewer and the viewed. The idea of a mutual exchange is central to altering the image of Ethiopia and I argue that contemporary artists and photographers working in Ethiopia are doing this by contributing more nuanced and alternative perspectives on social realities. These depictions can offer a rich corrective to the images presented by international media and aid organisations.

Photography in Ethiopia

The story of photography in Ethiopia is one of constant cultural exchange, with early experiments initiated largely by incomers, but slowing finding local consumers and audiences who adapted the art form for their own cultural practices and uses. Photography in Ethiopia can be traced back to 1859 when Henry Stern, a German Protestant missionary to the Ethiopian Jews visited Ethiopia with his camera. However, he soon displeased the then ruler Emperor Tewedros II and was imprisoned (Pankhurst, 1992: 234). During the reign of Emperor Yohannes IV (1872–89) and more significantly Menelik II (King of Shewa, 1865–89 and Emperor of Ethiopia, 1889–1913), photography played a major part in the life of the ruling class. Menelik II arranged for three Swiss craftsmen to come to his court to assist with modernisation of the country. Alfred Ilg, who served as technician and diplomatic adviser, was also a keen photographer (Pankhurst, 1976: 879; 1992: 234). Many foreign photographers who visited the country at this time photographed Menelik and his courtiers.

Photography remained in the hands of the nobility for decades to come. A custom that increased the medium's popularity among the nobility was its use during funeral processions. It had been customary for mourners to display an effigy of the deceased together with their valuable items. With the advent of photography, the effigy was replaced by a photograph, which mourners held high above their heads (Pankhurst 1992: 234). An example of this was evident at the funeral of Ras Makonnen in 1906, when it is reported that priests from churches in Addis Ababa spent the day mourning beside his portrait (Pankhurst and Gerard 1996: 30). This particular use, although limited to the aristocracy, increased the appeal of photography and it became widely used for formal occasions and celebrations such as weddings. Photographs were usually highly composed with the sitters in official dress. In group photographs, sitters were organised in hierarchical order in order to distinguish their relative importance and various relationships (Ibid: 25).

Greater accessibility and popularity of more informal photographs came when photographic studios opened their doors to the public. Bedros Boyadjian, an Armenian who arrived with an Armenian priest from Jerusalem in 1905, set up a studio in Addis Ababa. The studio was subsequently run by his son Hayjaz and then by another son, Tony, who served as court photographer to Haile Selassie (Ibid: 35). In 1909, Levon 'Leon' Yazedjian, an Armenian from Turkey, also set up a studio in Addis Ababa. This was followed by an Indian from Gujarat, G. Mody, who was based in Harar, who travelled to Addis Ababa in 1910 and founded a studio in the increasingly popular Ras Makonnen Avenue. In addition, Alex Dorflinger, a member of the Austro-Hungarian mission found himself stranded in Addis Ababa by the outbreak of the First World War. With the assistance of French resident, M. Stevenin, who provided him with accommodation as well as the necessary materials, he established a photographic studio. Outside of Addis Ababa, Megherditch Reissan, another Armenian, set up a studio in Dire Dawa (Pankhurst, 1976: 935, 952).

These studios provided photographs to the masses. Particularly popular were 'minute photographs', which were cheaper and increased the photography market further. While urban populations embraced photography eagerly, those living in the country still viewed it with suspicion (Pankhurst, 1992: 234–5). With little knowledge or explanation of the process of image creation, the medium may have appeared to have the kind of mystical qualities which had so far been reserved for religious practices. However, with the advent of the aforementioned 'minute photographs' in rural areas, a growing knowledge and its increasingly common place within society may have shifted views, making it more acceptable. A century later, photographic studios line the streets of Ethiopia's cities and can be found in even remote towns. Poses are more informal; yet remain constructed with a choice of backgrounds and props and endless possibilities provided by digital photography software packages. Groups of friends, families and couples often use studios when marking special occasions such as birthdays, graduations and almost always during wedding ceremonies where the bride and groom will have photographs taken and printed prior to the wedding day for distribution during the ceremony as wallet-sized prints.

It is against this backdrop that Aida Muluneh initiated the first edition of the Addis Foto Fest in 2010, and the second edition in 2012. A daughter of Ethiopia by birth and the daughter of the globe by circumstance, Muluneh's work has been guided by African-American photographers. It was during her participation in the Bamako Biennale 2007 in Dakar, that she found commonality between photographers in Africa and in the Diaspora (Muluneh 29.4.11 interview). The first Addis Foto Fest in Addis Ababa in 2010 presented a long-awaited opportunity for global discussion on the image of Africa and its Diaspora.

The second Foto Fest, in 2012, was much larger in scope and included international exhibitions, workshops, screenings and panel discussions throughout the city at various cultural institutions, local galleries and other venues. The opening exhibition, 'Addis Transformation' featured six Ethiopian photographers including Belete Tekele, Yemanie Gebremedhin, Goitom Habtemariam, Mulugeta Ayene, Samuel Habtab and Addis Belete, diaspora photographers Abate Damte and Addis-based Samuel Taye presenting works alongside international photographers Yo-Yo Gonthier, Alessandro Gandolfi, Karim Dridi, Kyle LaMere and Addis-based photographer Mario di Bari. Collectively, they provided a multi-faceted visual archive of the impacts of urbanisation on society and the radically transforming urban landscape. These extended from remote cultures in the south of the country, to urban fashion, and included intergenerational images by Belete Tekele who captured the city over twenty years ago alongside his son, Addis Belete who presented current panoramic images ranging from road constructions to thriving market scenes.

The Addis Foto Fest aimed to bring photography, which had yet to be fully accepted as an art form, to the masses in the same way that photographic studios brought to the public an activity that was once seen as restricted to the aristocracy. Several thousand people attended the exhibitions, aspiring photographers participated in workshops and portfolio reviews with established photographers, and new audiences found their way into galleries and cultural institutions for the first time (Muluneh, 2013).

Of particular interest is the work of Samuel Habtab. In the six months leading up to the Addis Foto Fest, he was one of a number of photographers who were assigned sections of the city and asked to document the rapid infrastructural development. With scaffolding and roadworks a fixed aspect of the cityscape for those navigating their way through Addis Ababa, these photographs provided a commentary on how these changes are affecting everyday life. Habtab combines his investigative skills as a photojournalist for *Fortune* newspaper in Addis Ababa with a creative intuition to provide images that explore the process of society's regeneration as a result of urbanisation, modernisation and socio-economic developments. Unlike his predecessors who found it easier to take photographs in urban settings compared to rural areas, he states that people in the city are often difficult to photograph, frequently demanding various forms of identification and accreditation before allowing him to take photographs (Habtab interview 25.2.13). It appears that people are more often suspicious when the photographer is Ethiopian whereas foreigners who were assumed to be tourists were less threatening. The curiosity of foreigners is perhaps more understandable and easier to accommodate because of its fleeting nature compared to the curiosity of one's counterparts, which can be seen as more invasive because of an unspoken yet shared understanding. There is also prohibition of photography in government buildings and in the interests of security, bags are checked for cameras and laptops prior to entry.

In figure 9.1, Habtab explores the tension that residents of Addis Ababa feel, pulled between increasing modernisation and tradition. The elderly man pictured observes the dramatic changes in his immediate surroundings, yet remains defiant in his grip on his home, which is subject to be demolished in order for infrastructural developments to take place. The man is placed in the centre of the frame as our attention is led

9.1 *Untitled* by Samuel Habtab, 2012.

to his eyes. He gazes softly ahead of him, unaware of the photographer, seemingly deep in thought. The image, which immortalises this period of transformation in Addis, speaks in a delicate but powerful way to the experience of many that are facing eviction from homes, schools and small businesses.

The investigative, yet humane manner in which Habtab presents this ongoing reality carries a delicate truth that does not dehumanise the subject, but lends an understanding based on shared experience. There is a need to nurture such an angle, particularly in the field of photography in a digital age where images are captured and distributed almost instantaneously in an insatiable market fed on mass communication, production and consumption.

Habtab feels a responsibility as an Ethiopian photographer to shed light on Ethiopia's rich history and natural resources, among other things, in order to counter previous associations with famine and poverty (Habtab interview 25.2.13). Through workshops, portfolio reviews and panel discussions, the Addis Foto Fest programme provided a much-needed platform for national and international audiences to contextualise image production within its historical and spatial contexts. Workshops were facilitated by leading educators, curators and practitioners including John Fleetwood, Head of Market Photo Workshop and Elvira Dyangani Ose, the Curator of International Art at Tate Modern, as well as photo-journalists Frederic Lafargue and Nick Danziger who brought years of experience to those establishing themselves in the industry.

The Addis Foto Fests were both largely funded with support from European sources, a situation that has generated difficult questions about its future. The first is the question of future financial viability, given the way in which recession in Europe is likely to cause cutbacks to all arts sponsorship. But the reliance on European funding is more than a financial dependency. Funding from national bodies often carries national agendas and conditions that shape programs in the interests of the particular funding body. Priorities and ambitions are dependent on the terms agreed upon with the funding body. In a level playing field these terms may be negotiated for the benefit of both parties. However, in many African countries with little or no support in terms of a cultural budget, the ball remains in the court of the funding body. Katharina von Ruckteschell of the Goethe Institut in South Africa explained Germany's increasing budget and stable grip on culture in Africa as a maintaining a foothold on the continent where other Western powers are being 'usurped' by the Chinese (Oforiatta-Ayim, 2012). Such a position begs the question of what Germany hopes to achieve by steering culture on the continent, and perhaps more curiously, what the cultural landscape on the continent would look like if China did decide to include culture alongside infrastructural development.

Drawing on the experiences of the Addis Foto Fest, it is clear that the value of images is not always enticing for local businesses and sponsors. This may alter when the role of photography and the inherent power of images is realised, challenged and owned on a national level. By presenting engaging and subversive images, photographers within Ethiopia and initiatives such as the Addis Foto Fest go some way towards making this a reality, but as long as foreign funding plays a significant role, this may be more difficult to achieve.

Visual arts in Ethiopia

Art extends beyond the confines of ethnography and grants access into other cultures, often acting as a 'museum without walls' (Malraux, 1947: 7). Contemporary Ethiopian art reflects realities facing individuals and offers a more tangible way of building understanding and sharing knowledge than imperial campaign traditions. Whilst African nations at the brink of independence found common ground in pan-African theories that aimed to revise imposed histories of colonialist powers, Ethiopia escaped this trajectory, a fact which helped establish it as the political capital of Africa. Emperor Haile Selassie with the then Foreign Minister Ketema Yifru played key roles in the establishment of the Organisation of African Unity in 1963, and today Addis Ababa still hosts the headquarters of the African Union and other notable institutions. Furthermore, the tricolour flag, which has origins in the Ethiopian Solomonic Dynasty, was the first national flag in Africa and inspired many flags that emerged from post-independent African nations (Ethiopian Millennium, 2011). Pan-African theories not only united African nations in reclaiming their own histories, but also forged a collective identity through struggle and liberation (Njami 2005: 54). This shared identity allows for further investigation through post colonial theories and criticism. However, the unique experience of Ethiopia presents a hurdle that distances contemporary Ethiopian art from beyond the comfortable confines of post colonial art theory, which can lead to its collective omission.

At the same time, Ethiopian artists can fall into the trap of using art to ignite the fires of Ethio-centric nationalism (Muluneh interview, 29.4.11). Locally-grown heroic, historically static images, or images that support political elites can be as disempowering and flattening as the imperialist and campaign imagery of the West. As Muluneh suggests, artists need to explore their affinity with their heritage and create work that represents honest accounts of humanity, including hunger, displacement and loss.

These are the issues that many Addis-based artists are confronting in their work. The support for contemporary artists stretches across local galleries and artist-run spaces such as Asni Gallery, Modern Art Museum/Gebre Kristos Desta Centre, Lela Art Gallery, Zoma Contemporary Art Centre Addis/Harla and Netsa Art Village, which facilitate a vibrant artistic community and support group and solo shows, premiering new work by local and international artists. In addition, various cultural institutions in the city including the Goethe Institut, Italian Cultural Institute, Alliance Francaise and the British Council provide cultural programming such as workshops, screenings, exhibitions and talks that support local artists' practices.

In a solo show entitled 'Beyond' (Italian Cultural Institute, 2009) artist Behailu Bezabih presented five collages made from newspaper found in people's homes, which had been destroyed to make way for road constructions in the city. He explores the way in which desired models of modernity, particularly infrastructure infiltrate everyday life (Georgis, 2010: 2). The view of modernity as a force that threatens non-Western traditions considers modernity to be exclusively Western (Mercer, 2008: 16). However, his work deconstructs identity; in particular its construction and loss.

Historically, there have been two related trends in Ethiopian cultural tradition; a keen interest in foreign models, as seen in the seventeenth century castles built by Indians and decorated by local artists in Gondar under the instruction of Emperor Fasilidas; and a firm commitment to established patterns (Chojnacki, 1989: vii; Pankhurst and Ingrams, 1988: 11). Escaping colonialism, as Muluneh points out, does not mean that Ethiopian art has not been influenced by Western concepts. A number of established artists were educated in Europe including Gebre Kristos Desta and Skunder Boghossian, both of whom later returned to teach in the former Alle School of Fine Arts and Design. Founded in 1958, it remains the oldest art school in Africa and is praised for developing the appreciation of art as a profession and also acting as a collector for valuable works (Tadesse, 1991: 3).

With a relatively small intake every year, the school provides an opportunity for students to focus on developing their practice, collaborate with other artists on different projects and learn from experienced teachers (Zeru, interview 30.4.11). In 2010, the art school joined the Yared Music School, and Theatrical Art Department under the newly formed Skunder Boghossian College of Visual and Performing Arts (Addis Ababa University, 2011). Although artists from different parts of the country have the opportunity to meet and transfer ideas, there is a lack of international exchange with those outside the country. This presents a void in the artistic dialogue enjoyed by many art students in Europe and America, who have professional networks and opportunities such as student exchange schemes.

The benefit of such exchanges can influence both national and international visual dialogue. An opportunity to learn from other artists allows exposure to alternative cultures and histories and allows for artists to engage with global issues and realise the similarities that transcend borders. Furthermore, when combined with a lack of marketing and post-art education professional practice, the visibility of contemporary Ethiopian art in the global art market remains unrepresentative of the volume of artistic practice within the country. This isolation brings to light the issue of authenticity because in a 'global world with fading traditions and borrowed ideas', the question of authenticity is never far behind (Muluneh, interview 29.4.11). By questioning authenticity, one must believe that tradition does not change. The idea that art from Africa needs to be rooted in tradition is naïve and unrealistic (Silva, 1997: 16), yet continues to influence wider audiences and collectors. Contemporary realities on the continent, including the increase in internet access, have contributed to an increased volume of information and exchange of ideas for many people living in cities. Tradition is subject to change; culture is fluid and evolves over time.

Digitisation and globalisation can be ambiguous. Trends show that internet and mobile phone penetration favours those in urban centres who are able to afford and access technology. Furthermore, the government monopoly on telecommunications means that Ethiopia has one of the lowest rates of internet and mobile phone penetration in Africa. Between 2000 and 2009, there was 0.5 per cent penetration, which translates to approximately 360,000 users out of a possible 85,237,388 (Freedom House, 2011: 1). Despite these figures, graduates from the Alle School of Fine Arts and Design and practicing artists are working in the midst of a digital age with ease. This generation of artists, living and working in the city, are able to navigate the chaos that comes with urban dwelling and retain the required distance that makes it possible to comment on one's surroundings, in much the same way Bakhtin suggests that one must locate oneself on the periphery in order to further one's understanding of a culture.

Contemporary Ethiopian art

Contemporary artists capturing images of Ethiopia explore themes that challenge nostalgia and inside/outsideness. They refuse to simplify or sanitise often painful themes about identity, belonging or the country's relationship with the wider world. Here I discuss four examples of works that provide thoughtful explorations of their locale, communicated through an international visual language that goes beyond the local and into the global.

In 2011, Zacharias Abubeker visited Ethiopia for the first time with his father. Things were vastly different from the United States where he grew up, and the urbanism that lay ahead of him was unexpected. He embraced the hospitality and warmth in a place where he 'had roots but more on a figurative level rather than a professional or practical level' (Abubeker, personal communication 11.6.13). In Addis Ababa, much like his experience in other cities, he is perceived as a foreigner, regardless of his cultural awareness or how much Amharic he speaks. His series *Ferengi* is a pictorial documentation of his initial relation to Ethiopia:

> Ferengi, meaning foreigner or someone of European descent – white. My father told me it was a term of endearment but I began to think otherwise. They are pointing me out as one who does not belong. Likely, no matter how much information I can tout about the country or its people, I will always be somewhat of an outsider. Strange to think that in the U.S. my race is in more of an ambiguous state, while in Ethiopia, I am not quite black enough (Abubeker, 2011).

Whilst navigating between the two places, he accepts the norms of each respective community. In the US, he is a source of first-hand information for fellow Americans on the state of Ethiopia. He sees it as his responsibility to change how Ethiopia is viewed from the outside. He regrets that some 'people still think there's no food in Ethiopia ... it seems really silly, but these are actual opinions [from] people I've met' (Abubeker, personal communication 11.6.13). He hopes his work will open people up to the current realities.

Figure 9.2 was taken during the photographer's first visit to Ethiopia, during a twelve–hour bus ride from the capital city to Harar. He identifies 'dual aspects of voyeurism' in the image whereby those on the outside, the children in the rural setting, are equally interested in the travelers inside the bus (Abubeker, personal communication 14.8.13). Various perspectives are captured in the frame; the scene outside of local children examining the bus, the view of those photographing outside, the boy to the bottom right of the frame, and that of the photographer. Abubeker sees this image as an embodiment of his 'initial desires to understand the country of Ethiopia ... placed inside ... on the ground' in order to foster understanding of daily realities (Ibid). Being on the outside of our own norms, as Bakhtin suggests, allows us to interpret and

9.2 *Untitled* by Zacharias Abubeker, 2011.

question the culture that we want to understand. In Abubeker's case, his position has both positive and negative outcomes, allowing him entry into a culture that finds it difficult to accept him as wholly one of its own. He uses this position to his advantage, discovering the nuances of people around him with the openness of an outsider and in turn learning about himself and his heritage. His work, which captures the social sentiments of those he observes, becomes a living and transforming archive that he can delve into to continually learn about Ethiopia and his dynamic relationship with the people who live there.

Through painting, local artist Kebreab Demeke shares in the everyday challenges brought on by a lack of sustainable development and effective environmental policies that lead to water shortages, pollution and soil erosion. Since graduating from the Alle School of Fine Arts and Design, Demeke has been preoccupied with the image of 'jerry cans', which are commonly used to transport water. Figure 9.3 shows 'jerry cans' in different sizes and colours from various perspectives. In reality, they are most commonly yellow, and are at times recycled cooking oil containers. His depiction appears to represent the people. The 'jerry cans' form a disorderly, yet recognisable queue in the same way that people may gather whilst waiting for something that might come, rather than form a queue for something that is certain. Water shortages affect those in rural areas as well as large cities. Faults in valves and

9.3 *Untitled* by Kebreab Demeke, 2011.

pipes inside bore holes as well as inappropriate pumping mechanisms are to blame with government funds allocated to address the problems (Capital, 2013). Evident in figure 9.3, the resulting abstract paintings are large and arresting. Bold brushwork covers large canvases with a delicate intuition that suggests that he is simultaneously observing from the periphery, watching as people queue for water, as well as being engaged in the act of waiting. Although a local, Demeke also explores the idea of outside/inside; his work strongly conveys the impression that the artist is always balanced between the two, simultaneously onlooker and participant.

Robel Temesgen explores the capture of the consumption of images of his own nation, and of Africa as a whole. His video *FotograF* (figure 9.4) provides us with a playful yet poignant look at the depiction of children. The eight-minute film documents the reaction of children and their teacher in Harla, a village near Dire Dawa. The artist records the participants' reaction to a camera. Instinctively posing for a still image, the participants jostle, obscuring other participants, trying to get to the foreground of the picture and inevitably becoming restless whilst they wait for the long-delayed click of the camera. The work

9.4 Still from *FotograF* by Robel Temesgen, 2011.

has developed into a series. In 'Fotograf III' the artist performs the same exercise with his students from Addis Ababa University. Their relationship to the camera appears to be more natural. Young women pose for the camera in the same way they would in one of the many photographic studios in the city. Some of the young men are playful, attracting attention to themselves as they might in the street. Although the environments are vastly different, from rural to urban, the actions of the participants are surprisingly similar. The duration of the work, which is determined by the diminishing figures from the frame, is similar at approximately eight minutes. It could be reflective of our general ability to concentrate, or could signify a similarity between people that transcends their environment and speaks to our relationship to images of ourselves and our dynamic relationship to the camera.

Reflecting on the urban experience, artist Helen Zeru's photographs capture the city's moments of frustration, ambiguity, doubts and certainties (Zeru interview, 30.4.11). It is believed the city still represents a utopia for a younger generation (Njami, 2005: 151), a place where everything is possible, where foreigners and strangers meet and opportunities stretch as far as one's individual threshold. Photography allows Zeru to make sense of these complexities, offering her a medium that enables her to reflect on both intimate concerns and those of the world around her.

In figure 9.5, she captures manual labourers in Konso digging the base for the first hospital in the town. Her current work laments the loss of her mother following an excavation of her burial site, which is reflected by the action of the men in *Hole Diggers*. Through a visual exploration of mortality and memory, Zeru intuitively captures not only a personal history, but also that of a nation often caught in the clutches of romanticised nostalgia as the only nation in Africa that escaped European colonialism. The fragility of memory, its openness to questions and inability to answer, allows for the creative exploration Zeru does through intimate reportage.

Conclusion

Global perceptions of Ethiopia may shift when images produced in Ethiopia from honest explorations are more widely recognised. This shift does not ignore the history of Ethiopia, which inspired many African nations in the anti-colonial movement, but actively refers to it and addresses its difficulties and ambiguities. The historical defiance to imperial rule in Ethiopia was a source of inspiration not only in the pan-African movement of the 1950s and 1960s, but also the

9.5 *Hole Diggers* by Helen Zeru, 2011.

African-American Civil Rights Movement in the early nineteenth century when leaders looked forward to the time when 'Ethiopia shall
stretch forth her hands; when the sun of liberty shall beam resplend-
ent on the whole African race; and its genial influences promote the
luxuriant growth and knowledge' (Royster, 2007: 24). This historical
appreciation and reverence can still be seen as Addis Ababa maintains
itself in a strategic diplomatic position within the Horn of Africa today.

If balanced with a mutual exchange, the influence of Ethiopian art
could benefit not only the growth of contemporary African art, but
art as a whole. Devoid of Ethio-centric nationalism, contemporary
Ethiopian art has the ability to probe contemporary realities and identity with a rich and intuitive visual language. It remains vitally important to document the changes that have taken place and continue to
occur in art introduced to Ethiopia, in the form of an accessible archive.
This would benefit present day visual art practice and future generations
too, leading to a fuller understanding of Ethiopia. Archives capture
images as they are made, and, as Mercer states, they do not allow us to
sentimentalise, a danger that can occur with works that focus strongly
on remembrance and memory. In addition, it is vital that Africans take
a firmer hand in the production and collection of such images. '[I]f this
history is written and produced by the West, the future image of Africa
will never change' (Mercer, personal communication, 5.11.10).

The role of an artist in society depends on that society's relationship to art. Nations that recognise the inherent nature of art to record, subvert and alter a nation's economic, social and cultural life and produce images that can be projected to the wider world are likely to understand the role of an artist in society. In Ethiopia, this role is yet to be fully realised and acknowledged (Zeru interview, 30.4.11). The role of photography, particularly in photojournalism, is an optimistic platform for altering the image of Ethiopia, if those who have previously monopolised it open it up to skilled Ethiopian photographers. Ethiopian artists appear to be in a position to define their role on a national and international stage and a number of emerging and established artists are already paving the way for greater understanding, exchange and appreciation.

References

Abubeker, Zacharias (2011): http://zachabubeker.com, 1.3.11, cited 30.6.13.

Abubeker, Zacharias (2013): Personal communication, 11.6.13.

Abubeker, Zacharias (2013): Personal communication, 14.8.13.

Addis Ababa University (2011): 'Fine Arts and Design', www.aau.edu.et/cpva/academics/ale-school-of-fine-arts-and-design/, cited 12.7.11.

Africa Watch (1991): 'Evil days: thirty years of war and famine in Ethiopia' (New York: Human Rights Watch).

Bakhtin, Mikhail (1986): 'Response to a question from the Novy Mir editorial staff (1970)', in Caryl Emerson and Michael Holquist (eds), *Speech Genres and Other Late Essays*, trans. by V. Austin McGee (University of Texas Press).

Band Aid Charitable Trust (2011): www.live8live.com/bat, cited 12.7.11.

Bekele, Daniel (2008): 'Daniel Bekele speaking at CIVICUS World Assembly, 18–21 June 2008. Glasgow, Scotland', http://hub.witness.org/en/CIVICUS/08/DanielBekele, cited 12.5.11.

Browne, Harry (2013): *The Frontman: Bono (in the Name of Power)* (London: Verso).

Capital (2013): 'Water shortages felt in Addis', http://www.ethiopiainvestor.com/index.php?option=com_content&task=view&id=2589&Itemid=88, cited 19.8.13.

Chojnacki, Stanislaw (1989): 'Proceedings from the First International Conference on the History of Ethiopian Art: Warburg Institute of the University of London, 21–22 October 1986' (London: The Pindar Press).

Eagleton, Terry (2013): '*The Frontman: Bono (In the Name of Power)* by Harry Browne – review', 26.6.13, http://www.guardian.co.uk/books/2013/jun/26/frontman-bono-harry-browne-review, cited 30.6.13.

Elsner, John and Roger Cardinal (1994): *The Cultures of Collecting* (London: Reaktion Books).

Ethiopian Millenium (2011): 'Questions and Answers', http://www. ethiopianmillennium.com/qanda.html, cited 12.7.11.

Freedom House (2011), 'Freedom on the Net', http://abbaymedia.com/News/? p=6658., cited 12.7.11.

Gamsom, William (1995): 'Constructing social protest' in Hank Johnston (ed.), *Social Movements and Culture* (London: UCL Press).

Geldof, Bob (1991): 'With love from Band Aid', http://www.live8live.com/docs/ bat-withlovefrombandaid%20.pdf, cited 3.5.11.

Georgis, Elizabeth (2010): 'Reason and emotion by Behailu Bezabih', exhibition catalogue for Goethe Institut, 11–25.11.10 (Goethe Institut: Addis Ababa).

Gill, Peter (2011): 'Food crisis in the horn of Africa: international response driven by image of Africa', Oxford University Press Blog, 8.7.11., http://blog. oup.com/2010/07/live-aid2/, cited 14.4.11.

Habtab, Samuel (2013): Interview with author, 25.2.13.

Harrison, Graham (2010): 'The Africanization of poverty: a retrospective in make poverty history', *African Affairs* 109(436): 391–418.

How To Archive Yourself (2011): BBC Radio 4, 11.4.11.

Jenden, Penny (1991): 'With Love from Band Aid', www.live8live.com/docs/ bat-withlovefrombandaid%20.pdf, cited 3.5.11.

Jones, Graham (2005): 'Live Aid 1985: a day of magic', CNN, 6.7.05, http:// edition.cnn.com/2005/SHOWBIZ/Music/07/01/liveaid.memories/index.html, cited 10.5.11.

Kifle, Elias (2009): 'Advocacy for Ethiopia holds press conference in Copenhagen', *Ethiopian Review*, 2.12.09, http://www.ethiopianreview. com/content/11694, cited 7.5.11.

Leroy, Jules (1964): *Ethiopian painting in the late Middle Ages and during the Gondar Dynasty*, trans. by C. Pace (London: Merlin Press).

Malraux, André (1947): *The Psychology of Art (Volume One): museum without walls* (London: Secker and Warburg): 7.

Mercer, Kobena (2008): *Exiles, Diasporas and Strangers* (London: Institute of New International Visual Arts).

Mercer, Kobena (2010): Personal communication, 5.11.10.

Monbiot, George (2013): 'Elevation', Monbiot, 17.6.13, www.monbiot. com/2013/06/17/elevation/, cited 20.6.13.

Muluneh, Aida (2011): Interview with author, 29.4.11.

Muluneh, Aida (2013): 'What happened during the Addis Foto Fest #2?: interview with Aida Muluneh, director of the Addis Foto Fest, preceded, by a short review of festival by Marian Nur Goni', *Africultures*, www.africultures.com/ php/index.php?nav=article&no=11453, cited 16.10.13.

Njami, Simon (2005): 'Africa remix: contemporary art of a continent', Catalogue of a travelling exhibition held at the Hayward Gallery, London, 10.2–17.4.05 (London: Hayward Gallery Publishing).

Oforiatta-Ayim, Nana (2012): 'A cultural encyclopedia', *Kaleidoscope* 15 (Summer 2012), http://kaleidoscope-press.com/issue-content/art-in-africa- words-by-nana-oforiatta-ayim/, cited 1.11.12.

O'Neill, Brendan (2005): 'What do pop stars know about the world?', BBC, 28.6.05, http://news.bbc.co.uk/1/hi/magazine/4629851.stm, cited 14.4.11.

Pankhurst, Richard (1976): 'The genesis of photography in Ethiopia and the Horn of Africa', *The British Journal of Photography* 8:878–957.

Pankhurst, Richard (1992): 'The political image: the impact of the camera in an ancient independent African state', in Elizabeth Edwards (ed.), *Anthropology and Photography 1860–1920* (Yale University Press. London: New Haven and Royal Anthropological Institute): 234–41.

Pankhurst, Richard and Denis Gerard (1996): *Ethiopia Photographed* (London: Kegan Paul International).

Pankhurst, Richard and Leila Ingrams (1988): *Ethiopia Engraved: an illustrated catalogue of engravings by foreign travellers from 1681 to 1900* (London: Kegan Paul International).

Rohter, Larry (2012): 'In Europe, where art is life, ax falls on public financing', *New York Times*, 24.3.12, http://www.nytimes.com/2012/03/25/world/europe/the-euro-crisis-is-hurting-cultural-groups.html?pagewanted=all&_r =0, cited 29.1.13.

Royster, Paul (2007): 'An oration on the abolition of the slave trade; delivered in the African Church in the city of New York, 1 January 1808' (Lincoln: University of Nebraska).

Sealy, Mark (2008): 'Disposable people: documenting contemporary global slavery', catalogue of a travelling exhibition held at the Southbank Centre, London, 26.9–9.11.08 (London: Hayward Publishing).

Silva, Olabisi (1997): 'Africa95: Cultural Colonialism or Cultural Celebration', in Katy Deepwell (ed.), *Art Criticism and Africa* (London: Saffron Books).

Tadesse, Taye (1991): *Short Biographies of Some Ethiopian Artists, 1869–1957*, second edition (Addis Ababa: Kuraz).

Zeru, Helen (2011): Interview with author, 30.4.11.

10

Silent bodies and dissident vernaculars: representations of the body in South African fiction and film

Lizzy Attree

Since 1999 South African writers have written about HIV/AIDS in their work, often avoiding any depiction of the 'sick' body, particularly the sick male body in relation to the HIV infection. The trajectory of the representation of HIV/AIDS in South African literature has crept closer and closer towards the personal in the last twelve years. There has also been a parallel movement towards the visual, towards descriptive representations of the body in pain. Silence, invisibility and the absence of the dead are slowly being eroded by narrative descriptions of suffering in fiction and at times explicit visual representations in South African film. Recent fiction such as Magona's *Beauty's Gift* (2008) and Kgebetli Moele's *The Book of the Dead* (2009) provide detailed descriptions of physical decline.

Literary fiction offers a counterpoint to sensationalist and spectacular photographic TV and newspaper images that dominated the representation of the HIV-positive person's body in the early years of coverage of the epidemic. However the film *Yesterday* (2004) is unusual in its graphic depiction of the suffering (heterosexual) male body and films such as *District 9* (2009) can also be read as a dystopian depiction of a future South Africa. All four examples, two literary texts and two feature films, provide prolonged contemplative spaces in which to consider subjectivity and the other, and how the representation and description of the external body can be counterbalanced in art, literary and filmic narrative.

In previous work (Attree, 2007) I have traced the development of representations of HIV/AIDS in literature in South African fiction. One of the most significant writers in South Africa is Sindiwe Magona who published the short story 'A State of Outrage' in 1999. Magona's fiction has consistently focused on HIV/AIDS in the last twelve years. Her second short story published in *Nobody Ever Said Aids* in 2004 is titled 'Leave-taking' referencing the funerary farewell which opens and closes the story. As in her most famous work *Mother to Mother*,

Magona's central character in 'Leave-taking' is a mother who tragically faces losing all of her adult children to HIV/AIDS. The space of death is expanded from the funerals featured in both her early short stories, to the funerals and death bed scenes of the extended narrative provided by the novel *Beauty's Gift* published in 2008.

Set primarily in Gugulethu, but also in and around Cape Town and the southern suburbs, *Beauty's Gift* begins with the eponymous heroine Beauty's funeral. The narrative then ranges back and forth over six weeks between the present in September 2002 and the past in order to explain how Beauty and her friends reached the point at which she gives them her gift:

> Toward the end, Beauty had had no peace at all. As far as Amanda was concerned, Beauty had just escaped from hell. Her mind spooled back to the moment in time she saw as the beginning of this whole sad mess, when Beauty had bestowed on her such a wonderful gift: 'Ukhule!' she had said, 'May you grow old!' (22)

Beauty's Gift builds on 'A State of Outrage' in which the scope and implications of the AIDS epidemic in South Africa are set out: '[B]y the year 2000 ... not a family in South Africa will be without one member who is either HIV-positive or suffering from AIDS' (125–6).

Beauty's Gift was Magona's fourth return to the subject of HIV/AIDS.[1] Once again using the public platform of a funeral to broach these views, the similarities of the message are striking: 'That is how it is going to be with AIDS. Very soon, all our families will have at least one person infected with HIV. One, if we are lucky' (85). As in 'A State of Outrage' the speaker, a community leader, effectively incorporates the awareness of danger, culpability, and susceptibility beyond the personal, to a sense of the whole community. One particular member of the community is singled out by the narrator as being the most to blame, and that is Beauty's husband who is described as a 'playboy'.

It is by using a dynamic elliptical, yet revelatory process that Magona writes the diseased female body into the text of *Beauty's Gift*, restoring subjectivity to the often objectified persona of the AIDS 'victim'. Beauty, at 35, is described as: 'Shrunken and skeletal'; 'Bone. Nothing but bone. That is what she has become'; 'But the voice is strong as ever' (57). Beauty's voice and her message are what become important, not the horror of her deteriorating body. The meaning of 'beauty' is shifted from the physical to the abstract, and yet Amanda continues to log the real extent of Beauty's physical suffering. The chapter opens with a description of diarrhoea, and the 'stench ... the suffocating smell [that] reigns supreme' (57). Magona deftly juxtaposes this initial sensory repugnance with the emotional pain and humiliation felt by Beauty: 'a tear rolls out of Beauty's eye. She is lying on her side, and the unchecked tear falls over the bridge of her nose and down into the other eye. Then, out it spills again, and sinks into the soft, pale yellow pillow cradling her gaunt cheek' (59), and the physical pain felt when dealing with her sick body: 'This is a major operation, as Amanda knows from previous visits. Covered in angry-looking, oozing sores, Beauty cries out and curses when touched anywhere except on her face, hands or neck. Everywhere else is a no go zone' (59).

This reclamation of the diseased body, and the traumatised, afflicted self is part of the still developing process of writing HIV/AIDS in postcolonial South Africa that mirrors what Gikandi has called 'territorial repossession' (Gikandi, 1992: 384). Destabilising the myth of the 'nation' as a unified, monolithic, naturally healthy entity, narratives about HIV/AIDS deconstruct hegemonic (often patriarchal) discourses of the postcolonial nation. Such reclamations have particularly significant implications for the patriarchal nation when the diseased body is either masculine or feminine. In this theorisation I draw on Meg Samuelson's illuminating work on the appropriation of women's bodies to bolster national imaginaries of 'wholeness and unity ... while repressing the ruptures that women's manifestly different experiences ... may reveal' (Samuelson, 2007: 232). It is the rupture caused by the unflinching description of the sick body that fractures national imaginaries, but it is the restoration of subjectivity to these sick bodies and those who interact with them, that confirms our humanity and creates space for utopian impulses to arise from the survival of hope and beauty in the face of death. This rupture breaks a long held silence in South African literature about HIV/AIDS and its effects on the body. Understanding this silence is an essential part of understanding the HIV epidemic in South Africa, part of understanding the 'story of AIDS in the Third World as a complex narrative' (Treichler, 1999: 99).

Amongst other academics, the Kenyan literary critic Simon Gikandi, has long theorised on the role of African literature in depicting and creating ideas of nation and national consciousness stating that: 'clearly, nation, national consciousness, and narration would walk hand in hand in African literature' (Gikandi, 1992: 378). Indeed the focus on literary representations of the nation in the context of decolonisation has dominated African literary theory for many years. Gikandi also astutely draws our attention to the emerging changes in depictions of the nation and a resurgence of other concerns of African literature in more recent times, asserting that 'our new global situation demands on narratives which face up to the task of representing the ambivalences of the post-colonial situation' (380). Gikandi also problematises the inevitable or natural relationship between nation and subject, suggesting that there are other spaces of belonging besides the nation: 'the nation does not naturally proffer identities, nor lead to the fulfilment of the desire to belong to a real or mythical community, but often comes between post-colonial subjects and their quest for a communal ideal, a *natio*, a space of belonging' (382).

I think it is productive to position the body between nation and subject and ask how health and ill-health figure in the formation of subjectivity and national consciousness. The body is, after all, the means through which we experience the world. Images of the body, in literature and film, enable readers and viewers to witness the physical manifestation of the 'health of the nation', or, when texts are less analogical, to be made aware of the discrepancies in the national imaginary, and experience the vulnerability of the nation to weakness, ill-health and suffering. In relation to HIV/AIDS, Treichler upholds the idea that 'every state has a "social imaginary", something it dreams itself to be' (Treichler, 1999: 108–9), and urges us to 'illuminate[s] the construction of AIDS as a complex narrative and raise[s] questions not so much about truth as about power and representation' (109). The way a nation represents HIV/AIDS should tell us something about the 'social imaginary' of that nation. HIV/AIDS in turn can alter the 'social imaginary', changing national consciousness to include a story of HIV/AIDS.

The power of the spectacle is crucial, the image of the infected patient, the sick body, does much to evoke empathy and elicit sympathy in the reader, as well as a certain amount of horror and fear. It is this spectacle, these images that have been most hidden in literature since the beginning of the epidemic, hidden in silent bodies and obfuscated by a reluctance to speak in the first person, taking full responsibility for the subject, or even to name HIV/AIDS directly. It is the power of anti-retrovirals (as they become more widely accessible) that will make the presence of HIV/AIDS more visible in South African society. But the very nature of HIV and the visible recovery of patients with low CD4 counts begins to blur the boundary between the sick and the healthy, life and death, suggesting that both can inhabit the same space in the human body. It is the very fact of the invisible location of HIV in the body that Kgebetli Moele exploits in his novel *The Book of the Dead* creating a first person narrative voice and a character out of the previously silent, hidden virus and locating 'it' inside the protagonist Khutso. It is exactly the 'moral credibility' of the male character that we call into question on hearing the voice of HIV, as we assume that as 'it' inhabits a male body, that the virus is male. It could be said then, that Moele's book demonises HIV and by extension the men in whose bodies it resides and conducts the murderous acts depicted in *The Book of the Dead*. Khutso effectively kills by infecting women with HIV, even hoping they will go on to infect their husbands and partners and so including those people's names in his body-count, recorded obsessively in the eponymous 'Book of the Dead' (reminiscent of a book at his high school which contained the names of blacklisted pupils) which he fills by the end of the novel. The power of the written word also seems crucial as it is important to Khutso (and one can assume the author too) to record the deeds committed in the story, as a record of his life, and its consequences, a form of narrative fulfilment which is enacted in completing both books; a clever narrative conceit. This demonisation is a form of displacement or othering which safely positions the reader in moral opposition to the repugnant acts Khutso embarks on in the second part of the novel.

Beginning in a pedestrian fashion *The Book of the Dead* seems at first to relate the simple story of a young boy who, after some truancy from school, decides to complete his education and escape his small town life. This section is entitled 'Book of the Living'. Once he achieves his goal and reaches university Khutso falls in love with Pretty, who is revealed to have come from a similarly impoverished background and paid for her education with sex, through generous boyfriends and ex-lovers. When they first meet, their fate is sealed in the sense that they begin a monogamous and loving relationship; the risk to Khutso is clearly apparent to the reader, as he has only experienced sex once before (during the shocking gang rape of a young girl at his school) and although they marry and have a son, it is a number of years before Pretty becomes ill and dies of AIDS. Although neglectful of his wife in later years due to excessive love of his son, when Khutso posthumously learns of her HIV positive status his grief and anger turn to bitter hatred and revenge. Abandoning his son, Khutso embarks on a terrible mission in the second half of the book which is marked by its new title 'Book of the Dead'. Khutso's HIV positive status has rendered him effectively dead, his narrative belongs to a character who no longer believes he is alive or has any reason to live, other than to do the bidding of the virus now thriving in his body.

Each section of the 'Book of the Dead' is divided into the names of his targets. Interspersed with these chapters are four sections penned by the virus and numbered I, II, III, IV. In fact the virus first appears in Chapter 12 of the 'Book of the Living':

> I live amongst you, waiting like a predator. I am faceless. I am mindless and thoughtless. But I am feared and despised. You hate me. But then I

put on a face – wear a human face – and I am respected, appreciated and valued. I am I. (77)

This eerie voice goes on to describe how 'you lovingly summon me. I don't break in … I am willingly invited in … I love my work – it is my work and I do it with pride – but I do it in the most gentle of ways' (77). Khutso also has his own dedicated section at the beginning of the 'Book of the Dead' when he is 41 years old, 107.6 kg and has a CD4 count of 650. Most interestingly for the question of authorship is the fact that although the reader initially believes Khutso records this information about himself, the virus actually pens this section: 'in the middle of the second golden page I wrote' (89). Of course the virus records Khutso in the 'Book of the Dead' as by the end he will also be one of his own victims, but this irony is very subtle on this first tentative page. The mission however becomes immediately clear: 'We were sitting in Khutso's study, both of us pondering the mission ahead, the mission that we were going to undertake together. We are going to fuck 'em dead, I told him, and he smiled' (89). Khutso's complicity with the virus is clear from here onwards, and yet after the relatively sympathetic portrayal of Khutso in the 'Book of the Living', it appears that the virus is the devil in this relationship, influencing Khutso's normal behaviour.

In Section II, most frighteningly, for those who advocate treatment, the virus also advocates treatment, but for nefarious ends, writing that:

I told Khutso that he must save his life, not for himself but for the cause. He didn't like it. He did not want to take the treatment, but I forced him to … ARVs. I like them. In fact, I love them. I want my soldiers to live as long as they can. I want them to have the freshest faces for the longest time, so that no one ever suspects that they are sick. (133)

It is in this second section, where Khutso records his age (44), weight (95kg) and CD4 count (400) for the second time that the virus refers to them both as 'we': 'Khutso went for an HIV test, just to check and see how far along we – Khutso and I – were' (133). By the final section, HIV is taking its leave of Khutso aged 47, whose weight is now recorded as only 65kg and CD4 count at 60, writing, 'It was a great honour knowing you, I tell him. I have had great soldiers, I have seen their great deeds, but you, you come second to none. But now, Khutso, your time is done, I tell him. You are dying and I have to move on' (165). By logging the physical deterioration of Khutso, Moele graphically brings to life the image of the emaciated, skeletal man Khutso has become, representing the ravages of the disease in cold hard facts, numbers, clinical representations of a disease which kills cruelly and slowly. It is worth noting

how significant this description of Khutso's decline is given that the
death of male characters from AIDS is very rarely represented in literature in South Africa. And yet the description is just facts, cold numbers,
it is Khutso's actions that are more horrifying and the ease with which
he carries them out.

In the final sentence Moele returns to the idea of authorship when the
virus writes as his parting shot: 'Somewhere out there I have conquered
another author of no mean talent, and we are starting another book
together for the cause' (165). In a very postmodern way, the author,
the virus and Khutso have inhabited this text (as has the reader) bringing this story and these voices to life on the page. Using the first person
to write parts of the novel from the perspective of the virus produces
an unnerving feeling of complicity in the intentional destruction of
so many lives. It points the finger very firmly at Khutso, who cannot
shirk the responsibility for his behaviour, but also at the reader, who,
like the author has completed this journey of imagination and stepped,
for the first time in South African fiction, inside the head of an HIV
positive character who has deliberately infected hundreds if not thousands of people. This is a very human, innovative and imaginative way
of expressing epidemiology, which gets absolutely under the reader's
skin. The feeling of displacement is unsettled by the realisation that as
stated in its title, the novel itself is its own Book of the Dead so that
although the floating voice of HIV has been separated from Khutso's
own embodied voice, removing responsibility from Khutso to a certain
extent for his actions, the voice has also subtly manipulated the reader
and authored its own story; the reader witnesses the death of hundreds
of people. This suggests a further displacement of another commonly
invisible presence in the novel, the author, Moele, by the virus, which is
of course even more unsettling.

In contrast, by focusing on a single family's life the Oscar nominated film *Yesterday* (2004) graphically shows how the AIDS patient is
shunned by a Zulu community. The film provides a unique counterpoint
to written literature, which rarely focuses on either the physical or rural
experience of HIV/AIDS, exposing the silent bodies of the rural poor
on screen to a much larger audience (it was selected for the Venice and
Toronto International Film Festivals in 2004, won Best Film at Pune
in India, and was nominated for both an Oscar and an Emmy in the
USA). It is with unflinching realism that the devastating effects of AIDS
on a single family are revealed. With its view firmly fixed on the future
the film both begins and ends with the eponymous heroine, Yesterday,
walking on a road. By the end of the film we understand that although
her past cannot be changed, Yesterday will do all she can to improve

the life of her daughter, Beauty, for the future, primarily by staying alive long enough to send her to school. Although Yesterday is the character whose story we trace as we learn that she is infected with HIV, it is her husband John's death that we are shown on screen. His return from the mines in Johannesburg where he has been living and working away from home is brutally but sympathetically portrayed such that his initial violent response to Yesterday's news that she is infected is tempered with the sad realisation that his role in infecting his wife will conclude with his premature, painful death.

John begs forgiveness for blaming Yesterday and explains that he has been fired because he is now incontinent with diarrhoea and can no longer work. The villagers protest at his presence among them and Yesterday is forced to build a house for him outside the village on a hill. John's decline while he is nursed by his wife is graphic and unflinching. He suffers on screen for us all to watch while we fear that his fate will soon be Yesterday's. The film contrasts with both *Beauty's Gift* and *The Book of the Dead* in that all three texts represent male characters who are culpable in infecting their wives and girlfriends, but each text treats that male subject in a different way. Most typically in South Africa we are shown women who are sick and suffering (in soap operas like *Isidingo* or *Scandal* for example), and *Beauty's Gift* depicts this injustice within a polemic against the dangerous way men live their lives, advocating that women abstain from sex or divorce their husbands in order to save their own lives. *The Book of the Dead* takes male culpability to an extreme, which although unrealistic, points the finger firmly at irresponsible men as murderers, even psychopathic serial killers. *Yesterday* takes the middle road, showing the intimate tragedy within a single marriage; the infidelity and secrecy which fuels the epidemic but which ultimately is not a criminal act, not an intentional act (John is shown to be a loving and hard-working husband and father) but a terrible betrayal nonetheless at the heart of many South African marriages. The consequences are shown in detail but the strength of Yesterday in fighting to survive means the film is more hopeful than *Beauty's Gift*, suggesting that whether Yesterday survives or not (which is not known by the end of the film), there is hope in the life and education of her daughter to live and become part of the much longed for 'HIV Free Generation' advertised on television.

In a conversation with her friend the Teacher about why she is keeping both her own and her husband's illness a secret, Yesterday reflects on a previous incident in Bergville, not far from the village of Rooihoek (meaning Red Corner, but which in reality is the village of Okhombe). 'What happened to that woman in Bergville? They killed her, threw stones until she was dead.' The cruelty of the disease itself is juxtaposed with the cruelty of the villagers, who on finding out that John has developed AIDS, demand that he leave the village in order to protect themselves. 'He will make us all sick,' and 'What if he bleeds all over us?' the villagers ask. 'He must go,' another villager agrees. The element of secrecy, misinformation and the shunning of the sick is not unusual in Zulu society or indeed South African society more widely. The title of the ground-breaking collection of short stories published in 2004 says as much, *Nobody Ever Said AIDS*, as does the euphemistic title of Johnny Steinberg's book about HIV/AIDS in Lusikisiki, the Eastern Cape, *Three Letter Plague*.

It is fascinating to note that the name of the disease itself is not mentioned for much of the film. John refers to his diagnosis in Johannesburg as 'he said just like you said'. Even Yesterday's doctor simply says: 'Your body is strong. It is keeping the disease in check.' It is more than half way through the film when the villagers are discussing how the disease is contracted that one person actually says: 'They say he has the virus HIV.' In this sense there is an element of complicity between the film makers and the viewers because if one has some knowledge of HIV and AIDS and the symptoms, particularly of tuberculosis, which is often the first opportunistic infection to take hold, then one will have realised that HIV is the virus being revealed to us in Yesterday's visits to the doctor. The film-maker relies on an assumption of this knowledge when we then follow the doctor's questions about sexual intercourse, protection and the fact that Yesterday must tell her husband about her status, to warn him that he is also infected. And yet at no point is the words HIV or AIDS used in transmitting this information. Even when John asks for forgiveness on his deathbed he only manages to articulate: 'I am sorry, for...'. Yesterday fills his silence with apparent absolution, or at best, wilful amnesia. 'Forget all that, it is in the past.'

The silences, the secrecy, are all part of the story of HIV in South Africa and despite the explicit nature of the film, its visual depiction of illness and pain, these integral elements of the disease, one of the reasons it has spread so quickly and so relentlessly, lie in the reluctance of individuals to confront or name the disease directly. It remains hidden, even in the words spoken on screen, just as it lies hidden in the body, until it develops into full blown AIDS, by which time it is often too late. AIDS is a non-image. It is solely through other visual cues that we interpret the devastation of the HIV virus: the dry skin, sores and marks on Yesterday's and John's faces, signs of Karposi's sarcoma, black cancerous lesions, the rapid loss of weight, coughing, weakness. And yet even these most visible symptoms are hidden from the village as John remains inside. The images of John in general are kept to a minimum, the film focuses primarily on Yesterday and her daughter Beauty, so that it is not until one villager comments, 'He is so thin the wind could blow him over', that we realise how serious John's condition is becoming and how obvious his illness is to outsiders. Is this the image that Westerners see when they think of Africa as the dark continent infested with HIV/AIDS? Do these ideas of skeletal men and women fit in right alongside the images of the Biafran and Ethiopian famines that once regularly appeared on the evening news?

In addition to the body of the people, the body of the country in the stunning landscape of the Drakensberg in KwaZulu Natal provides more than just the social and geographical context to the narrative, but juxtaposes the extremes of suffering, the relative hardship of rural life, with the epic beauty that surrounds the characters. It could be said that the 'wow factor' of the landscape, the image of South Africa's bounty and glory, the image sold to foreigners and tourists, hides the intricacies and difficulties of rural life. Not only does Yesterday visit the doctor three times before seeing anyone, but when she tries to get John in to the local hospital the nurse shows her rooms filled with ailing men, and describes a waiting list as long as both her arms. The brief contrast between the village and the city, seen when Yesterday visits her husband in Johannesburg, shows what different worlds the married couple inhabit, but also the almost bifurcated nature of South African culture, which contains locations so disparate and yet so interdependent economically. One cannot help but wonder if Yesterday's fate would be the same in the city, although it does not seem to offer a friendlier atmosphere. Testament to the alienation and isolation of inner-city Johannesburg, particularly in relation to HIV/AIDS, can be found in Phaswane Mpe's novel *Welcome to Our Hillbrow*.

I want to conclude by briefly looking at *District 9* (2009) as a counterpoint to the other three texts discussed in this chapter to see if the extremes offered by science fiction can be utilised to further emphasise my point. The film begins in 1982, when a space ship bearing a sick and malnourished alien population, nicknamed 'Prawns', appears over Johannesburg, South Africa. Twenty-eight years later, the initial welcome by the human population has faded. The refugee camp where the aliens were located has deteriorated into a militarised ghetto called District 9. In 2010, the munitions corporation, Multi-National United, is contracted to forcibly evict the population with operative Wikus van der Merwe in charge. In this operation, Wikus is exposed to an alien chemical which begins to mutate his body into alien form (beginning with his arm) and he must rely on the help of his two new 'Prawn'

friends. Obviously the film does not directly represent or feature HIV/
AIDS, and I have not come across any other analyses that look at the
film in this way, but I think it is interesting to view *District 9* as a
potential reflection of a society that in the future has segregated a large
proportion of the immigrant community for fear of contamination (the
aliens were originally discovered sick and malnourished aboard their
spaceship). The aliens are distinctly skeletal and depicted as living in
squalid conditions, shunned and treated poorly in a way that can perhaps be linked with the extremes experienced by those infected with
HIV in South Africa, who often live in informal settlements.

The dystopian element of the film can be read as an allegory of the
extremes of segregation, wherein barriers between the 'human' (white)
and 'non-human' (black) residents of Johannesburg becomes literally
interpreted as 'aliens' who are housed separately in the area referred to
as 'District 9', just as black citizens were removed from areas like District
6 in Cape Town to the Cape Flats or relegated to townships like Soweto
and Katlehong outside Johannesburg during apartheid. The allegory
also extends to the treatment of immigrants (*makwerekwere*) to South
Africa who are not integrated and are often treated badly, attacked and
blamed for spreading diseases such as HIV/AIDS. The classic representation of HIV in most societies shows that 'the epidemic's origin is often
identified with foreignness – Africa not the United States, the United
States not Russia' (Kruger, 1996: 80). This subliminal representation of
what some view as an invasion of HIV infection from outside the community is one way to read the film, demonstrating that the ubiquitous
visibility of otherwise 'silent bodies' can become de-familiarised through
the spectacular dissident vernacular of science fiction.

The infection of the central character Wikus with a fluid which begins
to turn him into a 'prawn' draws distinct parallels with HIV infection, although the fluid is only sprayed in his face rather than ingested
sexually or intravenously. When Wikus escapes from the scientists who
want to dissect him (echoing the notorious medical experiments connected to germ warfare performed during apartheid by Wouter Basson,
nicknamed 'Dr Death') a former colleague tells the press that Wikus is
infected with an alien STD and is highly contagious, once again making
links with HIV. The physical transformation of Wikus into an unrec-
ognisable alien being, a 'non-human', can be linked with fears about
HIV and AIDS which turns people into the 'living dead' or 'zombies'
and leads to the kind of inhuman treatment seen in the film *Yesterday*.[2]
The ultimate fear of contact with those who are sick is what has led to
the concealment of symptoms and the deferral of the voice of the first
person in narrative in order to create a distance between the disease and

the subject. We can see that in these four texts that distance has been closed and that by unveiling the hitherto silent body at length, creating space to think and write about the reality of the physical and mental suffering inflicted by HIV/AIDS, the truth about HIV and AIDS can be exposed.

The trajectory of the representation of HIV/AIDS in South African literature has become more graphic and crept closer and closer to the personal over the last twelve years. Images of HIV/AIDS also seem to be dependent on an element of cooperation, or co-creation between the author, film-maker, reader and subject. Signs and signals, words and metaphors are read in a particular way by a sympathetic audience in order to make sense of the narrative that is laid out before them, helping readers and viewers to understand the intricacies, idiosyncrasies, depth and detail of a disease which at times defies definition and comprehension. The literature and film discussed in this paper have broken boundaries, they have begun to create new languages, visual and linguistic codes: re-inventing genres for a new generation, and finding increasingly more complex ways of writing about and filming HIV/AIDS, for those who care to watch, listen or read the texts carefully.

Read together, the four texts I have analysed productively position depictions of the sick body between the mythologised ideas of nation and subject, and force us to reassess how images of ill-health enable us to re-imagine subjectivity and national consciousness. The images of the body, in *Beauty's Gift*, *The Book of the Dead*, *Yesterday* and *District 9*, enable readers and viewers to witness the physical manifestation of the 'health of the nation'. Through unflinching literary descriptions of the deterioration of the human body we are made aware by both Magona and Moele of the discrepancies in the national imaginary which is meant to be strong, healthy, invulnerable. By filming the suffering and death of Yesterday's husband in KwaZulu Natal and fantastically imagining a future in which the isolation of an individual by a village becomes the isolation of an alien 'infected' species by a city, or national government, as it does in *District 9*, we witness and experience for ourselves the vulnerability of the nation to weakness, ill-health and suffering. The power of representation in these four texts is clear. HIV/AIDS had not been represented in South Africa in these explicit ways until very recently, although, like the spaceship in *District 9*, it arrived in South Africa in the early 1980s. The way South Africa represents HIV/AIDS now should tell us something about the 'social imaginary' of the 'rainbow' nation and how much it has shifted, how much it has been subverted, and how much the incorporation of what has in the past been perceived as weakness and vulnerability, hidden within silent, hidden bodies, can now be read as a strength, a more realistic representation of what it means to be South African in a time of AIDS.

Notes

1 The third text not mentioned here is *Vukani! (Wake Up!)*, a play not yet published in English, first performed in Muizenberg on 17.8.06 and now published in Xhosa.
2 For more on 'death before dying' see Niehaus, 2007.

References

Attree, Lizzy (2007): 'The literary responses to HIV and AIDS in South Africa and Zimbabwe from 1990–2005' (SOAS, University of London).
District 9 (2009): Directed by Neill Blomkamp, South Africa.
Gikandi, Simon (1992): 'The politics and poetics of national formation: recent African Writing', in Anna Rutherford (ed.), *From Commonwealth to Post Colonial* (Sydney: Dangaroo Press).
Kruger Steven, F. (1996): *Aids Narratives: gender and sexuality, fiction and science* (New York: Garland Publishing).
Magona, Sindiwe (1998): *Mother to Mother (*South Africa: Beacon Press).
Magona, Sindiwe (1999): 'A State of Outrage', in Yvonne Vera (ed.), *Opening Spaces: an anthology of contemporary African women's writing*, (Oxford/Harare: Heinemann/Baobab Books): 114–27.
Magona, Sindiwe (2002): *Vukani! (Wake up!)*, unpublished, by email. First performed at the Masque Theatre, Muizenberg, Western Cape, South Africa, 17.8.06.
Magona, Sindiwe (2004): 'Leave-taking', in *Nobody Ever Said AIDS: Stories and Poems from Southern Africa* (Cape Town: Kwela Books): 124–41.
Magona, Sindiwe (2008): *Beauty's Gift* (Cape Town: Kwela Books).
Moele, Kgebetli (2009): *The Book of the Dead* (Cape Town: Kwela Books).
Mpe, Phaswane (2001): *Welcome to Our Hillbrow* (Pietermaritzburg: University of Natal Press).
Niehaus, Isak (2007): 'Death before dying: understanding of AIDS stigma in the South African Lowveld', *Journal of Southern African Studies* 33(4): 845–60.
Rasebotsa, Nobantu, Meg Samuelson and Kylie Thomas (eds) (2004): *Nobody Ever Said AIDS: Stories and Poems from Southern Africa* (Cape Town: Kwela Books).
Samuelson, Meg (2007): *Remembering the Nation, Dismembering Women?: stories of the South African transition* (Pietermaritzburg: University of KwaZulu-Natal Press).
Steinberg, Jonny (2008): *Three Letter Plague* (Johannesburg: Jonathan Ball).
Treichler, Paula (1999): *How to Have Theory in an Epidemic: cultural chronicles of AIDS* (Duke University Press).
Yesterday (2004): Directed by Darrell James Roodt, South Africa.

Index

EU authorised representative for GPSR:
Easy Access System Europe, Mustamäe tee 50,
10621 Tallinn, Estonia
gpsr.requests@easproject.com

www.ingramcontent.com/pod-product-compliance
Lightning Source LLC
Chambersburg PA
CBHW050646280326
41932CB00015B/2803